RIVER OF DOUBT

*Reliving the Epic Amazon Journey of Roosevelt
and Rondon on its Centennial*

MARC ANDRÉ MEYERS

"As I look back over my life's winding trails I realize that the journey down the River of Doubt overshadows all the rest; and when I recall the companions I have had, good, bad, and indifferent, Theodore Roosevelt stands apart."

George K. Cherrie, Dark Trails: Adventures of a Naturalist, 1930

PREFACE

When Theodore Roosevelt, former U. S. President, Nobel Peace Laureate, and hero of the Battle of Kettle Hill, Cuba, came to Latin America, he had been commissioned to give lectures in Argentina. He hoped to follow these by an adventurous journey filled with observation, discovery, and hunting. The fateful meeting in Rio de Janeiro, where he was offered the opportunity to be the first 'civilized' person to explore the River of Doubt, changed all that and brought him to the brink of death. The epic journey of 1914 down a river still inhabited by Indians that had never been contacted, co-led by Colonels Roosevelt and Rondon, has become the subject of legend.

This book describes our journey in the Parecis Plateau and down the River of Doubt in 2014 and 2015, comparing and contrasting it with the 1914 expedition. But Roosevelt and Rondon did not operate alone: they were deeply embedded in and the product of their societies. Indeed, they personified the highest traits of the U. S. and Brazil, respectively. The lives of Roosevelt and Rondon are also presented by analyzing their philosophies and guiding principles. A brief description of the indigenous inhabitants of the region, the Parecis, Nambikwaras, and Cinta Larga helps the reader to understand the surrounding environment and risks encountered by the expedition. Two chapters cover important events that happened and are happening in this region: the seminal 1939 anthropological voyage of Claude Lévi-Strauss following the same trek as the Roosevelt-Rondon expedition and the burning of the Amazon, a topic of great contemporary concern.

Finally, the first and last chapters relay the inspiration that led me to engage in this undertaking and the scientific studies that ensued from these recent explorations. Fascinating new aspects of piranhas, *arapaimas*, *tambaquis*, toucans, curassows, jarina seeds, and square lianas, which we encountered in the expeditions, are being revealed using analytical, computational and characterization tools of modern science and are guiding us to new, bioinspired materials and structures. Although these structures and features are in many cases not exclusive to the Amazonian flora and fauna, the creative process is a mysterious one and was triggered by this exploration. Is it the solitary time spent in this vastness leaving the mind to roam free? Is it the presence of these organisms in this unique biodiverse environment? We hope to transmit some of this knowledge and enthusiasm to the reader.

Áripuanā River

B R A Z I L

Utiariti Falls

Vilhena

Tapirapoan

Cáceres

B O L I V I A

P A R A G U A Y

Asuncion

300 miles

TABLE OF CONTENTS

1 | CHAPTER 1 Beginnings: Roots of Book
10 | CHAPTER 2 On the Rondon Project in the Purus River
24 | CHAPTER 3 Indigenous People: Parecis and Nambikwaras
33 | CHAPTER 4 Rondon
44 | CHAPTER 5 Positivism
51 | CHAPTER 6 Roosevelt
62 | CHAPTER 7 The Cinta Larga: Victims and Aggressors
66 | CHAPTER 8 Preparations and Expectations
88 | CHAPTER 9 Up the Sepotuba River
111 | CHAPTER 10 Through the Parecis Lands on Mules
141 | CHAPTER 11 Through the Nambikwara Lands
165 | CHAPTER 12 Down the River of Doubt
231 | CHAPTER 13 The Burning of the Amazon
239 | CHAPTER 14 Lévi-Strauss
251 | CHAPTER 15 Scientific Observations and Experiments

263 | Acknowledgement
265 | Selected Bibliography

CHAPTER 1

BEGINNINGS: ROOTS OF BOOK

When I closed the last page of Candice Millard's book, 'The River of Doubt,' about three years ago, an idea came to my mind: to follow on the footsteps of the 1913-1914 Roosevelt-Rondon Scientific Expedition using, as much as possible, similar means of transportation. This idea resonated with old dreams, which I carried within me all the way since 1969, when I participated in the Rondon Project, deep in the Amazon, on the Purus River. But the kernel was born even earlier, with fantastic stories brought back by fishing expeditions that left my home town of Monlevade and ventured farther and farther into the Amazon basin. Electric eels, fish with humongous teeth, blood-thirsty piranhas. So, I joined them once, in 1964, and spent 48 hours in the back of an old truck, cruising through the Brazilian highlands at 40 km per hour, enduring the bitterest cold of my entire life at 3 a.m. when the freezing night joined with the wind from the truck to torture us. We finally arrived, after being rescued from sinking in the swamps by the river by a train of oxen. The fishing was extremely poor, since we reached the Javaé, which was almost dry, instead of the fabled Araguaia River. The only Indian I saw was a lonely Carajá that visited our camp one day. The two rings tattooed on

1

his cheeks and his Asiatic eyes were the only sign differentiating him from the local river dwellers. But my undaunted enthusiasm and curiosity continued for these magical lands.

Roosevelt was the scion of a wealthy American family, tracing their lineage to the Dutch settlers of New Amsterdam, that later became New York. Rondon was an orphan of part Indian blood and rose in the military ranks by sheer willpower, discipline, and talent. A positivist, he adhered to a strict code of conduct and high ethical standards. Both were to meet glory. Roosevelt is one of the four American Greats whose head is displayed on Mount Rushmore for the centuries to admire. Rondon's name appears in a state, Rondonia, cities, airports, and avenues throughout the country. A soldier that never fired a shot and once took an Indian arrow on his chest, without flinching, Rondon matched Roosevelt's courage and bravado, displayed on many occasions, but never as dramatically as when he was shot at during a speech and continued his harangue after muttering: "It takes more than this to kill a bull moose." Both were intellectuals and carried with them, in the expedition, books that I read, to fully assess their intellects. In a fascinating twist, they conversed in French, the only language that they shared.

While Roosevelt was leading the world's most sanguine democracy into prominence, Rondon was traversing the most remote jungles of Western Brazil, establishing contact, for the first time, with indigenous tribes and integrating these vast expanses into the young nation. This was done at a high cost in lives and his expeditions matched, in duration, distance, and sacrifice, those by Stanley and Livingstone in Africa.

Brazil and the US are of almost equal size, if one does not include Alaska. The conquest of the West, which started in 1849 with the gold rush in the US, had been initiated much earlier in Brazil, in the 1700s and was marked by the construction of a massive fort in the Guaporé River, deep in the Amazon. However, endemic diseases such as malaria and yellow fever, leschimaniasis and an inclement climate caused the deaths of many thousands of immigrants, thereby slowing down economic development and integration of the Amazon into the nation that still favored coastal settlements and the contact with Europe.

So, the idea that rose in me was the resuscitation of a life-long dream. However, there is an enormous distance between dream and reality, and I did not know where to start. My attempts to enlist the Brazilian Army to reenact the momentous events failed initially, before logistic support was provided through a four-wheel drive vehicle and crew. However, in the whirlwind of random activity one lead, provided by my former student and colleague Col. Luis Henrique Leme Louro, changed everything. In an email he reported to me that he had heard of a legendary Brazilian officer that had kayaked 11,000 kilometers in the Amazon, being the first to descend several of the rivers. My hope turned to enthusiasm when Colonel Hiram Reis answered my email and supported the project enthusiastically. Here are his words:

"Dear friend,
We are "Ready to Go." This year, in principle, I have three more expeditions to conduct:
• 1st: Crossing the Patos Lagoon of Porto Alegre following the Rio Grande along the East Margin, starting on 02/04/2014;
• 2nd: Finishing my journeys through the Amazon basin (11,000 km) - - Santarem - Belem 08/01/2014;
• 3rd: Circumnavigation of Mirim Lagoon 09/17/2014
Nothing that cannot be rescheduled if you wish, Dr. Meyers. I will join you with my ocean kayak which can be shipped to the Roosevelt River. It would be an opportunity to honor Rondon, the human figure that I consider most important and charismatic of all our history."

From this moment on my hopes were up. He guided me through the process since I am, compared to him, a kayaking neophyte whose longest experience is eight hours straight, to equipment selection and strategy. Here in Del Mar, I received the enthusiastic support of Jeffrey Lehmann, producer of the 'Weekend Explorer.' We needed a fourth person and Col. Hiram found the ideal one: Col. Ivan Angonese. This was an unforgettable adventure since it represented not only our personal experience but also because of the historical aspects, which are of great importance. With patience, he saved me from the water three times and I owe him therefore a special gratitude. The first stage of our expedition was on horseback, through the Pareci and Nambikwara lands. The process of obtaining permission in the dense Brazilian bureaucracy took several months. The descent was not easy. Indeed, it posed challenges at times unsurmountable but Col. Hiram, just like his predecessor, used prudence where necessary and boldness when there was no other option. A few times I said a little prayer and, like knights of yesteryear, gave my soul to the Highest before moving down a rapid. We had three advantages over the 1914 Roosevelt-Rondon expedition:

1. Season. We arrived just before the beginning of the rainy season, when the Parecis Plateau was still dry and the rivers were at their lowest, whereas the 1914 expedition crossed the highlands in January-February and descended in February-March due to the many delays by Roosevelt.

2. Boats. Col. Hiram knows the Amazon rivers well and recommended the Ocean kayaks. This proved to be a wise choice. We complemented this with a supply canoe which was made of an aluminum frame covered by canvas. Although slower, with two

paddlers it moved rather briskly and faster than I on the kayak. Rondon had at his disposal heavy dugout canoes made by the local Indians.

3. Number of members and equipment. The original expedition had 22 members, of which 14 did most of the paddling, portaging, and camp travails. It also had almost 300 cases of equipment and supplies. We had four persons and a minimum of equipment and supplies, approximately 300 kg.

This river descent could not have taken place and importantly, would have failed had Col. Hiram not used all his knowledge and energy to guide us down this fascinating river. Roosevelt's admiration for Rondon, who was also a colonel at the time of the historic and tragic expedition, transpired in the many discussions in his book "Through the Brazilian Wilderness." This informed me of the complex interplay between history and adventure that converged on the 1913-1914 expedition and on the subsequent conquest of the Amazon. I, on the other hand, am a simple Second Lieutenant in the Brazilian Army.

This expedition was not only a journey into the Brazilian wilderness that is, one hundred years after Roosevelt, still fascinatingly dangerous and exotic. It represented the rediscovery of the dreams that drove these bright individuals, Roosevelt, Rondon and his gallant officers and courageous *camaradas*, and, twenty-five years later, the great French anthropologist Claude Lévi-Strauss. They left the comforts of their cities and their loved ones to embark on majestic adventures that expanded our knowledge, and we are fortunate to report this here. As I embarked on this adventure, I had three goals: to pay homage to these heroes, to compare the current environment with the one they encountered, and to expand my knowledge of biological species in this region.

July 2014. I stand here, deep in the jungle of Brazil, facing the swift current of clear water jutting into the forest. The afternoon shades already cover the shapes with a mantle of gray that dissolves the deep green. The river has the feel of an ominous mouth that will engulf me, a dark hole from which there is no return. Around me are a few rotten wooden stumps, all that is left of what was, one hundred years ago, a makeshift bridge. I made it here, to the source of the Roosevelt River, by a tortuous path which started two years earlier, through Candice Miller's book. As I commented earlier, the sudden inspiration to retrace Roosevelt's and Rondon's epic journey of 1914, has to take shape in a more concrete manner. One important decision was made: to follow their steps using means similar to the ones they had at their disposal: horses, mule trains, ox carts, and canoes.

I compare the scenery ahead of me with old photographs from the original expedition, and nothing has changed since Theodore Roosevelt, twice US president and celebrated hero, stood here. This is the starting point of the epic journey in which the Roosevelt-Rondon Scientific Expedition descended the River of Doubt. In so doing he almost lost his life, which was eventually shortened as a result of the superhuman travails that his aging body had to endure. A few moments ago, Manoel Sabanê, a Nambikwara Indian in his eighties, told me that the memories of Rondon and Roosevelt are still clear in his mind, from stories passed on by his father. Later, I discover that Claude Lévi-Strauss, the celebrated anthropologist who followed a similar path twenty-five years later, befriended a certain Sabanê tribe, close to the outpost of Vilhena. It was part of the large Nambikwara nation that covered a vast territory in the northern Parecis plateau. These Indians provided the material from which he would forge his grand theory of Structural Anthropology. Manoel was a child when he came by and befriended them. This is only his Christian name, Nambikwaras keeping zealously secret their real names from foreigners. Indians have lived in these parages since immemorial times, but successive epidemics and wars have brought their numbers to the brink of extinction. What I see in front of me, two houses with approximately fifteen Indians, represents the remains, spread through the region, of a 20,000-strong nation. A few thousand survived. Manoel Sabanê shows me his arm marked by an old scar of an arrow fired by a fierce tribe that also tracked the expedition, the feared Cinta Larga or Wide Belts.

And yet, everything has changed since that day, February 27, 1914, in which the expedition, 22 men, 3 dogs, and three hundred cases of materiel, on seven dugout canoes, started downstream to meet unforeseen challenges, death, disease and, ultimately, glory for the two leaders. The population of the earth has skyrocketed from one to seven billion. Two global conflicts racked hell in the lives of most. The airplane, a mere curiosity in 1914, crisscrosses the skies in ever greater frequency. The silicon chip has revolutionized our lives and billions of electromagnetic waves travel across space connecting our aspirations, ambitions, disappointments, and the multitude of stringed moments that make our modern lives. America became the muscular democracy with which Roosevelt dreamt, creating wealth, industry, new products, in an age of intense creativity that is becoming known as The American Century. Brazil followed its own course, less glorious perhaps but not less difficult, emerging as the sixth economy in this planet. Wide swaths of the Parecis Plateau have been transformed into mega farms, producing and exporting soy, cotton, and corn to the urban centers of Brazil and to other countries, fulfilling Roosevelt's prophecy but destroying the virgin beauty of the land.

This book is about Roosevelt and Rondon, their journey, and the changes that happened in these one hundred years. They personify the highest qualities of their cultures, the Anglo-Saxon and Latin, respectively. It is also about the Amazon, a region roughly the size of the US, and about the toll it exerted on those that tried to tame it, starting with Orellana's expedition of 1542, Aguirre's folly, the flailing dream by Henry Ford to create a modern city and to develop rubber tree plantations, the epic immigration in the 1940s in which hundreds of thousands of rubber tapers perished, and in recent times, the Jari project, led by US entrepreneur Ludwig, in an attempt to produce paper from the infinite supply of wood. The intrepid English explorer Fawcett was swallowed by this region, in a vain search for Eldorado, the magical city of gold. The German explorer Langsdorf became mad during his expedition. So did the Spaniard Aguirre. Why and how has the Amazon crushed these dreams?

But this book is also a little about me, my fascination with Indians that comes from my childhood, when I would spend hours looking at the photographs of Indians in their natural stage in the book "Tupari" by the Swiss ethnographer Franz Caspar. This was followed by encounters with the remains of Indian nations on several occasions, in which I had the opportunity to witness the sad decay of their life and culture. My fascination continued in the US, where I lived in South Dakota and met occasional Lakota Sioux. In New Mexico, a greater harmony had been reached and I observed from far these mysterious people, who periodically visited our small town of Socorro.

It is a fascination that represents for me the source of the conception of my inner being, devoid as some Native Americans are of the impositions of a complex hierarchical modern society. What is the effect of civilization, this complex construct, on our core, as humans? This theme also resonates in Lévi-Strauss' "Tristes Tropiques" account. He expresses this feeling as: "I had been looking for a society reduced to its simplest expression. That of the Nambikwara was so truly simple that all I could find in it was individual human beings."

One extended visit to the Purus River in 1969, as part of a student program called "Rondon Project", is the product of this desire. I could elaborate on other travels into the Amazon, but this journey represents a transformational step that created in me the conviction of the necessity of returning. This was more than a curiosity: it became a duty. Here is a brief report of this journey, seen through the haze of almost half a century.

CHAPTER 2

ON THE RONDON PROJECT IN THE PURUS RIVER

The absolute white. The white that blinds. I cannot take it anymore and turn away from it. The monstrous roar, accompanied by a vibration that penetrates the body, terrifies me. Two feet hang from a hole above me, and a human form sliding down through it confirms in a grave and nervous voice:

"Visibility Zero."

I turn to the front. Below the cockpit, a mechanic works with his back stuck to the ground, under the dashboard. In the center, beyond the pile of cardboard boxes, four pairs of afflicted eyes stare at the metal walls, which continue to vibrate from all screws and rivets, each emitting a high-frequency sound in a cacophony that reveals the old age of the Catalina, more than thirty years after retiring from WW2. This airplane was the workhorse of the Brazilian Air Force in the Amazon. Terror, which began in the morning with a growing concern, now comes to its height, as the captain's voice booms:

"We're going down. Hold on!"

I turn to the tiny window and the white invades me again. We are in a cloud that seems endless. In a few minutes, we crash on the trees. My faith in God grows stronger, and I pray to Our Lady for our salvation, promising her all my moments, my dedication, my sacrifices.

We had left Porto Velho, the sleepy town that was the capital of the territory of Rondonia in the morning after a sleepless night at the Fifth Battalion of Construction Engineering, and had loaded the seaplane with boxes of medical supplies, under the disapproving look of the Catalina team. Then we had slipped between the boxes and had squeezed onto the hard metal benches, twelve students eager to embark on the Rondon Project, about to live our greatest adventure. The airplane had accelerated on the runway, throwing up a cloud of dust. Through the windows, I had watched the treetops approaching. Suddenly, the slowdown and frantic braking. From the cockpit, had come the commanding voice:

"Excessive load. Abort the takeoff."

We had returned, raising again the red dust cloud and had jumped out into the heat, that was incandescent despite the early hour. The two medical students complained, saying that without the drugs they could not help the population. I assisted them in inspecting the boxes and selecting the most essential. Finally, we came to an agreement, as Major Boris, the airplane commander, had refused to make a second trip.

"Too much danger this time of year. We lost a Catalina a few months ago."

Suddenly, the white grows shallow and behind it I glimpse something dark. Trees!

The plane returns to its horizontal position as we watch, twenty meters below us, the jungle. It's my first view of this immensity, as the Catalina searches for something, like a dog sniffing for a prey. Finally, we cross a river, which our plane follows. It snails lazily through the forest and is our salvation. After a while, it ends in a brown colossus that we follow for about fifteen minutes. Ahead of us, by the river, is a clearing and some houses. Major Boris takes a turn, makes 180 degrees with the Catalina and points it upstream. We land on the water, sliding on its softness as if on a mattress. Forgotten the promises to God and the Holy Mary, I watch the pier, from which a canoe departs, coming our way. Is this our first day in Pauiní.

The days passed and we gradually adapted to the furnace infested by insects and drenched by daily rains that is the Purus River in January. From mythical curious beings coming from the South we had turned into heroes, healing the sick, extracting teeth, educating teachers and, in my case, helping the dentist and doctors and building a garbage collection system by following instructions in our manuals. Raul was a dentist and singer, and in the afternoons recited the eternal verses of Rubén Darío, whose book he had brought.

'Dichoso el árbol, que es apenas sensitivo,
y la piedra dura porque esa ya no siente,
pues no hay más grande el dolor dolor de ser vivo,
ni mayor pesadumbre que la vida consciente.'

'Lucky is the tree, that is just sensitive,
And the hard stone since it no longer feels,
'Cause there is no greater pain than to be alive,
Nor greater nightmare than a conscious life.'

The inspired poetry spread through the village and beyond, to the surrounding forest, enabled by the loudspeaker box that the mayor, Mario Said, had loaned us. It was the instrument that he carried along the river when on the campaign trail. Raul's soft accent from Nicaragua carried emotion and talent. Soon, we developed an evening show, and I recited poems, invented stories, made long descriptions of faraway places I had visited, and contributed to the general joy. Beneath our quarters, the only two-storied building in the town, which carried the idiosyncratic name of 'Bus Station,' the population gathered waiting for the vesper show. The mayor had obtained in Manaus resources to build a road, but there was only one trail linking Pauiní to a beautiful waterfall. The rest of the money had been used to build the single two-storied building and had probably been pocketed by him in the classic Brazilian fashion. We did all this under our nets that protected us from the myriads of mosquitoes of different sizes, *piuns* and *borrachudos*, and, especially, the feared malaria transmitters that were known to strike at sunset.

The doctors had become, despite their young age, serious and focused. Thus, they criticized our levity. Preparing for a professional life, they already showed the dull expression of medical doctors twenty years older. They exchanged medical secrets that they did not share with us lesser mortals. But the professor and the economist participated, but in a very passive way. When Raul tired of singing, I gave glorious descriptions of Europe, painting France, Germany, Italy, and United States in verbal colors. To our surprise the whole town was gathering in the minute square below our window, and we could not fail them. This was a heavy responsibility on our shoulders and our imagination was challenged. Raul's guitar was the saver every evening.

Having been a sharpshooter in my youth, I had brought with me, secretly, one Smith & Wesson Caliber K22 revolver. At the request of the mayor, I hit a vulture that had shown interest in my garbage bin, at a distance of thirty meters.

"This was just luck, *Doutor*," he said, from behind his thin mustache and sly eyes prematurely aged by his excessive smoking and drinking.

I handed him the gun and he tried unsuccessfully to hit one. We did this from the back window of our living quarters, the Bus Station, to the horror of the doctors. Finally, the last vulture flew off.

"Shoot that chicken there in the yard," challenged Mario Said, impatient and frustrated with his poor aim. I warned him that it was not a good idea. But his insistence left no option. Orders from the mayor! I aimed well, and let my finger slip softly on the trigger when the sighting of the barrel overlapped the chicken. I did this in a slow downward motion, thus eliminating any lateral inaccuracy. The shot was fired, without any twitch or instinctive muscle contraction. The soft noise that the bullet made upon hitting the target and the flying feathers left no doubt. It was a hit. The chicken shot through the yard, clucking desperately. A woman stormed out of her house, raging.

"The Mayor pays," shouted Mario Said, while the woman and her son chased the wounded chicken.

That night we ate a nice chicken soup, a change in our daily diet of turtle meat. The sad scene of the herd of live turtles in the mayor's yard, awaiting the fatal knife and gradually dwindling, made us suffer at each meal.

The problems encountered initially frightened us. Tetanus victims arriving by canoe, when we had a minimum of medicine. An isolated group on the other side of the river, a leper colony. Huge skin sores, that we later learned was leschimaniasis. Long lines with extraction requests for decayed teeth and even healthy ones. Raul had not brought the instruments, expecting a fully equipped dental office, which did not exist. It was up to me, the engineer, to build a foundation for the chair. We took the teacher's chair which we angled and used for patients. We got three forceps with a 'dental practitioner' that ran the river doing extractions. Instructed by Raul, whose hands had swelled after a few days of superhuman effort, the practitioner and I learned the modern principles of extraction of teeth and applied them mercilessly:

First, apply anesthesia sparingly to the blocking site. Don't pull right away. Then, using a forceps, rotate and loosen the tooth. Only when it is loose, pull! If the root is straight, tooth will come out. There were some dramatic cases of hook-shaped roots but in general the procedures were fast, since our anesthesia stocks were minimal.

We organized a football game, in which the inhabitants of Pauiní, I among them, played against the rubber tappers. These showed brute force and resistance, in addition to feet that seemed like mule hooves and left deep scars in our shins. I remember well how my nicotine filled lungs could not compete with these centaurs of the jungles. The result was unexpected but fair: victory for the rubber tappers.

We were told by the townspeople that the mayor was in the habit of inaugurating all constructions two or three times. True to form, he took advantage of our presence there to inaugurate a couple of buildings. The responsibility of representing the Rondon Project fell on my shoulders, and I weaved praise to his accomplishments in my speeches. Discovering this talent of mine, jokingly developed in drunken nights in Belo Horizonte, when I would imitate the fiery speeches of third rate politicians, he put it to use throughout the municipality, to the horror of doctors, who characterized me as a mercenary. These were nothing more than a few agglomerations of houses built on stilts scattered along the Purus River. Since the visits would be followed by celebratory libations, they were a welcome respite from my daily routine.

My mechanical engineering knowledge was also used to start up two brand new outboard motors that the mayor had brought from the tax-free zone of Manaus, where in fact he resided. So, I was asked daily to accompany the mayor in his boat runs to neighboring streams, which were followed by baths. One day, by pure spirit of curiosity, sticking my head in the water, I gave a loud roar. Within moments we were surrounded by dolphins. Then something unbelievable happened to me. As I dove from the boat into the black water, I ran into one of them. I do not know which one of us was more frightened, but the wild laughter of the mayor, his mind already altered by his favorite drink *cachaça* and *melado*, Brazilian rum with molasses, left no doubt as to the show.

One day, in describing over the loudspeaker the then recent film by Stanley Kubrick, Space Odyssey, I had an idea that I thought brilliant but our medical colleagues found ridiculous: to build a monolith at the harbor entrance, marking our passage through these shores. That night when we were having dinner with the mayor, I presented my plan. He looked at me curiously, somewhat puzzled. Then I threw the bait:

"Of course, your name will go on top."

Immediately, his sharp eyes lit up and his hooked nose danced in the space, a big smile on his lips. "When do you want to start, *Doutor*? But don't put my name. It is better to put Administration by Mario Said. Less personal."

Two angry stares across the table then shot at me while Raul roared. "Well let's put everyone's name!"

In a few days, the 'monument' was ready. The shape of the mythical monolith had been bastardized by including a lamp on top at the insistence of the mayor and our names in bold letters. It seems that we lacked the template for the S letter, and we had to improvise it by hand. On the other side of the monolith, we put the motto of the Rondon Project, Integrate not to Give Away, and the symbol consisting of a three-bladed propeller with arrow-shaped ends.

We visited an Indian village after going up the Aporinan River for two days. At the party, the Xingané, they aspired a mysterious powder through a hollow bone made from the leg of a curassow with rubber application at the end. The inhaled substance launched us into frantic dances in which the priest also participated. The purpose of this voyage was to baptize the children and therefore the priest had come with us.

The Indians had killed a Pauiní man a year earlier and so we kept some distance and decorum. But the story was more complicated; the man was the brother of Mario Said's mistress and gave himself all kinds of rights. Crazy drunk, he used to jump into the swollen river during the night when the rum tempted him, clinging to any uprooted tree passing by, and floating down until he reached a village five kilometers downstream. Living close to the Indians, also driven mad by rum, he had poked several of their buttocks with his knife. One day, the Indians had enough and got rid of him fairly and promptly. At night, when the macho was well soaked with *cachaça*, they called him out of the house, and as he stood at the door he received the full load of birdshot on the chest.

One Sunday, tired of the routine work in Pauiní, I got a canoe and went out to hunt. In the harbor a full canoe loaded with bunches of small purple coconuts had just arrived.

"*Açai, Doutor,* to make wine for us," said the boatman. This was the first time I came across these fruits, which became the rage of youth in our age of globalization. The Amazon contains many of these treasures: *cupuaçu, pupunha,* and others.

We paddled up a side arm, an *igarapé,* and entered the flooded forest, which had something eerie about it. A total silence descended upon us as we moored the canoe and walked through the forest that was, according to my partner, islanded land. We moved carefully, following the advice I had read in the adventure books, breaking branches and folding them back to indicate the return route if we got lost. The Amazon forest has throughout the ages swallowed countless unsuspecting people who were lost and often died of starvation. A few steps into the forest and all looked the same. There was no sun, nor any reference point. Suddenly my guide stopped.

"*Doutor,* let me see something here on your back." Using a branch, he performed several maneuvers without my knowing what he was doing. It was only when he gave a sigh of relief that he announced: "A huge scorpion."

I felt a shiver run through my body. We kept advancing into the forest for about two hours without seeing any game. The forest seemed a desert. I was getting ready to pull out a vine at the height of my chest when I realized it was actually a small snake that had positioned itself horizontally between two branches. One more step and my chest would have touched its head. I jumped back. We walked a little further and sat under a huge tree, that had buttresses as deep as a cathedral's, to give stability to the huge trunk, and ate our light lunch in silence.

"That snake was very poisonous, *doutor,*" said the boatman. "If it bites you ..."

I thought a little and I said. "This is definitely not my day. How about heading back?"

In the evening, Mario Said awaited us with his broad smile. "How about the hunt, *doutor?* We were expecting a good agouti or an *inhambu.*"

I told them our adventures as we accompanied our dinner with the *açai* extract, to which the mayor had added a good dose of rum. We could never have imagined that forty years later açai would go global and would be the rage of weight-conscious metrosexuals.

The mayor was the son of a Turkish merchant who had come up the Purus River in a *batelão,* a transport boat, and had penetrated into the Pauiní River, exchanging essential supplies such as gunpowder, kerosene, rum and alarm clocks, for rubber. In so doing he accumulated a small fortune. A local old-timer told me that he kept a gunman at the river mouth to prevent rubber tappers, all owing money, which represented most of the inhabitants of the Pauiní River, to escape without paying their debts. This system existed throughout the entire Amazon and is described by Euclydes da Cunha and Lévi-Strauss. It stems from two factors: (a) the exploitative nature of the merchants who financed the rubber tappers but controlled the rivers; (b) the low price of rubber, which fell precipitously after rubber tree plantations became productive in Asia. Low wages, high tree densities resulted in a dramatic increase in production. Thus, the rubber tappers could barely survive and the extraction of rubber did not produce any profits.

It was Sunday, and I enjoyed a stream of clear water exchanging warm looks and a shy kiss with Lindalva, a girl of the locality. Through Radio Rondonia, we had received firm orders three weeks earlier, to stay in Pauiní and wait for the plane, but on this Sunday the sun had been too pleasant and the invitation made to the almost pure Indian girl, to take a waterfall bath, had been accepted. The cold water mixed with our caresses created emotions in our bodies and a mysterious feeling, the blossoming of love.

I heard something in the distance, a light hum, which gradually, inexorably, rose and transformed into a roar, robbing us the enchantment of the moment.

The Catalina!

I received the rising noise with sadness, reflected in the beautiful almond-shaped eyes of Lindalva. Jumping out of the water as if waking from a dream, I shot down the trail, my revolver shaking at the waist. When I arrived at the harbor heaving, after half an hour of running, my mates from the Rondon Project screamed, afflicted with my delay. The luggage was already on the plane, whose engines turned at full force, in the middle of the Purus River, letting out a threatening roar. Trunks of trees floated downstream, ripped from the banks by the strong current, swollen by the rains. I unloaded the gun into the air, in a dramatic salvo, hugged my friends one last time, and boarded the canoe. The skipper pointed to the Catalina. From the back door, somebody threw a rope and we started the bailing operation. I was the penultimate in the canoe. Behind me was only one of the doctors, Jaime Balmes. I was almost at the door, obeying screams of the crew.

"Quick! We're taking off."

Then my turn came. The engines were already at full throttle and the plane started to move upstream, creating waves that overflowed the canoe. I felt my foot sinking as I stepped on the bow, but, in a sprightly jump, landed on my stomach, my torso in the plane.

"Hold on," I yelled, passing the rope to Jaime, who grabbed it at the last moment, when the bow of the canoe was already under water.

At this point the plane already had a considerable speed. The head of Jaime disappeared under the water to reappear moments later. This repeated itself with greater intensity, as the speed of the aircraft increased and the tension on the rope grew. I will never forget the despair in his eyes. The poor fellow was drowning. With all the force of my twenties I pulled the rope toward me, lying on the floor of the plane. I finally gained a few yards and grabbed Jaime by the back of his belt. With a quick movement, I flipped him inside. A quick thought ran through my mind: take this, doctor!

"What is that bullshit about shooting in the air? This is not a cowboy movie," warned the sergeant, asking me for the revolver. From inside the plane came the same rough voice that we already knew: Major Boris.

"I was about to leave you all here for a week longer. Didn't you hear our radio orders?" he screamed, while the airplane floated for a moment, avoiding a large tree trunk, and finally lifted off.

"Look at the river!"

I looked back and my last Pauiní vision was that of a capsized canoe floating downstream, the skipper grabbing the engine.

In Lábrea the plane boarded a rubber tapper who had been bitten by a snake. His swollen leg and sad look already foreshadowed death. A city dweller also entered the plane, frightened eyes and sweaty forehead.

"I was in the plane that went down here," he said, his nervous look staring at the river as if the fact were to repeat itself. "The hull was torn by a tree and I managed to escape through the hole, swimming."

The smell of the rubber tapper's leg, I'll never forget it even if I live one thousand years. It was a mixture of rotting flesh and poison, and we, the cowards, moved to the front part of the Catalina, leaving the man on a stretcher in the back, until the authoritative voice of Major Boris sent us back.

"Move back! Have to keep the airplane load balanced."

Upon arrival in Porto Velho, this time housed in the barracks of the Military Police, we began our wait for the second stage, transportation to São Paulo and from there to our home city of Belo Horizonte. The 5th BEC was receiving the return of the troops from the camps and many had malaria. An officer who served in these days told me that 30 percent of his troop was always under the effect of malaria during the rainy season. At the camps, he had to make a clearing with a 500-meter radius and mount the tents in the center to minimize the risk. Mosquitoes stayed away from clear areas. The mornings and evenings were the most dangerous hours.

The days followed in monotonous succession and every afternoon we would go to the local hotel, which was next to the governor's palace. There we met a rancher from my state of Minas

Gerais who was bringing cattle along the newly opened but almost impassable BR 364. The mud holes were long and deep and tractors had to be used to extract the trucks from them. The Vice Governor would join us and we would refresh the scorching afternoons with gin and tonic, the generous rancher financing us poor students. Also congregated with us were some gentle and elegant ladies from Rio de Janeiro, who made a living in the mining districts, and were flown there every two weeks, when the miners received their paycheck. Generous, they also paid drinks for our group of starving students. Needless to say, we were penniless.

The songs of Raul and our lively conversations satisfied everyone's curiosity and made a joyful get-together. When we returned to the barracks, we chatted into the night with the guard, an old soldier, pure Indian, who told us stories of the Madeira-Mamoré railroad construction, where so many suffered and many died for Brazil to win the state of Acre from Bolivia.

"The Cinta Larga raised a hell and many people died from their arrows," he would say, and follow with a fantastic story.

Sadly, the diary that I kept was stolen, together with my luggage, at the Denver Airport, and the stories that I had collected, together with the Aporinan dictionary that I had painfully assembled, are lost forever.

It was in Porto Velho that I learned that our grumpy Major Boris, who had taken us to the heart of the Amazon and brought us back with great difficulty and at considerable risk, had participated in a rescue operation. He had taken part in the search for the survivors of a C 47 loaded with soldiers in the previous year, lost in the jungle, and his insistence and shrewdness had been instrumental in their discovery. He had done this by landing along little known rivers and asked, personally, the riverine inhabitants if they had heard the roar of an airplane. Finally, he found someone, and it was thus that the search party identified the area where the airplane had fallen.

If there are heroes in Brazil, they are the explorers who criss-crossed this Amazonian wilderness with a minimum of equipment, many of whom left their life in these inhospitable shores. At the end of my stay in the Amazon, I made a solemn vow to return. I dreamt of traversing on foot the large distances between the rivers, that were the actual arteries of communications, braving dangers and discovering new Indian tribes. This secret promise stayed with me and was reawakened by the reading of "The River of Doubt." Many obstacles lay ahead of me but I knew where the beginning was.

CHAPTER 3

INDIGENOUS PEOPLE: PARECIS AND NAMBIKWARAS

Early Brazilians divided Indians into two groups: Tupi-Guarani and Tapuias. The first designation applied to all 'good' Indians who could be tamed, converted and transformed into labor in the new society. Tapuias were the wild Indians. The name 'Tapuia' comes from the Guarani language, meaning "cannot speak straight." During my school years, this denomination was still taught in our school.

Our understanding of the native inhabitants of the Americas has improved remarkably over the past thirty years. The drastic depopulation that took place shortly after the discovery of the Americas is one of the great tragedies of modern times. Although the estimates vary, it can be safely said that 80% of the Indians succumbed as a result of contact with the 'civilizers'. It is nowadays accepted that the Indian population in the Americas was in the range of 60-80 million. These numbers come from historical accounts as well as archeological evidence. Thus, the population compared with that of Europe, west of the Urals, during the time of the discovery. It is also reported that we know the population of the Americas more accurately than that of Europe.

The principal agents of change were diseases brought over, to which the Europeans had developed some immunity. Smallpox and measles ravaged entire populations. There was no cattle in the Americas and the closeness to it conferred some kind of protection to Europeans, since smallpox originated in it. Even the flu was mortal to the Indians. I recall well the reading of my history books placing the blame squarely on the Indians. The books stated that the Indians would combat fever by entering into cold water and that this led invariably to pneumonia and death. We know now that this is not the case. They would develop 'melancholy' when forced by the white colonizers to abandon their existence for that of the settler. They would rather die than subject to boring day-to-day labor. These were all false conclusions based on real facts: the Indians succumbed when in close contact with the colonizers. However, the real cause was their low immunity, which still plagues the Indians.

It should also be mentioned that the Roosevelt-Rondon expedition took place four hundred years after the discovery of America. For four centuries, Indians had been hunted for slave labor. This practice only ended in the early 20th century in the Amazon. Thus, populations had been displaced, wars started, migrations forced. Isolated Indian tribes had fair knowledge of civilized man long before they were contacted. Even their language incorporated Portuguese words, transmitted by a diffusion process. They were fully aware and coveted the steel implements carried by whites: knives, machetes, axes, and pots. In some cases, mixing of blood could already be perceived prior to direct contact.

But I should start with my own personal experiences, which shall set the stage for the subsequent description. I must have been seven years old when I went for the first time to the movies with my father. All I recall are brutal scenes of a circle of soldiers dressed in blue, protected behind dead horses, firing at Indians that galloped around them, emitting war cries. Much later, I realized that this was Custer's last stand, in Little Big Horn.

In my hometown of Monlevade, east of Belo Horizonte, and

not too far from the Doce River Valley, I overheard our gardener, Carlos Calixto Moreira, describe some people with brown skin and straight black hair that knew everything about the forest and had taught him to make bows and arrows, something that he repeated at my request. However, his bow was poor, although he claimed that he knew what wood he had to use: the stem of a coconut tree. I inquired whether they were Indians, and he simply answered: "Puri."

Monlevade was in an old gold mining region and the population was mainly composed of whites, blacks, and the many shades in between. Occasionally, one would see someone with Indian features, such as our maid, Raimundinha. Later, I learned that there was such a Puri tribe in the region, in the brink of extinction.

My fascination with this mysterious race continued unabated, and my readings led me to an idealized image of them, as presented in the novels by José de Alencar, one of the best known Brazilian writers from the romantic period. The noble savage Peri saves his beloved Ceci from being killed by a vicious Tamoio. Good Indians side with white men, and bad Indians are their enemies. In Brazil, those were the Tapuias. The greatest Brazilian opera, O Guarani, has the same theme: idealized noble Indians and nubile white maidens.

I had the chance to see my first Indian when we went fishing in the Araguaia River. On a second trip, we arrived in Aruanã and there I met a proud Xavante, who told me that he had walked three days to arrive at the town. Farther down the river, we came across Carajás that I already knew, recognizable by the circles tattooed on their cheeks. The Xavante had his hair cropped in front and carried it long in the back. Tall and lanky, he had strong Asiatic features and carried himself with great dignity.

During my visit to the Purus River, we went up the Aporinan

with the local priest on his yearly trip to baptize children. What I saw were the sad remains of a village that had been in the past probably a vibrant community. Several of the Indians had features that clearly showed mixed blood. The process of transformation from Indian to *Caboclo* was well under way. They performed their ritual dance, the *Xingané*, but the entire feast lacked enthusiasm and they were happier listening to country music on the radio. A number of them were extremely pale, and the priest explained to me that malaria was endemic in the area. Following the local tradition, we had fired shots before arriving, a well-accepted custom and etiquette. They did not appreciate visitors arriving without announcing themselves.

It was only many years later that I was able to see Indians in their natural habitat, preserved by FUNAI in the Xingu River. As we flew into the village where the Quarup festival would be held, we witnessed how deforestation had ravaged the land that surrounded their reservation. The head waters of the river were being logged and burned for agriculture. The Caiapós in the Xingu River are considered poster Indians of FUNAI and are routinely used as government propaganda for foreign dignitaries and journalists. Nevertheless, my impression was extremely positive and the Quarup celebrations were a touching event that I shall never forget.

So, other than the well protected Xingu Indians, I have only encountered, in my travels, and through my readings, the scattered remains of ancient cultures. In my state, Minas Gerais, the newspaper Estado de Minas periodically reported on poor and decaying villages in the north: the Maxacalis and Pataxós, reduced to poor *caboclos,* hillbillies. Thus, the current distribution of Indians in Brazil represents the crumbs found under the table after a meal. This meal was savored by the Portuguese invaders, who first used one tribe against another tribe, or against invaders (French and Dutch). Then, the expanding economy needed

The Roosevelt-Rondon expedition met Pareci Indians as the telegraph line was constructed. These Indians were employed by the Telegraph Commission. They were already dressed like average peasants in these regions, the *caboclos*. A number of Parecis worked for Rondon's outfit and at the telegraph stations; small settlements also existed, where they had agricultural subsistence plantations. Roosevelt describes the Pareci Indians as "cheerful, good-humored, pleasant-natured people", but remarks that they had bad teeth. Indeed, in all my travels through Brazil, this was uniformly the case and I attribute it to the large amounts of sugar in the diet of the *caboclo* and the virtual absence of dental hygiene and care. The dentists that traveled through these regions were self-taught practitioners and limited themselves to extractions. It was common to see people in their teens with a mouthful of rotten teeth. This tooth decay could have easily been prevented by brushing or by dental procedures. In contrast, the Indians in the natural state have good teeth since they only have occasional access to sugar, primarily through honey and fruit.

Roosevelt finds the Parecis 'strong and vigorous' and describes the gradual manner in which Rondon was bringing them to the civilized world. Rondon had guided them in the construction of houses similar to the ones used by the peasants. The men were dressed, but many of the women were stark naked, especially the young girls. They only had a loin cloth; however, they wore necklaces and bracelets. Roosevelt, always the scientist, observes that the women were well treated and that the boys did not bully the girls as they did with smaller boys.

The highlight of Roosevelt's visit to the Pareci village by the Utiarity Falls was a 'headball' game in which all the men took part with great enthusiasm. This is similar to our informal soccer games, except that the rubber ball, hollow and about 8 inches, could only be touched with the head. Similar to soccer, when the ball fell beyond the sidelines, it was retrieved and the game restarted. The Parecis showed great skill and stamina in these games. The number of players in each team was flexible. The game started with the ball on the ground. One of the players dived and hit it with the head, lifting it in the process.

Roosevelt refers to the Nambikwara for the first time at the Utiarity Falls. Apparently, there had been a raid by the latter against the Parecis, supposedly when the men were out. These raids were not uncommon, the purpose being the kidnapping of women and stealing of a variety of implements. Mané Manduca, our guide during the crossing of the Nambikwara lands, confirmed that in the old days they would close all the armadillo holes with branches and leaves prior to an attack. This was a meticulous job and prepared the raiding group against spirits that could eventually get out of the ground and defend the prospective victims. Roosevelt describes the incident, in which one Nambikwara was killed, and proceeds to provide details of the encounter. Roosevelt, like Rondon and all explorers at his time, considered the civilizing mission of the white man a sacred task.

A few days later, and in their trip north, close to the Juruena River, they met the first Nambikwara. These Indians had only been pacified by Rondon a few years earlier. Roosevelt describes their bows and arrows in some detail, the former being seven feet long and the latter, about five feet. These bows are larger than the English longbows, and it would be interesting to establish their performance in comparison. Since they are so large, the handle is not symmetrically placed. There were three types of arrow tips: blunt for birds, sharp for larger game and barbed arrows that would be poison-coated and protected in a long hollow guard. The latter were destined for humans, according to Roosevelt. Roosevelt was not impressed by the archery skills demonstrated by the Nambikwara.

Again, Roosevelt's comments were positive, and he describes how the women were as well fed as the men. He was preoccupied with abusive behavior and commented on how he did not see any brutality toward women or children. He also commends Rondon for having, in previous expeditions, instilled confidence and trust in the Indians.

The expedition encounters groups of Nambikwara again after Vilhena. In the latter group, different facial features are observed: beard and kinkier hair. Roosevelt was informed that mixing of blood with Negroes might have occurred earlier, through runaway slaves. The houses in the village resembled slightly the African beehive huts, reinforcing this hypothesis.

Apparently, several of the women had been taken from other villages after their husbands and/or fathers had been killed.

These Indians did not make hammocks, and slept on the ground. Their shelters were extremely simple and consisted of palm hatches tied together at an angle of about 45 degrees to the ground, forming a protection from the sun. On our trip back from the Roosevelt River, we stopped at a road side store. I could see a couple of kids at the door. At a distance, there was such a temporary camp by a stream showing that the habits of these Indians did not change significantly and that their desire for nomadism is still alive.

Twenty-five years after Roosevelt, in 1939, Claude Lévi-Strauss conducted a famous expedition throughout Brazil described in his classic book "Tristes Tropiques." He met the Nambikwara and documented their customs. The photographs shown in "Saudade do Brasil" confirm Roosevelt's description. Totally naked, they travel in small groups, carrying baskets that are attached to their heads by a strip of bark. Lévi-Strauss confirms the variation among the physical features of men, some of whom have a hooked nose and a significant amount of facial hair. The Nambikwaras lived in the *cerrado*, savannah-like vegetation consisting of sparsely distributed trees and grasses of the central Brazilian plateau.

These isolated groups of Indians, researched by Lévi-Strauss in the 1930s, are now recognized to be what remained after the triple tragedy that came upon the inhabitants from the Americas as a result of Columbus' discovery: diseases, slavery, and forced integration into the colonial society. The numbers are staggering. In Mexico, the population was reduced from 25 million to 700,000 in less than 200 years. The Indians in South America did not fare much better, and recent discoveries confirm the report by Frey Gaspar de Carbajal of the Orellana Expedition of 1542: the Amazon was heavily populated. Although the terrain, vegetation and climate are not proper for large-scale agriculture, archeological findings of specific regions of *terra preta* (black soil) and *terra mulata* (brown soil) suggest that the Indians had developed special methods of soil enrichment that stimulated increased fertility of the soil.

These are recent findings, but it is now clear that major population centers existed in the Beni region of Bolivia, in the Xingu basin, in the Tapajós, and in the Marajó Island. There is significant controversy in this respect, but Lévi-Strauss estimates the population of the Amazon basin to have been between 7 and 8 million in pre-Columbian times. Although this is still a matter of hot debate, it seems that the population of the Americas was equal to that of Europe. The city of Tenotchititlan, which became modern day Mexico City, at 100,000, was larger than London at the time of the conquest.

The Nambikwara suffered two major smallpox outbreaks, in 1945 and 1975, and their population was reduced to 700-800. However, they have now recovered from these catastrophic losses in reservations around the city of Vilhena, our operational base.

Roosevelt never met the Cinta Larga, and this was indeed fortuitous. The initial plan of the expedition was to descend the Ananás River after completing the mapping of the River of Doubt. The immense difficulties encountered in the first stage led to the postponement of the second stage. In 1915, the expedition led by Lieutenant Marques de Souza under the auspices of the Telegraph Commission, was attacked by the Indians and its commander killed. The same fate would have met Roosevelt and Rondon had they had attempted this descent.

CHAPTER 4

RONDON

I stand here, by the water that gently laps my feet. This beach is so different from Copacabana or Ipanema, where short waves slam hard on the sand and then retract, carrying with them the careless swimmer to the depths. Countless children have lost their lives, taken by the murderous waves as they advance on the sand.

Not here.

To my right and left, majestic rocks rise towards the sky. Their base is verdant with tropical plants and the tips are rounded like bald heads. The ocean ahead is blue and gentle.

This is the place, in the former Brazilian capital of Rio de Janeiro, where Rondon swam every morning during his military school days. This is where he transformed his fears into energy, his frustrations into action. While all the other cadets slept, he was up and in the water by moonlight. The frail body of a copper coloration cut through the water, guided by the determined mind. This discipline that he demanded of himself was a daily proof that his dreams would come true: he would return to his distant homeland to accomplish great deeds.

When the bugler called the awake at 6 a.m., he was already eager to go to classes, trying an impossible feat: to complete the two-year requirements in one year. Cândido Mariano da Silva Rondon was different from the other cadets, most of whom came from influential families in Brazil and belonged to the white aristocracy. Marked by his distinctive physical appearance, and devoid of the social graces that had been bred into the other cadets, he was somehow ostracized and nicknamed 'lowly brute.'

I, too, stared at this beach often, forty years ago, when I was a professor and researcher at the Military Institute of Engineering, built on the grounds of the Military Academy in the 50s. The latter was transferred to Resende, at the foothills of Black Needles, a dramatic basaltic affloration in the high mountains coasting the Atlantic. I swam these waters and dove into them, catching the occasional flounder and octopus on Saturday mornings, as the sun was rising in the ocean. So, Rondon was fortified by this daily vision and the sense of his special mission was reinforced.

The future in a comfortable setting would have been assured for him, probably in Rio de Janeiro, the Brazilian paradise for military officers, with its beautiful scenery, exciting night life, and cornucopia of military benefits. But his destiny was somewhere else, and the young boy swimming under the moonlight contemplated other horizons away from the comforts of privileged bureaucratic positions or teaching assignments, both of which he could have successfully landed, given his mathematical ability. I also dreamed on this beach, of distant parages, other places where my imagination would take flight, where my youth could find challenges. The hedonistic life of the *Carioca*, sitting on the beach, back to the nation, and turned toward Europe's latest fads, did not lure me with its siren's chant.

The boy born in Mimoso never met his parents. His father, one half Indian - as many of the people of Mato Grosso - died of smallpox before he was born. It was the year when Solano Lopez invaded Mato Grosso after access to the ocean of Paraguay, a land-locked country, was blocked by Uruguay. Rondon's mother moved to Cuiabá, the state capital, with a large number of refugees. Alas, she succumbed shortly after, also victim of smallpox. It is tragic how this disease has annihilated Indians in the Americas.

Apparently originating in camels and rodents, Europeans, Africans and Asians have developed certain immunity to its effects as the germ mutated and entered humans. But in the new hosts of the indigenous people, it wracked havoc.

Smallpox is still extremely dangerous and deadly. It is reported that in the early 2000, outbreaks decimated Yanomamo tribes and that vaccinations with live viruses actually created the disease, rather than protecting the Indians. Their extremely low immunity made them contract the virus through the vaccine.

So, the little boy was taken by his uncle and raised by him, who added his name, Rondon. This uncle had a certain status, and arranged for him to be registered in the Military Academy. Rondon refused the favor and joined the army as a regular soldier. After serving one year, he took the entrance examination and passed, in first place. The Academy was situated in Rio de Janeiro, on the shores of Praia Vermelha, the Red Beach. There, he took a deep interest in mathematics, under the tutelage of Benjamin Constant. The latter would have a significant effect on Brazil's development, since he was a follower of Auguste Comte, the father of positivism.

It is a fascinating story itself how this philosophy took hold in Brazil. Benjamin was a professor at the Military Academy. Brazil was at that time an Empire, ruled by Pedro II. He succeeded his father, who had declared independence from Portugal and was the son of the Portuguese king, Dom João VI. He belonged to the House of Orleans and Bragança, and was a fiery young man with an appetite for beautiful women, something that cost him dearly. A Habsburg princess was sent, dutifully married him and performed her marital obligations. She was serious and gifted and brought to Brazil a cohort of researchers.

The king, Dom Pedro, was called to Portugal after the death of his father. There, a war ensued with Dom Miguel, a pretender to the throne. Dom Pedro won the war but lost his life. In Brazil, his son Dom Pedro II was tutored by a brilliant scientist, José Bonifácio de Andrade, and absorbed all his advanced ideas. The situation can be likened to Alexander the Great, who was schooled by Aristoteles. José Bonifácio had a doctorate in Geology from Coimbra and had spent a good part of his life in Europe, making significant discoveries as a scientist. There is a mineral named after him, Andradite. He returned to Brazil in his fifties and was faced with many difficulties. The aristocracy was in favor of slavery, which was the motor of the Brazilian agrarian economy. Bonifácio was against it and instilled this direction in Dom Pedro II. Thus, the emperor was modern, reflecting Europe's development, while the populace was backwards. He stimulated industrial development, railroads, scientific studies, and other endeavors.

The Paraguay War was to change all. Wisely, Dom Pedro had kept the army at a minimum, knowing very well that it had the tendency to take the government by force. But the conflict necessitated rapid expansion of the military, and when that was over, it was used to maintain territorial integrity. Indeed, Brazil not only retained its unity, but expanded its borders in the west and north much beyond the initial agreements between Portugal and Spain. This process had already started much earlier, with the advances of the Brazilian *bandeirantes*. The Marquis of Pombal, who was the *de facto* ruler of Portugal from 1750 to 1780, ordered the construction of forts deep in the Amazon, in Manaus and the Guaporé River, on the current frontier with Bolivia. The construction of the forts in these inhospitable regions was a heroic feat, and the first leader died of malaria, being replaced by Ricardo Franco. His name will reappear in this book since he is considered the first great Brazilian explorer. The fact that Spain was mostly interested in controlling the regions of the Pacific also helped the Portuguese.

So, Brazil expanded and consolidated its borders under Dom Pedro, while the rest of the South and Central America, of Spanish colonization, fragmented into many countries, controlled by the local chieftains.

Many factors contributed to the more successful colonization by the Portuguese. First, the mercantile mind of the Lusitans created a global empire based on trade. The Portuguese presence was affirmed by forts along the African, Asian, and Brazilian coasts. The population of Portugal was only one million at the beginning of colonization, in the early 1500s. Of these, approximately 300,000 were able men. This diminutive contingent needed to integrate with the locals, and this was assured by early and prolific mixing. Thus, the descendants of these mixed marriages (actually, for the most part, liaisons) were catholic and therefore full parts of the nation. It is that small population that propelled the Portuguese to lead the greatest mass migration of human history, the transportation of slaves across the Atlantic. Up to the late 1600s, the tactic was to capture and enslave Indians. This depopulated the land and did not produce a reliable workforce. Diseases ravaged the Indians, the first account being that of Columbus, who brought 300 Indians to Spain in his third expedition, of which only three survived. Blacks were hardier, having been exposed to the Old-World viruses for eons. Captured by the warring factions along the Atlantic coast of Africa and kept in the forts, they were exported *en masse* in efficient but rather inhumane conditions, which the airlines are mimicking nowadays in the Economy class. The sardine can is the perfect example of tight packing, and the Portuguese seafarers devised techniques to transport a maximum load with a minimum of losses in human life. This is a sad story, but it is nothing new, slave trade being common in Africa and the Middle East before the discovery of America. The Vikings excelled at it, and Eastern European populations (Slavic comes from

Slaves) were a welcome supply for the Arab nations.

At the Military Academy in Praia Vermelha, Rondon excels in Mathematics and is guided by Benjamin Constant Magalhães, a military person with deep convictions and a disciple of Auguste Comte. The admiration of Rondon for Constant was so great that he named his first son after him. Benjamin Constant played an important role in the bloodless transition from Empire to Republic. He was the intellectual in a group of officers who succeeded in asking Dom Pedro II to resign, something he did in a most noble and dignified manner. Sent to exile in France, he died there as a commoner. This is a melancholic end to a brilliant life and a dark page in the history of Brazil. A lover of books and knowledge, he asked for his head to rest on a book at his funeral.

One more year at the Military Academy, and Rondon was promoted to Lieutenant at the age of 23. Rondon was 24 when the Republic was declared in December 1889, and he personally delivered the letter of resignation to Floriano Peixoto who was appointed the first president. Rondon taught advanced mathematics, rational mechanics, and astronomy at the Military Academy for a time and was attached to the newly formed Engineering Corps in 1890.

Positivism took root among the military class that wrestled power from Dom Pedro. The core of the Brazilian flag was changed with the removal of the imperial signs and their replacement by a globe with stars, each symbolizing a state. Across the globe, a banner with the words:

ORDER AND PROGRESS.

This was a positivist motto and its origins are in the foundation of this philosophical doctrine: Love as principle, order as foundation, progress as goal. In Brazil, Positivism became a religion and Rondon joined the Church of the Religion of Humanity in 1889. There is still one last positivist church in Brazil, a lone sentry to these high dreams. Alas, it is no longer frequented by the hedonistic atheists who have made shopping malls their cathedrals, where they worship Consumption, an important god in the new pantheon.

Unfortunately, the instauration of the republic in Brazil started a cycle of instability. A few years after being declared president, Floriano Peixoto had to renounce, passing the baton to another military, Deodoro da Fonseca. This period in Brazilian history is called "Republic of Swords." One of the reasons for the economic problems of this vast nation was its dependence on slave labor. Dom Pedro was an abolitionist and had freed his personal slaves. His daughter, Dona Isabel, had signed a law declaring that all children born of slaves would be free. However, he believed that a gradual transition would be the wisest process. Disgruntled landowners banded with the military to overthrow Dom Pedro when slavery was finally abolished one year prior to the abdication.

So, this was the political climate when Rondon, being a member of the newly-formed Corps of Engineers, was assigned the task of building a telegraph line from Goiás to Cuiabá. Shortly thereafter, he married Maria Francisca (Xiquinha) Xavier, who bore him seven children throughout the years.

From 1900 to1908, he extends the telegraph line to Bolivia and Peru. In the process, he meets Indian tribes and starts his lifelong mission of pacifying and protecting them. He might be criticized by some for having initiated the tragic cycle of neglect, disease and decadence undergone by the Indians. However, change was inevitable, the pressure of colonization stronger by the day as ranchers, gold-diggers, and other adventurers penetrated into the Brazilian west. Our current knowledge of their low immunity to our infectious diseases was absent in their days, and few realized the tragic effects of contact. It was customary, those days, to push away the Indians in order to occupy the land. Rondon was aware of this and wrote: "Hinterlands where civilized man never set foot are already included in public regions as if they belong to citizen A or B: sooner or later, according to where their personal interests be, these landowners will expel all the Indians who, by monstrous revised facts, reason and morals, will be thought of and treated as if they were intruders and thieves."

I can vouch for two episodes of my own experience.

When I was in the Purus River, in 1969, the following was relayed to me. The widow of the man who commanded the expedition was still in Pauní, but he had been assassinated by a group of Indians a few years earlier. He had been hired as a *bugreiro* (Indian hunter) to get rid of a village that conflicted with local rubber tappers. With his hired men, he arrived at night and surrounded the village from the forest. As dawn broke and the Indians went to the river to bathe, the fusillade from the forest started. The Indians were encircled and massacred. One incident that has stuck in my mind for close to half a century is the description of such barbarism against a child that held on to his moribund mother. He threw the toddler in the air and waited for him with his machete. When he came down, he was trespassed by the blade.

I witnessed a second, but less tragic report during the descent of the Roosevelt River. We stopped at a ranch on the left bank and while I guarded our equipment, my companions went to the house. They relayed to me on their return that the rancher had told them, as if he was reporting a wild story: "A few months ago, some Indians arrived and camped by the river. They claimed that this land belongs to them and that they were reclaiming it. Can you believe it?"

But today the FUNAI (National Indian Support Foundation) which represents the institution that was founded and first directed by Rondon under the name SPI (Indian Protection Institute) is present throughout the country and most Indian lands are being delineated and officialized. The wild days of *bugreiros*-the Indian hunters - are over now and this ugly wound in the colonization of Brazil is closed.

So, even prior to his major endeavor, the linking of Cáceres on the Paraguay border, to the northwest of Brazil, where Porto Velho lies, through 1,700 km of unknown jungle, Rondon had already acquired the fame as an Indian pacifier. He is called to the Rio Doce Valley, close to my hometown of Monlevade, where he pacifies the Botucudo, thus named because they used a large wooden disk inserted in a hole in their lower lip. He is sent to São Paulo for the Kaingang Indians.

The explorations that he undertakes from 1909 to 1915 have no parallel in the Brazilian history and represent one of the most extraordinary voyages undertaken in the 20th century. Three expeditions are mounted and directed by him, each one more difficult and challenging. In each one of them, approximately ten people lose their lives. He is not sent the best soldiers; to the contrary, in many cases the worst elements are transferred to him, either as punishment for their wrong doings in the army or as a good way to get rid of undesirable soldiers. Some prefer going to jail than to be sent into the jungle with him.

Rondon is, by virtue of his rigorous upbringing, a disciplinarian. He demands of his soldiers the same conduct in the jungle as in the military barracks. They line up in the morning and are read the orders. Around him congregates a cohort of superb officers, each with distinct characteristics, all imbued with the altruism and discipline that defines his mission. Several of them perish in the enterprises: Amarante, who marries his daughter and later dies of beriberi (the avenue where our hotel was located in Vilhena, was named after him); Lyra, who drowns in the Sepotuba

River; Lieutenant Marques de Souza, who dies in an Indian attack in 1915, descending the Ananás River.

These three expeditions extend the telegraph line, which in 1915 reaches a town a few kilometers from Porto Velho, on the Madeira River. Thus, the capital of Rio de Janeiro is now linked to the western frontier of the Amazon, and possession of this immense territory is ensured. Prior to this, information would take two months from the capital to Porto Velho, traveling by ocean, then up the Amazon, and finally up the Madeira River. The Madeira River is the largest affluent of the Amazon, navigable all the way to Porto Velho. Incredible difficulties were encountered by Rondon in these travels, which carried him from Tapirapoan, the operational base at the margin of the Sepotuba River, all the way to the Madeira River. In 1909 he discovers an unknown river, naming it River of Doubt. The exploration of this river, as well of that of the Papagaio and Ananás Rivers, is left for later. The visit by Roosevelt provides the unique opportunity for discovery.

In the first expedition, he made contact with the Nambikwara Indians who had never approached white men before. The Nambikwara Indians were enemies of the Parecis which already had significant contact with whites, and whose members were integrated into Rondon's teams and were hired to build the telegraph line. This was an exhausting task, with 11 posts per mile (7/km). Rondon had a team of approximately 100 soldiers under his command and progress was slow, since a wide trail had to be opened in the jungle prior to erecting the posts.

Not content with just building a telegraph line, he personally collects important ethnographic information, writes dictionaries of the various indigenous languages, of which he learned ten, and brings with him geologists, ethnographers, and naturalists. Thousands of specimens are sent to the National Museum in Rio de Janeiro. At the end of this major opus, he had laid 7,000 km of telegraph lines, crisscrossing Brazil. Alas, shortly after completion, the radio would supersede the telegraph.

CHAPTER 5

POSITIVISM

As I was strolling in Paris' left bank going towards the Luxembourg Gardens, I was faced with a large panel advertising a lotion that supposedly rendered the French women's breasts even more beautiful. There she stood, her perfect mammary glands radiating a diaphanous light. I paused for a moment, in awe. They were more feminine than those of the Venus of Milo, more elegant than the silicone contraptions so admired by Americans, more tangible than the purely functional breasts of the Asian women.

This is France!

I thought for a moment of Louis XIV's court women, who would send their babies to the countryside to be nourished by wet nurses so that their breasts would keep their perfect shape.

Ah! Gallic vanity!

Then, I continued one block and veered to my left, where I was surprised by a most dignified bust. My thoughts returned to my usual scholastic pursuits as I admired the Sorbonne portal that resembles, across the square, a chapel. A Church of Learning. I approached the bust which showed a serious person in deep thought. The eyes were fixed on infinity. Auguste Comte, the father of Positivism, stood before me. I turned to my colleague and told him that this man had a profound influence on Brazil. He smiled: "Marc, where do you get these ideas? Always exaggerating…"

And indeed, Rondon remained a positivist all his life. This philosophical doctrine came to him through Benjamin Constant

Botelho de Magalhães. A military man, he served in the Paraguay War, where he took part in armed combat. The fact that he tried to commit suicide at the early age of twelve presaged a turbulent life. I suspect that his name is a homage to the Swiss teacher and philosopher Benjamin Constant, given that the two subsequent surnames are Portuguese. This is a Brazilian custom, and Washington, Jefferson, Roosevelt, and their Soviet counterparts, Lenin and Stalin are a precious presence in the telephone directory. In my engineering school, I had two classmates named Stalin and Roosevelt. A third was called Marconi. All wonderful fellows. The numerous Brazilian families allowed for such flights of fancy. Parents could experiment with names, because there was always another baby on the way.

Benjamin, an intellectual at heart, and of the French school, was a brilliant mathematician and became an instructor at the Praia Vermelha Military Academy. Being also an ardent follower of Auguste Comte, he imparted his philosophy on his students.

So, what are the precepts of this doctrine that Benjamin Constant attempted to transform into a religion in Brazil, by founding the Church of the Religion of Humanity?

The man and his works are intimately connected. A brilliant mathematician, a condition to be a respected scholar in France, Auguste Comte (born 1798) had passed the rigorous entrance examination to the prestigious École Polytechnique at the precocious age of fourteen. Being too young, he had to wait until he was sixteen. However, Comte and his entire class were expelled before they graduated (in 1816) for political reasons and could not join the ranks of France's military elite. Thus, he had to work to support himself and therefore entered into the services of a famous philosopher and social theorist-scholar, Saint-Simon. Comte absorbed the knowledge of Saint-Simon but, at a point in their life, there was a bitter breakup, as so often happens between teacher and pupil, or father and son, when the strength of the latter ceases to accept the wisdom of the former. Comte is on his own again, and he does not have an academic position. So, he supports himself with his lectures, which are well accepted. He has been accused of stealing the teachings of his mentor, Saint-Simon, but this is a natural process. The student learns from the master and extends his thoughts. He bases the positivist philosophy on three stages of the evolution of thought.

• Theological Stage. Gods and religions dictate the thoughts of man in his attempt to comprehend the world around himself.

• Metaphysical Stage. Man, not content with his gods, seeks rational thought in his pursuit of order in the apparent chaos of the universe. Thus, the currents and ideas that evolved from Platonic to Aristotelian thinking, to modern philosophies, fall under this category.

• Positive Stage. Science rules! Comte organized the sciences in a hierarchical fashion, from a most fundamental (mathematics) to astronomy, physics, chemistry, physiology (equivalent to our biology) and, finally, the study of entire human societies. As science increases in complexity, the ability of mathematics to capture all its phenomena decreases. Hence, sciences become less mathematical as one ascends the hierarchical scale. We are still faced by this conundrum today.

Like Benjamin Constant, Comte had a fragile mind, wavering at the edge of instability. He abhorred his first wife and divorced her when he was 44, and had a breakdown following the separation. Later, he met a lady, Clotilde de Vaux, who was to become the love of his life. For her he abandoned the pursuit of the beautiful-breasted women of Paris, for which he was well known. He adored Clotilde and put her on a pedestal, but she refused to share her bed with him, challenging him to transform his love for her into a spiritual guiding energy in his life. Alas, she died at 31, four years after he met her. We are not aware of the consummation of their union. He became increasingly religious, although he did not believe in the conventional God of Christianity. His mysticism is a strange feeling and his attempt to unite science and religion represents a formidable intellectual undertaking. This last stage of Comte's thoughts, under the spiritual influence of Clotilde de Vaux, was redacted in the book "Catéchisme Positiviste", published in 1852.

Comte had abandoned any belief in God by the time he was fourteen. Thus, it is ironic that, in his later years, he was consumed by a broad attempt to create the equivalent of a modern religion based on science, while shedding a belief in the supernatural. He accepted ritual and tried to achieve a mystical synthesis with science and knowledge. In this sense, he was different from the post-revolution rationalists that rampaged the churches desecrating holy sites, digging up the bones of saints, and abhorred all form of worship. Even Mary Magdalene was a victim of their wrath. Comte replaced the calendar of saints with scientists (positive heroes) and established meditative periods as a replacement for prayer. At the age of sixty, exhausted and destitute, he becomes sick and dies. The Englishman John Stuart Mills and wealthy patrons supported his meager existence.

It should be mentioned that Brazil has always been a profoundly religious country, one in which sin (a frequent event) is juxtaposed with virtue (often a vain attempt to reach higher spiritual levels). The strong influence of the Catholic faith has been often countered by other movements that also acquired religious characteristics. Thus, the teachings of Alan Kardek and spiritualism took a stronger hold in Brazil than in Europe. The Brazilian Spiritual Union is well-organized, with churches and followers in every town. The African religions were transformed and blended with Christianity, and *macumba* rituals are common place and well accepted by society. It is perfectly accepted to take part in *macumba* rituals, usually at night, and to attend Catholic Church in the morning. The African religions are usually known as "Low Spiritualism", in contrast with "High Spiritualism". More recently, the evangelical churches have made deep inroads into Brazil, and a variety of millionaire bishops command vast churches that have become economic empires. However, the Catholic Church has counterattacked, modernizing its rituals and imbuing them with the fresher aspects of the evangelical rites. Masonry continues to be popular in Brazil with many loges throughout the country. This is a more vibrant environment than the religious indifference displayed by the blasé Europeans, intent only at seeking their hedonistic pleasures. They usually worship the Sun God on the beaches of the south during their sacrosanct vacations.

Hence, Rondon's joining of the Church of the Religion of Humanity in 1898, most probably at the insistence of Benjamin Constant, is completely normal in Brazilian society. He adhered to its principles until the end of his life. Such was his admiration for his tutor that he named his son by the name of Benjamin Constant Rondon. It is ironic but also typical of Brazil, that one of his grandsons became a Catholic priest.

Benjamin Constant was an ardent republican and plotted tirelessly to remove the Emperor, Dom Pedro II, whom he considered archaic. He created the Military Club, an assembly of officers that paved the way for the republic. This represented the future, the logic extension of the positivist thought. This was accomplished peacefully in December 1889. Two years later, Benjamin Constant, the father of the republic, dies at the early age of 53. There is a city in the Amazon by this name and it is probable that this was done at the instigation of Rondon. The trust that Benjamin Constant deposited in him is demonstrated when he was asked to carry the Proclamation.

In order to put into perspective the diffusion of positivism in Brazil, one should consider that Benjamin Constant was born in 1836, only thirty-eight years after Comte. Thus, positivism was still a young and fresh philosophy when it was absorbed by the young soldier, who had also other important tasks, such as fighting a war in distant Paraguay. The introduction of these new ideas into Brazil, and more importantly, into Rondon's bright mind, was a wind of fresh air that had lasting consequences. When Rondon marched into the west and started his life-long mission, he carried inside the intellectual framework to which he would adhere throughout his life:

Love as principle
Order as foundation
Progress as goal.

It is fitting that these words are carved in his tombstone. Curiously, Rondon died on Comte's birthday.

This intellectual framework manifested itself in the most poignant manner throughout his life, dedicated to the welfare of the Indians. Out of this came the lemma of his mission: "Die, if necessary. Never kill." It might be paradoxical for a military officer, but it sums his belief, that has unfortunately not been shared by Brazilians.

It is rumored in the recondite areas of Brazil that Rondon had many liaisons in his explorations. This was told me during my Rondon Project days, in 1969, when we went up the Aporinan River. A teacher in a Pareci village, Sandra Azomaizokero, confided to us:

"I met an old lady in the Sacre village, 115 years old, who told me that she became Rondon's girlfriend when she was twelve."

I did the mathematics: 2010-115+12=1907. So, this would indeed be possible.

"She would follow Rondon on his travels through our lands after this," she said.

Later, I saw a couple of photographs of Rondon at Utiarity Falls. Indeed, a young girl had her hand on his shoulder to indicate, perhaps, possession, or at least an emotional closeness.

"But she did not bear him a baby," she concluded. It is was also whispered to me that he has descendants in Jatobá village.

A local inhabitant of the Purus River told me, in 1969: "The Amazon is full of Rondonzinhos, little Rondons." But these unions, accepted in the past, represent the continuation of a process of formation of the Brazilian nation. Were it not for these, homogeneous population blocks would have formed and eventually would lead to segregation, which is opposite to integration. These bonds of blood consolidated the Brazilian nation and gave it its unique character.

CHAPTER 6

ROOSEVELT

A parallel can be traced between Rondon and Roosevelt, although they differ in almost everything. The contrast that they present is fascinating, for both reached unequaled fame in their respective countries, and both are heroes worshipped by millions. Rondon has a state named after him, Rondonia, and three cities: Rondonópolis, Marechal Cândido Rondon, and Rondon do Pará. He is also the patron of the Brazilian Army Communications Service.

Roosevelt is a hero on his own, and in a country that abhors monuments, the naming of streets, cities and parks, he shines above all other presidents. There is a shrine in South Dakota, Mount Rushmore, where the heads of four great American presidents are carved: Washington, Lincoln, Jefferson, and Roosevelt. Thus, through radically different paths, in two cultures that have often antagonic characteristics, the Anglo-Saxon and the Latin, these two men forged paths that led them to the pantheon of heroes.

Roosevelt was born in 1858, seven years prior to Rondon (1865). Whereas Rondon came from a small town, Mimoso, in the Brazilian hinterland, Roosevelt was the scion of a wealthy New York family and was raised in the cosmopolitan environment of that city.

Both men took an active part in momentous events in their respective countries: Rondon by delivering the letter that would declare Brazil a Republic at the young age of 24, Roosevelt, by being a Rough Rider in the Spanish-American War and personally commanding and leading an attack riding a horse in Cuba. This marked the beginning of American global hegemony. Both Rondon and Roosevelt were to reach early fame and were, in their lifetime, put on high pedestals. However, this did not deter them from pursuing their explorations into unknown lands, for the entirety of their lives, driven by their adventurous spirits.

On the personal side, both were prolific procreators: Roosevelt had six children, whereas Rondon had seven, not counting the children he left throughout the Amazon. Both were avid readers and favored classics. Rondon would take books on his expedition, tearing each page as he finished reading it, to lighten the load. Roosevelt describes with a certain pride the books that he read, including Dante. In his report about the River of Doubt expedition, Roosevelt names the Oxford Book of French Verse, Ronsard, Joaquim De Bellay, Eustache Deschamps, brought by his son, Kermit. These books, more entertaining, relieved him from heavier reading that he had brought on the expedition: Gibbon, "La chanson de Roland," "Quentin Dunant."

Throughout his life, Roosevelt was an avid reader. This passion manifested itself early. Already a scholar during his university days, he studied the naval battles of the 1812 independence war and published "The Independence War of 1812" which is a treatise that is still read today. It is a detailed analysis and systematic study of the U.S. and British navies during the war. As a historian, he read the primary sources from the U.S. Navy records. The book contains detailed sketches and technical evaluations of high caliber.

After Harvard—where he entered with a primary interest in biology—he was accepted at the Columbia Law School. Bored with the irrationality of law, he never finished his studies and went into politics, instead.

Roosevelt was home-schooled and developed an early interest for biology as he observed a dead seal at the local market in New York. He obtained the head and created, in his house, the 'Roosevelt Museum of Natural History' filling it with animals that he had caught. He learned the rudiments of taxidermy. At nine years of age, he wrote a paper entitled 'The Natural History of Insects.'

But Roosevelt and Rondon's ancestors couldn't have been any more different.

Roosevelt's grand-father was Dutch (Cornelius Van Schaack Roosevelt) and furthermore, he had Welsh, English, Irish and French ancestry. In contrast, Rondon was Indian, Portuguese, and Spanish. Roosevelt's father had risen to prominence in New York, having helped to found the Metropolitan Museum of Art. Rondon's parents were dead before he knew them.

Roosevelt was a weak and sickly child and was diagnosed as being asthmatic. Vigorous exercise throughout his life minimized its effects. On a camping trip, he was bullied by two boys. This stimulated him to take up boxing, a sport he practiced throughout his life. At Harvard, he was the runner-up in the boxing championships. If one looks carefully at his photographs, one can distinguish a 'boxer nose.' Even as president in the White House, he practiced the 'sweet science' with sparring partners. A well-placed punch blinded one of his eyes, something he kept secret. Thus, the sickly boy became an athlete. Once entering a bar, he was challenged by a couple of patrons. He took them out and beat them both. Rondon became seriously ill during his Military Academy days and almost died.

We find a parallel with Rondon, who was also a highly-disciplined man and showed great personal courage on a few occasions. This was demonstrated in a couple of revolts of his troops that he squelched with great energy, riding his horse back to the barracks and asking the troops 'to get in form.' He delivered corporal punishment by caning the culprits. This was done so energetically once, that one of them succumbed, having his lung perforated by the bamboo. In one of his expeditions, Rondon contracted malaria and was weakened to the point that he was put on a horse. After a while, he refused, preferring to march with his sick soldiers.

The traits of personal, physical courage of these two men manifested themselves throughout their lives.

Roosevelt helped to form the "Rough Riders" unit during the Spanish-American War. This was an assembly of volunteers made up of Eastern gentlemen, hunters, armchair athletes, Western cowboys, and Indians. They were transported to Cuba on June 23, 1898 after training in Texas. This is a legendary period in Roosevelt's life, and the heroism displayed by the troops is inscribed in the history books. After a few short skirmishes, the Rough Riders had a major confrontation in Kettle Hill on July 1st. Roosevelt commanded the assault, which was almost suicidal. The U.S. lost 200 men and had 1,000 wounded; however, the hill was taken. Roosevelt had the only horse and rode from fire pit to fire pit, encouraging the troops. He had been promoted to colonel prior to this engagement, a title that he appreciated all his life, since he abhorred his nickname Teddy.

The Spanish troops were protected by trenches and Roosevelt commented on the battle in the following manner: "On the day of the big fight I had to ask my men to do a deed that European military writers consider utterly impossible of performance, that is, to attack over open ground on unshaken infantry armed with the best modern repeating rifles behind a formidable system of entrenchments. The only way to get them to do it in the way to be done was to lead them myself."

He was denied the Medal of Honor because regular army officials were ensconced by his bravado and by the publicity of the stunt and blocked it. This medal was finally given posthumously, in 2004.

Much later, during WWI and after his descent of the River of Doubt, Roosevelt tried hard to reform the Rough Riders unit and planned to take it to Europe. He was an early supporter of the Allies. The isolationist policy of President Wilson was severely criticized by him. The honor of riding into Europe was denied him by jealous politicians, and the regular Army was sent to Europe in 1917.

In this, his sanguine approach to conflict, he differs greatly from Rondon, who was a pacifist at heart and had as a principal concern throughout his life the protection of the Indians. Rondon considered the civilized man as an intruder into the Indians' lives. Roosevelt was an energetic representative of Anglo-Saxon puritanism and his moral and ethical values are admirable but nevertheless harsh to the less gifted. He was in favor of sterilization of criminals and his words are:

"I wish very much that the wrong people could be prevented entirely from breeding; and when the evil nature of these people is sufficiently flagrant, they should be sterilized and feeble-minded people forbidden to leave offspring behind them."

It should be emphasized that eugenics was widely accepted as a scientific approach to social evolution in the beginning of the 20th century. After the Nazi excesses of WWII, it took a more ominous connotation.

In his life, Roosevelt authored about 18 books and his style is, in places, poetic. Indeed, Robert Frost considered Roosevelt 'of our kind.' Roosevelt also read poetry, which made him explore the mysterious recesses of our spirit. Here is an excerpt from 'Through the Brazilian Wilderness.'

"Great azure butterflies flitted through the open sunny glades, and the bellbirds, sitting motionless, uttered their ringing calls from the dark stillness of the columned groves".

The love of nature and freedom which permeated Roosevelt's life also was a guiding light for Rondon, who continued his explorations after completing the construction of the telegraph, in 1915. He was given the job of mapping Mato Grosso, which he concluded in 1919. Later, when already a general, he was given the task of checking the entire length of the Brazilian borders. He conducted his extensive travels in his late 50s. However, in Rondon's case, the concern was primarily with Indians. He endeavored to find a way to bring them into the civilized society while preserving their well-being. He is singularly responsible for avoiding the total obliteration of the native populations in Brazil. In the 1950s, Rondon supported the creation of the Xingu National Park, which protected the Indians that had been pacified by the Villas-Boas brothers. I personally visited one of their villages in 2010 and I can vouch for the energy and health of their communities. The participation in their yearly celebrations, the Quarup, was a momentous event for me. Had it not been for the protection by FUNAI, these communities would have followed the disintegration and decadence of so many other Indian groups whose fragmented remains are a sad testament to the destructive activity of the *civilizados* as the Brazilian colonists call themselves euphemistically. Greedy, yes, ruthless, yes, but civilized, no. Rondon also understood that the protection of indigenous tribes required the demarcation of their territories. In this manner, nature was and is being simultaneously preserved through the strategy of creating indigenous areas.

Roosevelt's approach to nature was quite different. He did not show great admiration for the Indians in the U.S., and some of his comments are, actually, quite derogatory. He said, in his youth: "I don't go so far as to think that only good Indians are dead Indians, but I believe nine out of ten are, and I shouldn't like to inquire too closely into the case of the tenth."

This attitude is the result of the Anglo-Saxon Protestant vision of the world, conflicting radically with the Indian Cosmology. I have witnessed it in South Dakota in the 1970s. There is no middle ground between the Northern European settlers and Indians. Their worlds are utterly incompatible.

However, in his book on Brazil, Roosevelt refrains from any pejorative remarks about the different races. On the contrary, he shows admiration and approval for the manner in which Brazilians show acceptance of each other and about the harmony among the *camaradas* in the expedition, which represented the Brazilian mix. Indeed, a white man was the worst of the bunch, shooting Paixão, a black man, in the back, in a most cowardly fashion.

About the Indians, Roosevelt discusses the Pareci and Nambikwara. The latter had only established contact with the previous Rondon expeditions a few years before. With an ethnologist's eye for detail, he describes their features, habits, dances and other characteristics with no prejudice. During the descent of the river, he is more sanguine than Rondon, and states that, faced with the dilemma of being trespassed by arrows and defending himself he would, without hesitation, choose the latter. But his main interests are animals, and he describes in detail the birds, reptiles, mammals, and fish encountered by the expedition. With him are Cherrie and Miller, accomplished ornithologist and naturalist (mammologist is the term used by Roosevelt), respectively. They use the standard techniques of the time. A 16-caliber shotgun for birds, bringing them down from their branches, and well-placed bullets from Kermit's and Teddy's rifles for the large game. It is interesting how Roosevelt masks his passion for hunting, whose excitement he clearly enjoys, with a final statement of justification: "Splendid specimens that will be sent to the Museum."

However, although modern readers criticize this behavior, it should be understood in the context of the time. The immense Amazon basin, equal in the size to the U.S., contained at that time uncountable numbers of animals, and the collection of a few specimens did not alter the ecology in any manner. Indeed, the scientific knowledge gained from this task had, in the long run, a beneficial effect on these species because of the documenting factor.

The destruction of habitat is by far the greatest danger to animal species, and the inexorable advance of our civilization into these areas is the largest threat. Roosevelt did a great deal in this respect. At an early age, he had the opportunity to visit the American West. Shortly after the double tragedy that marked him for life, the loss of his first wife, Alice, and mother, Mettie, on the same day, February 12, 1884, he retired, at 26, to a ranch in North Dakota. But a year later, he returned to political life, his cattle having died in the 1886-87 winter, and he moved to the East. However, the ranching days in North Dakota had left an indelible impression on him. He lost most of his investment when his cattle died, but gained an extraordinary conception of the vastness of the US and of the necessity to preserve its nature.

In North Dakota, he formed the Boone and Crockett Club and worked toward the conservation of large game and its habitat. This knowledge and concern would later lead to his support of the national parks in the US.

The schooling of Rondon and Roosevelt was quite different, and they gravitated towards different disciplines. While Roosevelt was strong in Geography, History, Biology and Literature, he struggled with Mathematics. Rondon was the opposite, excelling in the latter discipline, considered by the French as the foundation of science. If we compare the two, Roosevelt had a broader reach, which he expanded as he governed the U.S. and was its president for almost two terms. Politically, he proposed the Square Deal, and attacked trusts and the corrupt practices of big business. This put him on the left of the Republican Party. Rondon, being a military officer, stayed far from politics in spite of his early involvement in the formation of the republic and a brief period in which he was imprisoned for siding with the legal forces after the Getulio Vargas coup.

Prior to 1913, when they met, Roosevelt had had a mercurial career, being the youngest president of the United States. At age 42, he had had a major involvement in the Spanish-American War, and supported the occupation of the Philippines; he had masterminded the political moves that created the Panama Canal; he had been shot in the chest during a political campaign. His breadth of activity was wider and his fame had reached the Nobel Commission, which awarded him the Peace Prize for negotiating the Japan-Russia agreement that ended their conflict. He had widely traveled and visited Europe and Egypt as an adolescent. Rondon did not have these opportunities. He was crisscrossing some of the most difficult regions of the world, and his vision was, by necessity, a narrower one. In his later years, he was given the task to delimit the northwest borders of Brazil with the Guianas, Venezuela, Colombia, Peru, and Bolivia, a difficult and important job. Eventually, he also nominated for the Nobel Prize, but did not reach this honor, unjustly.

During the years preceding their meeting in Porto Murtinho, Rondon had become a legendary explorer and fierce defender of the rights of the Indians. His work was vastly ignored in the world. This reflected Brazil's isolationism. Wrestling with a country of continental dimensions, the young Brazilian republic had turned inwards. The empire had fostered a great era of collaboration with Europe, that unfortunately waned as the new elite stepped up. And so, Rondon was a man of the Brazilian hinterland, deeply embedded into its vastness, struggling with a superhuman task of building a telegraph line covering the territory never traversed before by civilized man.

Religiously, Rondon abandoned the Catholic faith to embrace Positivism with all his fervor. He stayed loyal to the Positivist vision to the end, with love, order, and progress as his guiding values. Roosevelt was a product of the Protestant faith, which had strong puritanical foundations. He saw the effects of alcoholism in his bright and handsome older brother, who would die at 35. His son, Kermit, who would commit suicide in his forties, was also an alcoholic. Thus, Roosevelt was a strong believer in religion for the survival of communities.

In 'Through the Brazilian Wilderness' he writes: "A very short experience of communities where there is no church ought to convince the most heterodox of the absolute need of a church."

Later in the book, he states, after commenting that Brazil's major religion is Catholicism: "...but the spiritual needs of a more or less considerable minority will best be met by the establishment of Protestant churches, or in places, even the Positivist Church or Ethical Culture Society."

He argues that conduct is of much greater importance than dogma, concluding that "...no democracy can afford to overlook the vital importance of the ethical and spiritual, the truly religious element in life."

These two sentences, of their own coining, perhaps best summarize the beliefs of these men:

Roosevelt: "Speak softly and carry a big stick, and you will go far."

Rondon: "Die, if necessary, but never kill."

Roosevelt's muscular approach to democracy laid the foundation for American hegemony in the 20th century. He was courageous, kind, intelligent, and disciplined. One can hardly fathom a modern U.S. president undertaking such a perilous journey. Had he been allowed to take his Rough Riders into the Great War in Europe, the entire drawn-out battle could have been shortened and WW2 averted. But these are speculations. Although he did not start the national parks, he was a strong supporter and these monuments of nature will remain forever a collective ownership of all Americans.

CHAPTER 7

THE CINTA LARGA: VICTIMS AND AGGRESSORS

The Cinta Larga derive their name from a broad belt made of the bark of a tree that they used in the past, to wrap around their waist and forearms. Although the Roosevelt-Rondon expedition never encountered them directly, gifts for them were left during their descent of the river and collected, and vestiges of their existence were found in primitive bridges over narrows in the river and abandoned villages and plantations. There was also an incident in which one of Rondon's dogs was shot with arrows as its owner entered the riverine forest following what he thought were bird calls. Had Rondon been ahead of the dog, he would have been shot and, most probably, eaten by the Indians.

One year later, in 1915, an expedition led by Lieutenant Marques de Souza and part of the Rondon's commission, was attacked on the Ananás River. The Ananás runs parallel to the River of Doubt and is an affluent of the Aripuanã River. Marques and one of his soldiers were killed. The marauding Indians had macaw feather as ornaments and therefore were called Arara Indians (macaw, in Portuguese). In the following years, rubber tappers, gold and diamond miners sporadically had encounters with them. There were a series of violent incidents, massacres of rubber tappers and Indians following each other. They are hunter-gatherers and semi-nomadic, like most original Brazilian tribes, and cover a vast territory loosely bound by the Aripuanã and Roosevelt rivers.

As early as 1928, *bugreiros* under the direction of Julio Torres, the rubber-tapper who controlled the Aripuanã River, massacred a village of the Iamé Indians on that river. In the Cinta Larga language this is a greeting. The conflict with the rubber tappers reached a climax in 1963, when Antonio Mascarenhas Junqueira, head of the rubber-tapping enterprise Arruda Junqueira and Co. planned and executed a barbaric attack on Cinta Larga villages using dynamite thrown from Cessna airplanes, followed by an armed invasion on foot. The acts of cruelty were of a magnitude such that there was international repercussion. Apparently, there had been punitive expeditions before, in 1958, 59, 60 and 62 that went unnoticed by the press. The viewpoint of the rubber tappers is simple. They were there, carrying an important mission for the civilized society, and were periodically attacked by Indians. The fact that Indians do not take to the work of the settler-invader is another detriment, in their eyes. Rubber tappers live isolated in the forest and are easy prey to Indians that can kill them, take their pots, pans and knives and also, in the case of the Cinta Larga, eat them.

A few of these incidents in a good rubber-tree region are sufficient to trigger a violent reaction. This has occurred throughout the entire Amazon basin. It is interesting that these conflicts arose in the Aripuanã and Roosevelt rivers in the waning days of the rubber tapping, a practice which is practically extinct nowadays.

The pressure on the Cinta Larga territories along the Aripuanã and Junqueira rivers increased with the opening of the Cuiabá-Porto Velho highway, currently known as BR364. This is the major axis of development of Rondonia, and important cities sprung up along this road. Rapid development through massive immigration from the south created a booming economy, with vast plantations of soy and corn on the Pareci highlands, and large industrial ranches dedicated to cattle farther north. Rondonia has 13 million head of cattle and this transformation required massive removal of the forest. The years 1970-2000 were marked by enormous fires that generated global protests about "the burning of the Amazon." This process has now decreased due to government intervention and enforcement.

In the 1960s, as during Roosevelt's expedition, most Cinta Larga villages were located near small streams. The telegraph post in Vilhena, headed by the Pareci Indian Marciano Zonoecê, was visited by the Cinta Larga in 1965. They carried no weapons, indicating a peaceful mission, and were fed by Marciano's daughter and by the Air Force support group. The following year they returned, but apparently an accidental gunshot triggered a violent reaction. Marciano's daughter was wounded but returned fire with a shotgun. The Cinta Larga claim that their population was decimated from attacks and reduced from 6,000 to 3,000. The SPI (Indian Protection Service) founded by Rondon, and its newer version, FUNAI (Fundação Nacional de Auxilio ao Indio) intervened and created an outpost. The initial doctrine was to group the Indians into larger settlements in order to disrupt their nomadic lifestyle. This was, essentially, a way to conquer them.

In 1976, the photographer Jusco von Puttkammer recorded 16 villages and 2 FUNAI posts. In 1987, a FUNAI post in the Aripuanã River named Ouro Preto, after a deactivated gold mine, concentrated half the Indian population in that river. Sadly, a flu epidemic decimated the Cinta Larga population in the FUNAI post on the Roosevelt River. This was followed by Indian attacks, since they claimed to have been poisoned. Indeed, this is not far from the truth, although the infection was involuntary.

The rocky formation of these rivers, responsible for the marvelous waterfalls, contains kimberlite. The mineral also exists in South Africa and is of volcanic origin. A curse to the Cinta Larga, it contains diamonds. The invasion by diamond miners is the last chapter in the turbulent history of this tribe. Thousands of miners invaded their lands, some with prior agreements with the Indians, many without. This led to a number of conflicts. In 2004, the Indians killed a number of miners and expelled them from their lands. The official number is 29, although the Federal Police and persons in Vilhena claim that actually over 100 were killed. In some places, the miners were simply tied up and led to the boundary of the Cinta Larga territory, where they were released.

It is a wicked web where Indian chiefs, FUNAI employees, and miners play various roles. Greed is the guiding principle, and agreement is followed by dissension in a strange dance. The government has intervened and the Federal Police has posts near the reservations. Compounding this, logging, both legal and illegal, is an important component in the local economy. The Cinta Larga population is again growing and their number is perhaps 2,000. Massacres are no longer permitted and the Indians are increasingly assertive. Measles and smallpox vaccination campaigns have freed them from this scourge. Our hope is that the income from the diamonds will benefit the entire population, not a few rapacious chiefs.

CHAPTER 8

PREPARATIONS AND EXPECTATIONS

March 2013. General Villas Boas, the head of the Amazon Military Command, in Manaus, received me as I entered the vast salon that led to his office. His sharp bluish-gray eyes and athletic built were smoothed by an affable personality. His handshake was firm but gentle. Col. Gilmar had guided me up and I was asked to sit and to explain my case, which I did, nervous as a young soldier in front of his superior officers. My insecurity returned, the shyness and fear, as the gray eyes scrutinized me. I proceeded, stumbling on every sentence, yearning for some help that did not come. We walked into another vast room and I prepared myself for the PowerPoint presentation. As bullfighters before facing the arena, I asked for the last piss.

As I progressed in my talk, the confidence returned. The questions were pointed, intelligent. Then, the grey eyes looked at me and the expression of the general mellowed.

"We will support your project, but no foreign NGOs."

As we separated, his broad smile and strong chin expressed support. "Every venture starts with a dream," he said encouragingly.

The young ROTC student of forty years ago gave way to the confident professor. The omen was right, the Villas Boas name shared by my 94-year old nanny, Alaide Maria Villas Boas, was positive.

Here I sit, in a new Manaus transformed by progress, a city

of skyscrapers, monster malls, and traffic-clogged streets embedded in the Amazon jungle, facing the next months, in which the dream will become reality.

Pieces of my past, fragments of my life paraded: a momentous Rondon Project adventure, service in the Brazilian Army, my love for the Amazon basin and many fishing expeditions of which I partook, the waning years of a life marked more by the elusive emotion of teaching and of having my research results published.

My admiration for these great men, Roosevelt and Rondon, grew as I pondered over their superhuman feats. I looked at the calendar: in one year, we will have the centennial.

I talked to my family, friends and procrastinated. But now the hour had come, and the project was kick started due to Jeffrey Lehmann's constant insistence. We met a few times, after I laid out, in Cartesian symmetry, the three stages of the expedition, its three goals, and the three principal mistakes made by the Roosevelt-Rondon expedition, not to be repeated. Albert Lin, former student and National Geographic explorer, played an important role in helping me to focus the energy, establish the goals, and develop a plan.

On March 19, I met with Col. Barros, soon to be General and commander of the São Gabriel da Cachoeira detachment in the northwest of the Amazon, where the border line draws a dog's head and fierce Yanomami still roam the forests. Col. Barros was the Public Relations Chief of the Amazon Command and Col. Alcimar was getting ready to take his place. Lunch was fascinating, and Col. Barros provided us with a view of the military in the Brazilian society, a heritage of the Portuguese. I was surprised to learn of the fort built in the 1700s by the Portuguese in the Guaporé River, in the far reaches of the Amazon. Its function was to establish and defend the borders on the west. The Portuguese, often ridiculed in Brazil for a lack of intelligence, are indeed an intrepid race. The northern part is populated by the descendants of Visigoth invaders. These barbarian tribes crossed Europe at the end of the Roman Empire and settled the provinces of Douro. This is the origin for the blue-eyed kind. In the south, the Moorish influence was strong and left indelible marks. A poor country having a powerful neighbor to the east, Portugal threw itself into the sea, mastering it. The School of Sagres, founded by Prince D. Henriques, was a university where the ways of ocean navigation were learned. While other European nations were busy with internal fights, Portugal was exploring the seas, descending lower and lower along Africa's coast, and finally turning back up, after Vasco da Gama's epic crossing of Cape Horn. All the while, forts were built to defend Portugal's commerce. This adventure led all the way to India and beyond, to Taiwan, Japan and China.

Shortly after Columbus discovered the Americas, launching off from the Portuguese Azores, a treaty was signed between Portugal and Brazil: the Tordesilhas Treaty, which limited Portugal to East of 47°, measured from Greenwich (370 leagues west of the main Cabo Verde island of Goma). Dom Pedro Alvares' official discovery of Brazil was an accidental occurrence, but the real story is a little different, since Spanish ships had already been in the Amazon and Brazilian Northwest. Cabral had brought with him a stone marker and deposited it in Porto Seguro, in the state of Bahia. After erecting it on the beach, claiming the land for the Portuguese crown, he proceeded to India, where the real riches were. His was a trading mission, not one of conquest and exploration.

Magalhães' heroic journey, the discovery and charting of California by João Domingues Cabrilho, and other feats of navigation demonstrate the courage of the Portuguese that had the apogee in the 1500s. A nephew of Vasco da Gama launched a last crusade against the Moors and saved Ethiopia from Islam. Another expedition into Africa by Dom Sebastião met disaster in the

Battle of Alcácer Quibir. The loss of Dom Sebastião's life in the battle led to the occupation (or unification with, in Spanish viewpoint) by Spain, which lasted 80 years. Portugal had accepted and absorbed a considerable portion of the Jews expelled by Queen Isabella of Castile. Later, during the Spanish occupation, they met the same tragic fate, many of them escaping to the Netherlands, while a fraction came to Brazil.

There was a unique aspect of the Portuguese colonization that distinguishes itself from the British and the Spanish: the incorporation of other races. This was both a necessity, because the Portuguese population was only 1 million in the 16th century, but was also a defining trait of the Portuguese character. The importance of both military and church ratified this. So, in the new lands, the rapid incorporation of the sons and daughters of mixed liaisons into the mainstream of society provided the needed population.

The ability and willingness to procreate was a trait considered very positive, and men freely took mistresses, lovers, girlfriends wherever they went. Even priests were not immune to the local culture, and many of them fathered children. This created the Brazilian race, and provided manpower for the immense enterprise of populating, organizing, and exploiting a large territory. Not content with sticking with the Tordesilhas Treaty lands, the Portuguese advanced resolutely west, south and north, doubling the size of this prized possession. The system was, of course, a feudal one, one that Europe was shaking off with the emergence of an urban bourgeoisie. In Brazil, the *Fazenda,* the feudal land holding, was the economic basis. Within the *Fazenda* there was a hierarchy of responsibility and authority, the slave being at the bottom of the scale.

But there were, also, significant differences with the antebellum plantations of southern United States. In the U.S., the breeding of slaves was done on an industrial scale, whereas in Brazil the slave was an integral part of the economic unit and protected by the Catholic Church. Slaves had the right of buying their freedom and the most enterprising did. In the gold cities, such as Ouro Preto, between 80 and 90 percent of the population was of African origin. Thus, the African retained his/her culture, music, food, much more than in the U.S. This society is masterfully described in the book 'Casa Grande e Senzala' by Gilberto Freire.

After my positive visit to Manaus and a tentative acceptance of support by General Villas Boas, Col. Alcimar told me to wait for three months while the Army considered my request and evaluated the needs of the expedition. He had told me that power boats would be required and that my initial idea of using just human power, paddles, was not realistic. Since I had seen several helicopters in the headquarters, I asked about the possibility of air support. He told me that this was extremely costly and quoted a figure of Re 10,000 per hour.

I returned to the US and waited two months before contacting Colonel Alcimar again. After several unsuccessful attempts, I finally was able to reach him. In a somewhat tortuous and indirect manner, he told me that shortly after my visit, a Brazilian author, accompanied by one of Rondon's grandchildren, had been at the Amazon Command and launched a book on the 1913-1914 expedition there. Upon learning that the Army was considering taking part in our expedition, the gentlemen reacted in a negative manner, stating that even the use of the Rondon name had to be cleared with the family. His threat to use legal means was met with indecisiveness by the new commander, who scrapped the entire project. The Army should not support a foreigner. Apparently, there were legal aspects involved and the publishing of the book was tied to some filming rights from which the family would receive royalties.

Faced with this disappointing news, I had to dig deep inside and seek other alternatives. Fortunately, my contacts with Col. Hiram Reis, the experienced kayaker that had descended some of the longest Amazon rivers, had been positive and we decided to pursue our goals independently of the Army. So, in the first days of August I flew to Cuiabá, which was the staging place for many past expeditions and is the *de facto* birthplace of Rondon. My plan was to scout out the different sites that the expedition had traveled to assess the challenges and needs. Upon Hiram's advice, two kayaks were ordered from São Paulo, with an October delivery date. I was hoping that Hiram could bring his kayak also. The plan included Corporal Mario, who had followed Hiram in previous expeditions. He usually followed with the supplies in a small motorized boat. However, Corporal Mario worked for the Amazon Command and permission had to be requested for his release from duty for the extent of the trip.

In Cuiabá, I made a last attempt of obtaining permission from the Brazilian Army in August 2013. Part of our expedition covered terrain that falls under the jurisdiction of the Military Command of the West. One of the brigades of this command is headquartered in Cuiabá and its new commander, General Avellar, is the nephew of a close family friend, the retired Air Force officer Avellar. He received me in his home and was very affable but told me clearly that he could not make this decision. It had to come from his chief. We looked at the Tapirapoan-Vilhena stage that was covered on horseback by the original expedition and General Avellar commented that several Indian reservations had to be traversed, requiring permission from FUNAI.

I arrived in Cáceres in the middle of the night, at 1 a.m. by bus from Cuiabá. There was a horrible accident in the mountains one hour from Cáceres. A semi filled with wood logs rammed into a long line of cars that were waiting for the road to reopen after a first accident. Interestingly, I had originally rented a car in Cuiabá but returned it in utter frustration or after getting lost in the exit three times and listening to countless cars honking behind me. My nerves were raw and my decision, which looked silly at first, proved to be the right one. The initial report was of 21 deaths, which was later revised to five, with a number of heavy injuries. The long wait on the highway, several hours, was nothing compared to the possibility of an accident. Brazilian highways are among the most dangerous in the world because of their poor condition and the heavy traffic. BR 364, originally built in 1969, is a two-lane highway with minimal curb space and, in many places, a dangerous drop. The entire flow of goods and persons to Brazil's northwestern state of Rondonia passes through this road, and the traffic is intense. The highway leading to my home city of Monlevade has been nicknamed Highway of Death, being the most dangerous in Brazil. Every week two or three horrible accidents exact their toll of fatalities. I suspect that BR 364 is not much behind. The socialist governments in Brazil have been more preoccupied in filling the pockets of their politicians and fostering a chimeric equality than in developing the infrastructure.

Fortunately, I found a hotel, with the unique name of Gasparin, close to the bus station, and I slept well. In the morning, I stopped at the local church, a concrete copy of a European Gothic cathedral, and thanked the Lord for guiding me back to Localisa, where my Fiat Uno was reluctantly accepted back. After surveying the wreckage of cars and buses and trucks, my enthusiasm for driving in these deadly Brazilian highways is considerably dampened. And I thought that the Highway of Death that connects Monlevade to Belo Horizonte was the most dangerous one!

The deadly cocktail of semis, large buses and minuscule cars produce these horrific accidents. I have seen too many of them, and the senselessness befuddles me. Who is to be blamed? The drivers, but primarily, the present and past governments that have not addressed the road system problems. All investment has gone to the eradication of poverty and support of political campaigns, but now is the time for addressing the infrastructure because it is negatively impacting economic development.

But what brought me to Cáceres and Vilhena? I am scouting out the area. The Roosevelt-Rondon expedition left the well-traveled waterways (Paraguay, São Lourenço, and Sepotuba rivers) in Tapirapoan and initiated a long journey using pack mules and oxen, trucks, and riding horses. The first part of the expedition was straightforward, as they used a small yacht, the Riquelmo, while Rondon's crew used the Ñyoac, up to a certain point, and then continued on smaller boats. The journey became more challenging when they connected the Paraguay to the Amazon basins following the telegraph line erected by Rondon a few years earlier (from 1905 to 1913). The topography and vegetation vary widely in this region that separates the two basins.

Cáceres is a typical city in western Brazil. But, in addition to the streets lined with small stores and dental offices it has a sprinkling of old houses, a reminder of the early days of the 20th century. The monument in the central square is a stone marker dating from 1750 and has the Portuguese coat of arms with seven castles on one side and the name of Dom Ferdinando on the other. An arm of the Paraguay River borders the town and a couple dozens of long boats surrounded by small aluminum fishing boats indicate that there is the staging point for fishing trips to the *Pantanal*. Groups of obese middle class fishermen load these boats and travel to the smaller rivers in search of the plentiful fish, filling their stomachs with excessive meals and their souls with alcohol, while they exchange scatological jokes. This is a Brazilian ritual reserved only for men. I, too, took part in these events in my youth, but I dreamt of crossing lands and conquering mountains while watching the moon at night and listening to the multitude of sounds coming from the forest.

That same afternoon, I continued my journey north by bus and this is the most comfortable option. The road first traverses a marshy area that transforms gently into a plateau that represents the western-most part of the very Brazilian highlands. The vegetation becomes a savannah-like *cerrado* with occasional small and tortuous tress and then gradually evolves into forest. The countryside has been transformed by farming. The land is much more fertile than the western U.S. My conclusion is that the horseback portion should be a 'walk in the park.'

As one moves north toward Vilhena, the plains give place to gently rolling hills, and patches of forest are left among vast expanses that have been turned into pasture. The land is fertile, and we pass some sugar cane plantations. There is a monotonous uniformity in the Brazilian countryside, and what I see here could be in Rio de Janeiro, Minas Gerais or Goiás. The earth is red, hematitic. The pastures are, in places, covered with termite mounds, called *cupim* in Portuguese. The cattle are the same mixture of European and Indian, Gir, Zigurá, Nelore, races that were developed in Brazil by mixing the climate-resistant Indian with European cattle to produce meat.

The soil turns white and the road rises gently, straight as an arrow. Three hours have passed since we left. In the distance, a mountain range. Coconut trees alternate with pastures and a low forest. We are moving west. There are patches of trees everywhere. The cattle are fat and the large *fazendas* succeed each other. We drive parallel to a mountain range that is on our left. The highway consists of two lanes and a minimum of curb space on each side. If a vehicle has to move to the right, it will roll out. Electrical posts are on our right and left. Do they follow the original Rondon telegraph line? We now approach a town called Pontes e Lacerda, a strange juxtaposition of names. Couldn't the local inhabitants decide on a name? We pass a university building, a surreal site in this vast expanse. A large swath of the original vegetation has been removed on the mountain, evidence of mining. We cross a high voltage electrical line that goes towards the mountain range.

In Pontes e Lacerda we stop for some time. It is a new community and it seems to be growing rapidly, built in the mold of Cáceres. The lots are about 400 m² and neatly organized. Many of them are walled and the houses are modest but neat. The bus stations are the life of these small communities. Farther south the road forks and goes towards Mirasol. A girl with a broom cleans the area in front of the bus station which is well organized. We had left at 12:30 and it is already 4:45. The next large town ahead is Comodoro. In one hour, it will be dark. This region is the vast Parecis plateau. It is here that the Nambikwara freely when Rondon crossed this region and twenty-five years later, when Lévi-Strauss followed on his footsteps. There must be Nambikwara villages in these areas.

So, what will I do in Vilhena? First, I had to find a roof under my head. Then I set three basic goals:
• Check the River of Doubt. Can it take kayaks there? How far north do I have to go?
• Talk to some local ranchers. Where can I find horses that we could take to the south to initiate the journey from Cáceres to Vilhena?
• Try to find a place to store the kayaks. Is there a warehouse? A local military detachment?

We arrived in Vilhena at around 10 p.m. on August 7. The bus ride was extremely comfortable in the spacious double-deck-er. This is the primary mode of transportation for the Brazilian of the poorer class. One can travel anywhere cheaply if one is patient and one gets a perspective of the people that is real and not artificially filtered by airports and five-star hotels.

The bus continued on to Porto Velho, another 700 km north, but I stepped out. The Vilhena bus station was clean and filled with the same faces one finds everywhere in Brazil. Women with babies, young, tough-looking guys, and a few older folks like me. The taxi driver informed me that Vilhena has a population of 80,000 to my surprise. As he drove into town, I was surprised by the regular pattern of streets. Highway 364 passes through the middle of town, and one has to cross it on foot to go from one side to the other, a dangerous maneuver. I was dropped off on Major Amarante Avenue, a major artery. I chose Hotel Colorado because of my emotional connection to that state: my children were born in the state of Colorado. I would learn later that the hotel was named after the town of Colorado, which, in its turn, was given by immigrants from southern Brazil, gauchos as they are called here. Colorado means 'red' and is the name of an old political party and the color of the soccer team 'Internacional.'

A second surprise was the agreeable temperature. My jacket helped to keep me warm in the walk to find a place to eat. An important thing to remember: bring a light jacket. The region between Cáceres and Vilhena is called Chapada dos Parecis, named after the Indians that lived there in Rondon's days. The altitude of Vilhena is 600 meters, making it one of the best climates in the Amazon region. In contrast, the altitude in Manaus is 10 meters!

I was fortunate to meet a local historian, Professor Emmanuel, who is an enthusiast of the Rondon expeditions. He was a high school teacher and his name was given to me by the girl working in the travel agency. He was an affable person, wearing a white hat and light suit. He demonstrated deep knowledge and promised to take me to the spot from where the expedition had launched into the river. He gave me his phone number and asked me to call him the next day to confirm the appointment. I was thrilled with my early success about the prospect of driving to the River of Doubt.

The next morning I went to the *Prefeitura* (City Hall), an expansive complex of buildings, flanked by a gaudy monument showing three prongs pointing to the air. I searched tentatively for somebody that could help me and a secretary pointed me to another building on Major Amarante Avenue. So, I returned to my original avenue. There I met the Secretary of Industry, Commerce and Tourism, Eliar Negri. He told me that Rondon's house still exists and offered to take me there. Vilhena also has an Air Force Base and an airport. The city was incorporated about 40 years ago, and has grown by 40% in the last ten years.

Vilhena is a good place to invest, since I predict that it will continue growing. The economy of the area is based on cattle and grains (primarily soy beans and corn). The city seems to be wealthy and the population came from the south, starting in the 60s when Juscelino Kubitchek opened up the road. Pick-up trucks roam about and the atmosphere is definitely "Western". The U.S. cowboy attire has been copied and adopted in Brazil. One sees, in the better restaurants, tall, blue-eyed people. This is a reflection of the Italian and German descendants, who also provide dynamism to the local community. Eliar Negri personally took me to visit Rondon's house. It is a whitewashed construction with a front porch and has obviously received a new roof. We had to enter into an area of exclusive use of the Brazilian Air Force but were able to penetrate through a gap in the fence. This is most probably a place where Roosevelt stayed before embarking down the River of Doubt expedition. In front of the house there was a strange steel contraption with a crank and a set of gears. There were also six-foot high steel circles that probably were the rims of the oxcarts used in the construction of the telegraph line. Eliar informed me that inside of the house one can still find some of his personal effects but it was locked. There used to be a cemetery in front of the house but no markers. These must be Rondon's *camaradas* (the Civilian workers), soldiers, and Indians that died in these parages. There was a rumor (as there is often) that he had buried gold in the yard and this was followed by furious digging I inspected the heavy steel contraption, probably weighing a ton, and completely corroded, in front of the house and tried to establish its function. It has a hand crank and a set of gears. Could it be a machine to stretch the steel wires that comprised the telegraph lines? The 2-meter diameter rims of the ox cart wheels showed that the carts were more sophisticated than the ones I saw in Minas Gerais during my childhood. The latter had wood wheels that were extremely heavy. This better technology came for the south, where the gauchos manufactured them through a technique that was relayed to me later by one of my expeditionary companions, Col. Angonese. These oxcarts brought the necessities all the way from Cáceres along the trail opened by Rondon. Rondon's house was actually a telegraph station, and I later learned that it was manned by the Indian Zonoecê and his family for many years. These stations were spaced about 70 km apart.

Afterwards, he took me to the fairgrounds and introduced me to its president, an Italian named Agostinho Pastore. He informed us that there are very few horses in Vilhena, except for expensive purebreds kept by rich ranchers. We are in the middle of soy territory, and this is the local gold. It is transported by truck to Porto Velho, 500 miles north, and then by barge down the Amazon to satiate the ever-growing need of an expanding Asia. Soy is the most important component of the local economy. Mr. Pastore also told me: "Forget about horses! What you need are mules.

78

Much more endurance."

And much less pleasant to ride, I thought to myself.

He told me that farther south, close to the beginning of our planned land journey, there are plenty of horses and mules. He offered to keep them in his corrals, once we make it to Vilhena, and informed us that it would be a simple matter to repatriate them to their point of origin, since there are large numbers of cattle trucks in the area.

Prof. Emmanuel had informed me that one of Roosevelt's abandoned steel boats was still somewhere on the trail. He will hopefully join our effort and enrich us with his knowledge. This area has also been visited by Claude Lévi-Strauss who studied the Nambikwara Indians. It is possible that Fawcett found his end somewhere not far from this parages, in a mysterious way.

Eliar confirmed to me the information passed on by Emmanuel, that one of Roosevelt's steel boats was around a few years ago. He did not know its whereabouts, and I promised myself to inquire further. Apparently, there is a secretary in the mayor's office who knows a gentleman who knows where the boat is. It would be wonderful to photograph it.

I could not contact the person that knows about the steel boat that the Roosevelt-Rondon expedition brought and resigned myself, in the afternoon, to watch one of the most boring matches of my life, Netherlands vs. Argentina. The historian never called back and probably changed his mind about his offer to help. This put me in a difficult position. Thus, I contacted a car rental agency. I had to find a way reach my destination: the headwaters of the Roosevelt River.

The World Cup was in full swing and I found a bar to watch the Brazil-Germany game. I got there early and secured a table not too far from a huge screen. There I witnessed the hideous defeat of Brazil by a powerful German squad in the soccer World Cup semi-finals. Brazil had, to this point, advanced in a shaky manner, luck on its side in the game against Chile. Having lost its best players, Thiago Silva and Neymar, the defense crumbled completely in the first half and in a period of 30 minutes Brazil took 5 goals, something unheard of in modern soccer. The goalie, Julio Cesar, was definitely past his prime and his slow reflexes contributed to the debacle. The bar congregated Vilhena's elite, some of them dressed in cowboy garb.

The second largest Brazilian soy grower, Bisetti, lives in Vilhena. Soy is the local gold and the rush consisted of burning down the forest to plant it. Eliar told me that the glorious days are past, and that the indiscriminate cutting of the forest is now much more difficult. The road started in 1960 and completed in one year, linking Cuiabá to Porto Velho, unleashed a rapid flow of immigrants from the south, eager to receive a piece of land from the government. Similar to the parcels in the American west, land was given to these settlers. I was in Porto Velho in 1969 and met, at the hotel where we would have drinks every afternoon, a rancher from Minas Gerais. He was transporting his cattle to the region, using the dirt road, and described to us his colonization efforts. He had to cut down the forest in time for the cattle to arrive.

I was informed by the local FUNAI Office that I have to make an official request to go down the river, since this is indigenous territory. The same applies to the Nambikwara villages, which are primarily in the Comodoro District. The information is available through the FUNAI site. The participation of the Brazilian Army in this endeavor will be very important since it would, undoubtedly, assist me on this.

It was a disappointment to hear the recording over the phone without being able to get in touch with the historian. However, through sheer luck, I found an enterprising partner, Naif, who owns a car rental agency. He promised rent me a car for the hefty price of Re 500. My plan is to visit three places: the point where the river starts; Lago Azul, the blue lake; and a place where the Roosevelt River is already navigable and where there is a small Nambikwara Village.

Through Nacif my principal objective in Vilhena would be accomplished: make it to the headwaters of the Roosevelt River. I don't know the reasons for the historian's change of heart, but my mentioning of the Brazilian Army could have given him a sour taste. In any case, I explained my situation, after he inquisitively asked me where I wanted to take the car, and informed me that I needed a four-wheel drive. I suggested that he join me, something he had done 4 years ago. He remembered watching the Brazil-Netherlands game in the Indian village in 2010. We have a game coming on Saturday! My luck is that he accepted to join me on such a short notice and inquired about the road. Fortunately, he did not trust his sense of direction and obtained the help of Roberto, from the mayor's office, through the intercession of Rita Marta, a most efficient and competent person and the Chief of Ceremonial.

We started after lunch in his truck and soon abandoned the paved road, crossing immense corn and soy fields. I thought I was living a nightmare: a tropical version of the US Corn Belt. The *cerrado*, thin vegetation, had been cleared on this immense plateau to give rise to modern mechanized agriculture. This area has become one of the major corn and soy producers in Brazil. The combines were neatly parked in the large garages of Fazenda Independencia. As the road got sandier and narrower, we penetrated into a forest that gradually grew denser. We were now in the Indian reservation. The wooden bridges grew more and more primitive and the long sandy stretches could have never been crossed by a two-wheeled vehicle. After a couple hours and many forks with no explanation, the road dipped further and we approached a slope that was too irregular even for our seasoned driver, with Rally experience. We walked down a few hundred yards and saw the river between the trees. Exactly as described by Candice Millard, it had an ominous look. I crossed it with some emotion, since it is from there that Roosevelt and Rondon launched their dramatic expedition one hundred years ago. The trees hung over the rapid water like ghosts over a child. The water was clear and innocent, but the movement had a disquieting nature. This is the stream that had taken them down, to suffering, death and, eventually, glory.

On the other side, a band of kids played in the afternoon. They quickly ran out of the water as the girls covered themselves. We asked for permission, which was given by the woman accompanying the kids, crossed the wooden bridge, and entered the minute village, two houses and a dozen people. She told us that she was a Nambikwara, but that this was a Sabanê village. The name Nambikwara awakened a host of feelings, since these were the Indians studied by Lévi-Strauss in the 1930s; this study led to his classic book 'Tristes Tropiques.' These Indians were also described by Roosevelt in his account of the expedition.

A crew from Vilhena was there, checking the health of the Indians and measuring their pressure and blood sugar. Two boys played soccer while a pair of parrots squawked with infernal dissonance. An old man sat at a chair and chatted with us, telling us, in a barely understandable voice, that he remembered Rondon and that his father used to tell him stories. Showing his arm, which had an old scar, he explained that he used to work in the pacification of Indians and that he would be sent ahead of the white men to establish contact with wild tribes. A poisoned arrow had hit him there. "They rub the tip in shit," he said with disdain and anger. He went on, telling some other stories about Rondon's love of nature: "He never allowed his workers to kill snakes." Then, he told us that the remnants of the old telegraph line still could be seen, a short distance from the village.

A beautiful little girl passed by, followed by a baby peccary. I tried to fetch it and got a good bite. She ran into the hut, and the pet followed her as if she was the mother. Then, she brought the little critter out, holding it in her arms. "I have a monkey inside," she said, and her mother authorized us to step inside. Indeed, the shy little marmoset was hiding under the roof.

I went down and contemplated the river again. This time, it looked like a hole in the forest, pointing to countless dangers. The Indian lady had told me that it was impossible to go down. "We tried," she said, "but the river disappears into marshes, reappears, and then drops."

We wanted more information, but the old man referred us to Lino, the chief. "But he is in Vilhena with his sick wife."

So, we called Lino and were finally able to meet him in a poor neighborhood in Vilhena, upon our return at night. His instructions were somewhat vague: "...just in front of a tractor, one block after a bicycle shop..." We finally identified three men in the dark, one just arriving home. A friendly dog received one of them, promptly carrying his baseball cap into the house, dropping it off, and returning for the backpack. The mutt struggled but was able to drag it through the dirt and into the doorway.

We took Lino to a local bar. He is already a city slicker, baseball cap, cell phone, and other trappings of urban life. His Portuguese, although heavily accented, was more easily understood than his father's, Manuel. He assessed his father's age as early eighties, a more modest figure than the number given by his daughter, 95, and wife, later on: 105! Lino gave us more detailed explanations about the river. His wife was undergoing treatment for a disease that he could not explain well, but was out of the hospital already.

Rondon's bridge was not at the village but a few kilometers downstream. Two tree trunks crossing the river are still there apparently, but the length, 20 m, is the same. He confirmed that the river turned into a marsh downstream and then reemerged, a couple of meters wide at first. This was also described by Candice Millard and Roosevelt: the river went underground in places. Beyond the true Rondon Bridge, he could go down by motor boat for about one day until a major waterfall is reached. His tribe tried to go down from the village but got stuck in the marsh, and the old woman had said, peremptorily: "It cannot be crossed. The legs sink until the knees. We took two days."

Lino accepted to take us to the waterfall. He knew a fellow that lives there and apparently, the larger fish cannot get upstream past that point. But I was interested in the entire journey, all the way to the Aripuanã River, following the memorable expedition. He looked at me for an instant, fear in his little eyes hiding behind the baseball cap: "I can't go there. The Cinta Larga live there."

So, things had changed much and yet so little in one hundred years. The Parecis plateau had become one of the richest agricultural expanses of Brazil. In Vilhena, personal trainers sculpted the derrieres of the local belles and happy kids returned from karate classes in the evening and wolfed down pizza slices. And 200 km from there, the Cinta Larga, the same ones that had killed Rondon's dog and trailed the original expedition, still terrorized the less belligerent Indian tribes. "But if we can transport my boat beyond the marsh, we can go to the waterfall," he said.

He sipped on the beer, hoping that we would offer him a second bottle, and eyed the scantily clad waitress. Naif complimented her on her hardiness, since the night was chilly. We took her picture, as her father, the bar owner, watched us with an expression that was less than friendly. Then, we bailed out and took Nilo back to his wife. Before parting, he asked for some help to pay for her medicine, and we obliged. I also gave him some chocolates for the peccary girl and promised that we would return. I committed myself to plant ten orange trees in the village, a habit that I have acquired over the years.

Back in the truck and on our way to a sophisticated restaurant, Naif explained that the Cinta Larga occupied a large swath of land along the river. It is called the Roosevelt Reserve. He confirmed that that this region was rich in diamonds and that South African geologists were scouting the area in rented pickup trucks.

"The Cinta Larga know about the illegal miners and come by their camps every now and then. They ask for money or diamonds and usually get them. If not…"

He then told me a story that was fascinating for its sheer terror. In a recent incident, a miner tried to cheat the Indians and swallowed his diamonds. They simply slaughtered him, then field dressed him, and retrieved the gems from his stomach.

"Many cases like this take place. We never hear from them," he continued after I mentioned a massacre that had taken place a few years ago.

"They are the pit bulls of the Indians," he concluded philosophically. I thought of Lino's father and the deep scar in his arm. So, we have a plan to go down the first 150 km of the river. What about the other 600 km? I close my eyes and imagine the scene, perfect for a Tarantino movie. A Cinta Larga, painted in red and black, clubs down a miner and systematically inspects the entrails until the pebbles are found. Definitely, luck was on Roosevelt's side, since only a dog was killed. Or perhaps it was Rondon's gifts left hanging at their campsites as a proper payment for passage.

In August 2015, after the successful descent of the Roosevelt River, and after planning Phase 2 of the expedition, the trek from Cáceres to the bridge on the river where the 1914 expedition launched off, I returned to the area, this time with Col. Angonese, with the following goals: to scout out the entire region, finding the original trail, to assess the places where we could camp, to visit the Indian villages that we would cross and to ensure a good reception, and to establish how we could cross the many rivers along our path. Most importantly, we needed to hire boats to go up the Sepotuba River and a mule train to take us from Tapirapoan as far north and west as possible. The second phase of the expedition, nearly 800 km crossing two large Indigenous areas, necessitated permission by FUNAI, the Brazilian Indian Support Foundation. An extensive proposal was submitted with all the required documents, including medical examinations and vaccines of all expedition members as well as official documents. In parallel with this, our attempts to obtain official military support continued. Once all these organizational steps had been fulfilled we started, from Cáceres, where the original expedition entered into its challenging stage after a comfortable and leisurely cruise up the Paraguay River in the yacht loaned by the president of Paraguay, Adolfo Riquelmo.

I flew to Campo Grande, where I visited the commander of the Western Military Command after the Roosevelt River descent, and was again well received and informed that my request would be considered. My pleas to the Military Institute of Engineering were heard but a lack of commitment was clear in the evasive answers and refusal to sign a simple letter of reference. It should be mentioned that the new timidity of the Brazilian Army is the result of the political climate. The power is in the hands of the leftist Workers Party that is intent on minimizing the reach and influence of the military, staunch enemies of communism in the past. In an ironic twist, Dilma Rousseff, former guerrilla fighter and the President, appointed a member of the Communist Party of Brazil as Minister of Defense.

In the end, as we were ready to start our journey from Cáceres, we obtained logistic support from the Brazilian Army, and our expedition became an official mission. This was enabled by Col. Hiram, who has close colleagues in high places in the Army. This is important because it reflects the spirit of the original 1913-1914 expedition, which was an amalgam of military, researchers, and explorers from both countries.

In the next four chapters, we follow the 1914 expedition, ignoring the fact that we did the river portion in 2014 and the land portion in 2015. We number the days sequentially in each chapter without specifying the exact date.

CHAPTER 9

UP THE SEPOTUBA RIVER: JOURNAL AND COMMENTARY

Day 1

As I sit here, in the cool lobby of Hotel Tainá, sheltered from the cauldron of Cuiabá, I reflect that this is my fourth stay at this place and that it became the *de facto* hub of this exploration. Roosevelt, Rondon, Lévi-Strauss, Fawcett, and others used Cuiabá as an operational base for incursions into the wild North. Now, paved highways replace trails and some of the sense of adventure is lost as industrial mega farms and immense cattle ranches are in place of deserted swaths of virgin land where the occasional human being had the exoticism and uniqueness that are still etched in my mind from childhood.

Yesterday I arrived in São Paulo and, as I crossed the extensive taxfree stores before exiting the airport, I pondered over the irony of it all, the advertisements bombarding me with invitations to purchase. Winged beauties wearing underwear paraded on the large TV screen creating a surreal world in which Victoria's Secrets, now fully exposed, are an invitation for aerial sex. An impeccably dressed Beckham sipping some unknown scotch distracts me at left and aggressive sales ladies demand that I get a cart to fill with goods. My tired eyes move to other travelers weary from the night in the plane, seeping through the products. This chasm hits me hard. The world of illusion, toward which we strive, and the mundane reality of fat bellies, short legs, and scraggly hairdos pushing and poking as if the mere fact of purchasing would endeavor them with the esthetic qualities of the ads.

I continue, like a zombie, through this gallery of consumerism, intent on my goal: to embark on this expedition and honor our heroes who, one hundred years ago, faced the unknown Brazilian hinterland to find pain, death, and glory.

I open the local newspaper and the new reality that we seek in this distant land sinks in. One entire page is dedicated to a region close to Pontes e Lacerda where gold was discovered a few weeks ago. The photo shows a terrain covered with holes, as if gophers had dug it, each protected by a blue tarp. The other photo shows a woman dragging two suitcases followed by a man carrying a 50-gallon water container. The headline says: "Hookers find fortune in gold camp."

The reporter interviews several. The first claims that she brought two cousins over, that work in the same trade. They are paid in gold, 20 grams per trick. Since the miners spend two or more weeks without bathing, the ladies provide water to them and bring ample supplies of underwear to the camp. The atmosphere is upbeat and one of them, a part time university student with a boyfriend in the city, states that she can make Re 5000 a month. She likes the financial independence. Other hookers have found boyfriends in the camp and are taken on trips. This material, presented in a lighthearted tone, would hardly be the subject of a newspaper article in the puritan US. The roles in the camp are clearly defined: the men dig for gold and the women provide relief from the dreadful and dangerous life.

Soon my travel companions, Col. Angonese and Col. Hiram will arrive from Porto Alegre, in the extreme south of Brazil, and the team will be complete.

Day 2

We had a successful meeting at FUNAI, the Brazilian Indian Protection Foundation. The situation is more complex than we envisaged in our proposal. The Federal Government has limited power over the indigenous areas. The permission, requested through our proposal to FUNAI, has to be asked again to the various indigenous areas involved after FUNAI has approved the project. Marcio Carlos, a pleasant FUNAI employee, received us well and provided all the required documents, telephone numbers, and contacts. Slightly built, he did not have any wrinkle to distract his simple and pleasant smile. He confessed that he was 48. We inquired about the Parecis and Nambikwara, and he told us that he had worked for FUNAI for 30 years.

"I started at 17, and they dropped me in the middle of the Nambikwara territory for 30 days. They gave me a shotgun, some ammunition, and food, and I was never as scared in my life."

He confirmed that the small group, close to which he was left, slept on the ground in the ashes of the fire.

"They were covered in ashes and their hair was waxy from something they put on it. After five days, they told us that they were leaving. I was terrified."

They took him with them, after loading all their possessions into baskets that they carried on their backs, attached to a strap that they passed on the forehead: a few pots, bows, arrows, even their pets."

After a few days, they decided to return. Marcio had been marking the trees all along with his machete.

"The happiest people I've ever met," he said with a twinkle in his eyes. "Because they only own what fits in their *xiri*, their basket." He explained that one of them told him that 'if it does not fit into the *xiri*, we don't need it.'

This lack of attachment for material goods is, according to Marcio, the source of their happiness.

This description matches the one by Lévi-Strauss who was looking for a people devoid of objects, a culture reduced to its utter simplicity.

He relayed his other experience to us when he was sent with a priest to visit the Miki Indians. They walked seven days in the forest and the priest, having injured himself with the machete, returned to the base. Marcio continued alone and finally arrived at the village semi starved. He had not eaten for a few days and dug up some mandioc roots, proceeding to cook them in a tin can that he found in the village. He was boiling it when the Indians came and yelled at him, kicking the can off the fire. Delirious, from hunger and exhaustion, Marcio felt that he would get killed. He looked around and found a shotgun hanging in the hut. He then started to plan his next move as he put the mandioc back in the fire.

"The Indians returned and kicked it up again, yelling at me," he said. "Then, I became sure of what I had to do."

He checked the gun but realized that the reloading would not be simple, since he would need a knife to extract the shell. So, he would only be able to kill the first one and the second and third would club him to death. As evening approached one of the Indians came by and threw him a quarter of a monkey.

"I was sure that it was poisoned," he said. "So, I did not roast it."

Fortunately, the priest arrived that night having been duly sewed up. He knew the language of the Miki Indians which belongs to an isolated group, and relayed the message. The mandioc was the wild kind, which contains cyanuric acid.

"The Indians were trying to tell me that I would die if I ate it." A smile came back to him.

"I had to spend fifteen days under psychiatric treatment. This really messed with my mind."

I sympathize with him. These stories are interesting when told, even entertaining. But the experience, when lived, leaves permanent memories, often scars.

As we parted, he had one last and surprising revelation. He had been raised by Dona Nair, the chief of the Jatobá Pareci village.

"If you meet a fellow that looks just like me and does not return your greeting, don't worry. It is my twin brother, Carlos Marcio, who also works for FUNAI."

Day 3

We are heading to Cáceres by van and our driver, Jair, is full of fantastic stories that he relays to us in an interminable staccato. His life, from his sailor days to his recent forays as a tourist guide, is paraded in front of us. Time passes rapidly as we mentally calculate whether the number given by the hooker for a trick, 20 grams of gold, is correct. We debate the price of gold and conclude that it is Re 2,000, or U$ 500, ten times the going rate in Brazil. So, the reporter is off by an order of magnitude... The conversation drifts to the local fauna. In the mountain range that we cross there is a lodge where tourists come to photograph the Brazilian harpy.

"There is an observation platform 40 meters from the nest," he says with pride, "and I watched the babies." Then, he tells us about the jaguar tour he hosted last season, where eight were seen, one a repeat.

When we arrived at the Transit Hotel of the Frontier Battalion in Cáceres the soldiers already awaited us. Our first job after lunch, which proved to be challenging, was to exchange my 10,000 dollars. Dollar João, the local trader, was out of town and the banks were on strike. Somebody informed us that the owner of the Martins Boot Store used to buy dollars, and we headed there. After a twenty-minute walk in the sweltering afternoon heat we found the store, an empty place with an office in the middle. In the side, remnants of a boot factory. The man, a portly Portuguese-looking gent in his fifties, informed us that there was a shortage of Reais in Cáceres. "It's the damned bank strike."

Blood turned cold in my veins since I know that the expedition depended critically on cash.

"Nobody wants dollars," he said. "Perhaps the Indians." Then, he offered us his exchange: 3. 6 Reais per dollar, slightly above the official rate but below the black-market value, which fluctuated between 3.8 and 4.2.

Having no choice, I agreed.

"How many?" he asked.

"Four thousand."

He scratched his three-day beard, grabbed his minuscule cell phone, and spoke to somebody. A time later a tall guy with a gold chain wearing a wife beater shirt and shorts entered the store. He looked every bit like a drug dealer.

"Let me see the bills," he asked. I showed him a couple brand new hundred dollar bills, and he inspected them.

"You must have a really good printing machine at home, my friend," he said. Looking at my desperate expression, he laughed: "Just joking."

He took a hand-held calculator, struggled with it for some five minutes, until he uttered, looking at me puzzled:

"14,400 reais for your 4,000 dollars."

I gave him the money, which he counted before slipping out and mumbling: "Wait a little."

The fellow at the desk, seeing my anguish, comforted me: "My younger brother."

Then, he went on to explain that he no longer made boots, since it did not pay sufficiently. When I asked about alligator boots, he went on a long harangue against the government. The system of taxation and controls increased the price of alligator leather beyond any commercial value. And worst, tanning was no longer allowed in the region.

Half an hour later the brother reappeared and called me to the side. I counted the money while the fellow on the door told us that this was a criminal activity and that we could get arrested. I winked to the colonels while I peeled an additional 1,000 to the drug dealer-looking fellow.

"We travel to Bolivia every couple weeks," he told me.

I did not question further the nature of his import-export business, but his desire for dollars was made clear. My beloved greenbacks will probably be exchanged for some illegal merchandise like cocaine, I thought.

Money in hand we proceeded to firm up three deals: boats, mules, and a support truck. Col. Hiram periodically called higher ups in the military, former classmates at the Military Academy. These ties form an informal network that is a powerful way to get things done in the Army. We obtained the boats through Sergeant Luna, an energetic and handsome fellow that would be a top soldier in the best armies in the world: he was dynamic, intelligent and has a sense of initiative. On top of it, he has the looks of a movie star.

The cook was arranged through him and will double as a pickup driver. Brazilians pay a lot of attention to food. For me, the utter simplicity of our REI rations would suffice, but not for my colleague Angonese. The cook/driver is a soldier in the battalion, Eder. A tall and dark fellow with fine features, he is bright, responsive, and resourceful. On top of this, he shows me respect, addressing me by 'colonel.'

Next, we went shopping, following the detailed list prepared by Angonese. We still needed to see Manoel the mule guy, but it was already past 11 p.m. and we could not find his house.

Day 4

Preparations continued with periodic visits to the bank to extract cash from the machines. All banks had big paper ribbons printed GREVE. The strike had been going on for two weeks but the machines were replenished with cash every day. Only BRAD-ESCO took my card and the limit was Re 800. Our calculations finally showed that we had enough for the trip.

We visited the commander of the battalion, Lt. Col. Braga. He received us in his vast office, the size of a classroom. It was lined with pictures of former commanders, back to a Portuguese officer. The transition from colony to empire and then to republic was rather smooth in Brazil, and the wall below which we met to discuss our plan had the picture of Dilma Rousseff in full regalia.

He told us that he would support us but needed official orders, which Hiram assured us were on their way. Quite a difference from the young, adventurous, and dynamic army that Roosevelt encountered in 1914. The current cadre of officers is also dedicated, but much timider. One small slip can alter an officer's career and impede his/her advance to the supreme dream of becoming a general. Thus, caution is the most important quality, the best way to advance. So, as we waited we decided to look into a pickup truck at the local agency, LocalIZA.

As soon as I had signed all the papers and my debit card had been approved and charged, a call came from the upper echelon confirming the Army support. From this moment on, our expedition becomes an official mission.

Eder was disappointed because his freedom as a civilian will be replaced by military discipline and a sergeant that will come along as his superior because a military regulation of two persons per vehicle. He also warned us that the Marruá, the Brazilian equivalent to the US Humvee, often left people stranded. But the advantages of greater space, four-wheel drive and a military presence outweighed the inconvenience. We finally went to Manoel's house and found our gargantuan cattle drive leader with sleepy eyes. He pointed to a bottle of *cachaça* and mentioned that he had asked his wife to buy one the previous night. Our negotiations continued for one hour, and all prices, except the mules, rose. Instead of a peon, his brother, nicknamed Boi, would be our mule train boss. He complained that we were three, and not four as originally indicated. In spite of the fact that we had already committed to two mules per person, he insisted that we rent a ninth mule, just in case. And the little 'godmother' horse was an absolute necessity. Of course, Boi was not a regular peon, but his brother, and would require Re150, and not the regular Re100 per day.

He had slaughtered a cow to sell us his *charque*. These are thick slabs of beef that are salted and dried for a few days. The meat is rehydrated and at the same time most of the salt dissolves away prior to cooking. This means of meat preservation was learned from the Incas and actually the word is originally Inca. We use the term jerky in the US, but the original *charque* is much thicker, about 1 to 2 cm. The Inca used to dry lama meat to preserve it.

In walked another rotund fellow, a former sergeant named Murtinho. He realized that the pickup place was 120 km beyond the initially arranged place. He would drive the mules to Tapirapoan and pick them up at the Juína River, but there would be an additional cost.

Finally, the total came to Re 21,000, a good chunk of cash, even in dollars. Manoel has batrachian features, a stomach that droops like a skirt, and a broad face that made sense to me after he told me that his mother was Bolivian. They are five brothers, of which I met four. Manoel's face, a mixture of shrewdness and bestiality does have beauty, and he carves a living out of taking large cattle herds across the vast swamps of Mato Grosso, known as *pantanal*. He and his brothers described the beauty and challenges of their trade, and I hope to follow them one day, emulating Guimarães Rosa, a writer which I have admired since my youth.

We returned in the evening and the entire group was sitting outside, shirtless all, sipping beer. Each one had a story, and Angonese took a shot of their *cachaça* as they extoled their tales.

"Before we start the drive, we herd all the cows and keep them together for a few days," said Manoel. "Then they will start acting as one group."

His eyes glistened behind the fatty folds of his broad face. "They act like one. You can move them wherever you want."

"But sometimes they run off," I said, remembering the cowboy movies of my childhood.

"They still do this," he answered.

Commentary:

Roosevelt describes the city of São Luiz de Cáceres in his characteristic lively manner, presenting it as beautiful and ancient. The houses had red tile roofs and the latticed windows, that come from the Moorish days of Portugal. We call them *moujubi* and they no longer adorn the streets of Cáceres. He also mentions an important public building, the new school. We walked by the historic site that was illuminated at night and has not lost anything from its ancient glory. It is still the best school in Cáceres.

Since Cáceres is not the capital of the state and is neither at important cross roads, it did not explode in size like many other Brazilian cities. Hence, we were able to enjoy its charms and struggle with the narrow sidewalks already mentioned by Roosevelt.

Roosevelt stayed at the comfortable house of Lt. Lyra, one of Rondon's officers. He comments on the spacious house and mentions that Lyra was a member of the expedition. He lost his life tragically in the Sepotuba River three years later when his canoe filled with water and they jumped into the river to keep it afloat.

He still had time to throw the annotated field books to the margin before being dragged by the strong current and succumbing to the rapids.

Day 6

We spent the morning on the last errands, while we waited for written orders from the Western Military Command. They did not arrive until noon, when work stops on Fridays. We decided to return our pickup truck and start the expedition. At 2 p.m. we embarked on two power boats with 25 and 20HP motors. The temperature had risen to 37 degrees C in Cáceres, but we soon felt refreshed by the breeze. The Paraguay River was lined with fishing huts and we met fishermen every few hundred yards.

"The economy is bad these days and many people are unemployed," said Alemão, our guide on the river. "So, they fish not only for relaxation, but to make an extra *contos*."

He still used the old term, *contos*, which had been superseded by cruzeiros, cruzados, and now reais, each worth one thousand of the previous one. The huts gradually thinned out and after one hour we entered the Sepotuba River. This river runs faster than the Paraguay but our boats advanced rapidly. Our first destination: Alemão's mother-in-law, 70 km up the river. The margins were covered with forest, but the maps showed that there were large ranches in the eastern bank and that only one thin sliver of wood was left. This river has in the past been a major source of wood, and the opening of ranches required the cutting of the forest.

We saw one *tuiuiu*, a large bird, a couple of macaws, and varied egrets along the way, and a surprised capybara jumped into the river, which has an undeniable beauty. Although Roosevelt states that the name means 'River of Tapirs' this was not confirmed by Col. Hiram who states that it is 'River of Lianas' in the Pareci language.

We arrived at Alemão's mother-in-law at around 5:30 and had plenty of time for socializing after we set up our tents under a large thatch-covered structure with open sides. Dona Josefina prepared us a nice meal of *pacu*, rice, beans, and mandioc, and the other guests, a group of weekenders that included a tall black man who was a 33-year veteran of the Army. He entertained us with stories and offered us *cachaça* with *fedegoso*, an interesting herb that has, according to him, marvelous medicinal properties.

The evening breeze and sun lighted the west with reddish hues filtering through the trees. Two macaws circled us in garrulous chatter, sat on the palm tree for an instant, and then flew home. The clucking of chicken stopped and a rooster jumped up to roost in our shed. He was promptly grabbed by one of the men who locked him up. He would have been an infernal presence among us keeping us awake.

At some point, Alemão repeated his story to us, his sad childhood where he was abandoned by the mother and adopted by a rich Lebanese rancher who had, at some time, 2,000 workers and families working under conditions of quasi-slavery. Everybody owed money to the *patrão* and if somebody tried to escape he would send his *capangas*, armed guards, after him and summarily shoot him.

The sale of a native medicinal plant was at the time a major source of income. I heard similar stories in the book about Fawcett. As deforestation progressed, the supply of this herb decreased and economic conditions changed. The collection of *ipecacuanha*, or *coalha*, as it is known locally, and that of other medicinal and aphrodisiac plants, was an important economic activity in early Brazil.

"The man had a store where he provided food and clothing for the workers, and I and his brother wrote everything down.

Everybody was scared of him, but I helped the poor souls, who would only get 70 pounds of rice a month, per family.

"One day when I was 14, he called me a thief. I asked him for two Reis to take the bus, after telling him that I was leaving. He gave me only one." Alemão's face turned bitter.

"I walked out and one of his employees gave me 45 Reis, all his savings."

He then told us that he found a job in Cáceres as a fisherman's helper. "After catching a ride on a truck, I set up my hammock in a tree in the center of town."

Soon he was employed as an alligator hunter, in a team of twenty. They would enter the *Pantanal* and set up camp, illegally. Three hunters and fifteen skinners. His story reminded me of Jack London's famous novel about sealing, Seawolf.

"Every week we would get six to seven hundred skins. I shot them with a 22LR in the head, between the eyes, and the gaffer would bring it into the boat."

But things changed with the prohibition. They still hunted illegally, but both the ranchers and police would meet them with bullets. They made an airstrip and a Cessna would come and fly the hides to Paraguay every week, six hundred of them. One day his boss decided to go with the plane, which increased the weight. At the end of the makeshift runway the plane hit the water and capsized, burning passenger and pilot alive. The police came, attracted by the smoke, and that was the end of it.

He also told the story of the ambush in which the police killed all twenty-two alligator hunters. One of them had gone hunting and heard the firefight. He got on a tree and waited. When the police boat came by he shot the pilot. As the boat veered aimlessly, he methodically shot the other five. A meticulous fellow, he got down, slit the bellies of the six, took a machine gun from one of the soldiers and emptied it on the boat. It readily sank and the feast of the piranhas was the last thing he saw of them as he motored away.

Vengeance is dealt rapidly in this country, and Alemão told us another hair rising tale of his youth.

"I had been partying with my friends in town for the entire night when we ran out of *cachaça*. I volunteered to get another bottle at the corner store. I was getting it from the old man, whose daughter had been my girlfriend in the past, when two policemen arrived. I knew one of them, who asked me in the typical aggressive police talk: 'You should not have dumped Felicia.'

"This was my previous girlfriend, the sister of his. I answered rather abruptly and he came toward me. I ran from him and went straight to the jailhouse, informing the police chief of the incident. He offered protection. I was walking home accompanied by two policemen when the fellow reappeared, now wearing civilian clothes.

"Fortified by the presence of the other two, he proceeded to attack me, kicking me several times. At some point, I punched and dropped him. He came to me six times and six times I dropped him."

Alemão now squinted and his eyes were replaced by two narrow slits on his flushed face.

"He pulled out his gun but before he could shoot me I took it out of his hand and shot him in the middle of the forehead. He dropped to the ground and the policemen arrested me. I thought I was done for but he got up and stumbled home. The bullet had ricocheted in his skull and was lodged in the back of his head. It was a 32-caliber pistol, a piece of shit."

Thrown in jail, he was only freed after his stepfather came and talked the police chief into letting him go.

"This is to show you how powerful the man was," he told me. "I would have caught over one year of jail time, at least. And if there were no bystanders, the police would have killed me for sure.

"Life has been good to me," he said, but there was bitterness in his determined look.

Later he told me that he had eleven children, all doing well.

"And how many wives?"

"Five." He laughed, the sadness gone from his eyes. "They all like me."

The mother-in-law, sitting by his side, confirmed. She had had sixteen pregnancies but looked happy and lively. A small woman with dark skin, she was full of energy and wore a sexy negligee the next morning. The music that blared from the boom box announced her happiness and flirtaceous nature.

We went to bed after having a couple shots of the *fedegoso* laced *cachaça*, only to be awakened every two hours by the three roosters that took turns announcing the distant morning.

Commentary:

We used two aluminum boats with smallish outboard motors and this was not too different from Roosevelt. Interestingly, they had Evinrude outboard motors, which were still produced in my youth. Although the details are not provided, we know that they went up to the river with one boat pulling two small barges and stopped at the Porto do Campo ranch. This was and is a large *fazenda*. There, the equipment and part of the crew left for Tapirapoan, while the remainder of the member stayed back for 5 days hunting and collecting specimens. The owner of the property, Argen, tells us that a box with materials for embalming animals was unearthed at the *fazenda*. He believes that this material is from the original Roosevelt Rondon expedition. Roosevelt reports that the ranch is located 110 to 130 km upriver from Cáceres. The expedition mounted tents in front of the ranch and the US and Brazilian flags were raised every morning and brought down every evening while the entire troop was at attention.

Tapir hunts were organized for Roosevelt, who would wait for them in the boat while the dogs would chase them and flush them into the river. Roosevelt has a famous photograph on the beach in front of the ranch with the tapir and white-lipped peccaries shot that day. He also shot a deer, something he was proud of because it was a challenging shot. Argen, the owner of the ranch, tells me that there is still a profusion of game in his ranch and I believe him, because hunting is prohibited in Brazil. Roosevelt intermeshes his description of the hunts with detailed analyses of the classification, habitat, and habits of the animals.

Little escapes Roosevelt's eyes as he observes the vegetation and focuses on the *babaçu* and *buriti* palms. The hunting party explored the area on horseback and Roosevelt had ample opportunity to know the region adjoining the river. Now, except for a strip of forest along the river, it is all pasture.

Day 7

Twenty minutes after leaving Josefina's ranch, where we listened to more fantastic jaguar stories by her sister-in-law, we arrived at *Fazenda* Porto do Campo, a place of historic significance where Roosevelt and Rondon spent a few days hunting tapir, peccaries, and deer. The owner and patriarch, Argen Fogliatto, is one of the largest ranchers of the region and raises some of the purest Nelore cattle. The ranch is 48 km long along the river and has about the same width, going all the way to the Bacaval River. The three hours we spent talking with him were most interesting. His tall blue eyed appearance contrasts with the locals and denotes his gaucho roots, which are traced from Northern Italy, Venice.

Argen entertained us with stories of his life, proudly announcing that he was one of the first to create wildlife corridors between the two rivers. Spaced 5 km apart and 200 meters wide, they allow animals to move from one river to the other.

"Now it's a law, but I did it before them," he announced proudly.

I remember Germany and Luxembourg, where wildlife bridges allow animals to cross highways without risking death. The animals quickly learn the safe paths and use them.

Argen was part of the immigration wave from the south. He bought the ranch at Porto do Carmo in 19984 and made large investments farther north, between the Juína and Formiga Rivers. Mentioning a figure of 400,000 hectares, shared between him and his friend Mazut, he explained that he parceled off the large property and sold it. These were indeed frontier times, and vast expanses changed hands in the first days, when the plateau was only poorly productive. It was only after special strains were created and the soil corrected that the fertility improved. The huge extension of land was owned by a corporation, Montepio da Familia Militar, who sold it at a loss at an auction. But the original owners were the Pareci and Nambikwara.

The purchase was not accepted by some, and Mazut made enemies in town, one of whom hired a *pistoleiro* to kill him. He survived four bullet wounds and Argen, his trusted friend, asked the man how much he was paid. He pulled out his wallet and paid him the amount. "This is not to shoot him again, since you haven't finished your job," he said, and the hired gun complied.

But one day the complications got bigger as he faced a corporation, Pandovani, that wanted to take his land by force. Mazut walked towards the squatters and was received by a shower of bullets, 32 of which ended in his body. This time, he could not get any help. His widow asked Argen who had done it, and he indicated, correctly, Pandovani.

A couple days later he gets a phone call from a gentleman. "Please don't mention anything anymore to the widow," said the voice.

Argen inquired the mysterious voice and he told him that he had, years ago, walked into his house and demonstrated kindness to his family. "I was hired to kill you, Mr. Argen."

Again, Argen gave him the agreed upon sum, a proven technique in the area, and realized that the widow's lawyer was connected to the Pandovani Group.

He was called by the group in Cuiabá to negotiate the sale of his portion of the land and was told that he owed Pandovani a large amount of soy. The following threat was made: "If you don't sell the land, we'll kill you."

At this, Argen became mad and riposted: "If you kill me, your wives and children will die and this building will be blown apart."

He continued and mentioned his personal friendship to the Governor of Mato Grosso, Julio Campos, and other important dignitaries.

At the end, he concluded: "You may be bad but I am much, much worse. You just watch out for your lives."

After this the Pandovani group left him alone. Argen continued to digress about Mazut, this colorful character that he had known in the South.

Mazut was a poor boy and had courted a girl from a better family. Resourceful, he would take a shower at a nearby gas station, and catch a taxi to visit his beloved. When he proposed to her, shortly thereafter, he came to Argen and asked to borrow his pickup truck and driver. The girl was enchanted with his looks and truck, and accepted.

Then came the wedding, Argen again stepping in. Argen suggested that he open a construction company, and he got him a loan through the bank. At the signing, Mazut looked at him terrified. Argen took him outside and asked him: "What's your problem? No courage to sign?"

Mazut explained that he did not know how to, being illiterate.

"Practice here on this paper, quickly", instructed Argen.

They went back inside and Mazut scribbled something that the banker readily accepted.

So, the two buddies came to Mato Grosso, became large landowners, and remained friends till the end. Interestingly, the road that leads from Campos de Julio to the small hydroelectric power station named Telegráfica is called Mazut.

We continue up the river which flows at an increasingly fast pace, and in places is so shallow that we risk hitting the bottom stones with the propeller. Our pace slows down considerably. There are pristine areas followed by sequences of little harbors with fishing boats. Small fishing lodges abound in this area and we saw a number of fishermen.

A *bacuri,* a palm whose trunk is partially in the water, appeared, and *buritis* are a common sight. In front of the ranch there was a solitary majestic *jatobá,* that is, apparently, the model for a Brazilian stamp.

The afternoon sun and heat cooks us, after 2.5 hours up the river. Neither nature nor the ranches are too different from Roosevelt's days and we are happy to see that the water flow is swift in spite of the season, the end of the dry period. Alemão was worried that the boats could not make it up the low river. The explanation given by Argen and also heard before is that the Parecis Plateau has subsurface aquifers. It acts like a sponge that takes in the rainwater during the rainy season. This feeds the rivers year long, both the north-flowing as well as south-flowing rivers.

But the winds on the Parecis Plateau sometimes change. The ones from the north bring humidity from the Amazon. When they turn and come from the west, little moisture is left on the way from the Andes.

From the Porto do Carmo Ranch we moved up 70 km to reach an island where the RR expedition also stopped. The number of river rapids increases steadily, and our propeller hit a number of rocks. The vegetation is certainly very similar to the one of one hundred years ago, but we meet fishing boats every hundreds of yards. It is Saturday and people from the surrounding towns came to the fishing cabins and platforms all along the river. The favorite catch: *pacu,* a 3-6 lb. fish resembling a piranha, and most probably of the pigocentris or serrasalmus family.

We stopped at the island mentioned by Roosevelt and found a house, apparently empty. By the time Hiram and Angonese had set up the tents on the porch, a fellow arrived by boat. José was initially suspicious but became cordial soon. He was neat and the place around the house had been cleaned of leaves. A storyteller like most local people, he explained that he was a professional fisherman from March until November, and then would move to his city house. Dark skinned, he had white and Indian features.

He explained that a rancher had sold lots 35 meters wide, along the river, and that there were 150 fishing lodges and harbors along the area from there to the Tapirapoan. Indeed, the succession of makeshift landing docks took away the majesty of the river.

Commentary:

After five days of resting and hunting at the ranch, the powerboat and pull boat arrived and the team embarked, heading north. And indeed, it was a team: 30 men, five dogs, tents, provisions and fresh meat, that every day became less fresh, as Roosevelt puts it. The rainy season was already in full swing and they did not have our problems with the low level of the river, bringing danger to the outboard motors. It is also possible that the level of the river has decreased due to deforestation. The motorboat was pulling the large boat and the advance was slow, estimated to be 2 km per hour. Every now and then they passed a ranch. These ranches were owned by Cáceres people. Roosevelt refers to his reading that included Quentin Durward, Gibbon, and Chanson de Roland. I am familiar with the last two, but the first is a mystery to me.

They camped outside and Roosevelt describes the *babaçu* branches that can be up to 13 meters, in a detailed technical manner stating that the lateral spatulas join the trunk in pairs forming an angle of 90 degrees.

He also comments on nature saying that it is not benevolent, as people say, but is absolutely indifferent to good or bad, progressing in its goal with total disdain for the pain and suffering that it inflicts. This writing was done under the influence of the hornet stings that he and Rondon endured during one of their hunts at the ranch. The horses, also stung, took off at high speed through the forest.

Day 8

I had set up my tent outside and was getting ready for a quiet night when the *curiango* that I had seen earlier, started calling and singing ten yards away. These are small owl-like birds that prefer to sit on the ground. I probably intruded in its territory and it felt as disturbed as I. The songs had a special clangor, as if he had metal in his vocal chords. Another one answered in the distance. The *curiango* was sitting on the ground and was my jungle lullaby. Before the sun rose, at the first sign of light, the cicadas started their songs, which repeated themselves in the distance. Then, light came and nature returned to its silence.

We are heading north, passing the succession of boating wharfs 35 meters apart. The river provides a leisure place for the people from the surrounding cities. José complained that fishing was poor, but this is understandable since we saw many lines tied to trees on our way up and a collection of plastic bottles floating around. A line and hook is attached to each and the fisherman follows them on his boat. José told me that he feels that the dam being built 70 km upriver is to blame. But the pressure from excessive fishing is the main culprit.

After we passed the bridge, the forest returned to its original beauty. The mornings are cool and pleasant. The forest is thick in places and intermeshed with *buritis* (a palmate) and *babaçu* palms (a pinnate).

Two macaws fly over us and for fifteen minutes we are again immersed in the untouched beauty of the river as we approach Tapirapoan. It took the Roosevelt Rondon expedition nine days what we covered in 2.5 days. From now on, on horseback, our pace will be similar.

We find two trees covered with yellow flowers over which butterflies fly. The morass of our travel is broken by these sights. The beauty only reveals itself over in periodic surprises. The *babaçu* trees have clusters of nuts that are used to make oil.

We pass a *buriti*-like plant where the trunk penetrates into the water, the *palmito*.

Large bands of yellow butterflies cross the river. Their flight, random in a Brownian-like motion, seems to prefer the east-west direction. These are the same butterflies that congregate in light posts, on the beach, and fly off when we approach them. Could this be a migration similar to the Monarch butterflies on the west coast of the United States?

We pass a *tucum* palm tree with ripe yellow nuts of approximately one inch. These are a favorite food of the wild pigs, and in his book, Roosevelt reports that upon observation of the stomach contents, entire nuts were found. Thus, the flesh is digested and the nut is expelled.

The preponderance of palm trees gives the forest an eerie primeval appearance. I recall a painting at home of a lake or river that was backed by palm trees. *Tesoureiros,* scissor birds fly over us. Their tail is shaped like a swallow's, and this must give them some advantage in maneuvering. An entire flock of them fly over the water and from time to time one of them skirts the surface, seeming to catch something, a yellow butterfly perhaps. Roosevelt also describes them.

CHAPTER 10

THROUGH THE PARECIS LANDS ON MULES: JOURNAL AND COMMENTARY

We arrived at Tapirapoan by noon and were given a room at the middle school Marechal Cândido Rondon. The old ranch house that housed the headquarters of the Telegraphic Commission headed by Rondon is still there, and is part of the school complex. I visited it, imagining the original expedition. The school director showed us a high pole which had a ring on top. According to him, corporal punishment was delivered there. The steel ring had been removed but its emplacement was still visible.

Soon we went to *Senhora* Walda, who owns a bar 20 yards from the school, and ordered dinner. We had two beautiful *pacus* which she promised to prepare in two styles: fried and stewed. At 3 p.m. the mule truck arrived. The truck backed up on a dirt mound and they happily jumped down staying together because of their mysterious attraction to the little horse. It is known that they become attached to either mares or geldings and follow them everywhere. All Boi had to do was to tie up the paint gelding. The mules stayed around.

In such an expedition, one plans for everything—nine mules for four riders—but the paint cut himself as it jumped out, had a deep gash over the hoof and was limping badly. Let us hope that this will not be the Achilles heel of the expedition.

While the mules grazed happily after having taken their fill of water in the river, we watched the local cowboys practicing their skills with calves. The object is to lasso the calf between the ears, and the lasso has to be open around 8 "braces". This is a southern Brazilian rodeo competition. The local boys lacked skills but made up for it in enthusiasm. The Nelore calves are wild and fast, and one in each four attempts resulted in a lassoing. Of these, only a minority were caught between the horns.

Later, we were surprised by a magnificent dinner by Dona Walda, a skinny smiling lady approximately 60 years old. She kept shaking her head explaining that we were absolutely crazy; that by car we could get to Vilhena in ten hours.

"You know that Rondon's house is haunted?" she asked with a twinkle in her eyes.

"When I was a little girl, everybody believed that he would carry the slaves that he killed and would throw them in the river. There used to be a long tunnel from the house to the river."

I had just returned from the house and had not seen such tunnel.

"The director of the school had it sealed with concrete because the students would go down there."

Angonese explained that many old farms had a secret tunnel so that the occupiers could escape in case of a siege by Indians or Spaniards.

"This house is much older than Rondon, and the ring in the pole was not used by him but was there for the slaves, way before his time", Angonese concluded, defending our hero.

Hiram confirmed, though, that the Army in those days followed Count Lipp's discipline, which included corporal punishment. So, it is very probable that recalcitrant soldiers would be attached to the pole, just like in the days of the slaves. Rondon was sent the worse soldiers and troublemakers, and had to use a rigid discipline in order to conduct his important task of building the telegraph line.

Commentary:

The two boats with the Roosevelt Rondon team also arrived at noon and then the long process of assembling the team of riding mules, pack mules, pack oxen, and oxcarts started. Roosevelt describes the large corrals, employee houses, and the headquarters of the Telegraph Commission. This was a striving ranch at the time, with corrals, houses for the employees, and cultivated areas. Up to that point Cherrie and Miller had collected one thousand birds and two hundred and fifty mammals to be sent to the US through the Paraguay River. One of the Americans, Harper, was in charge of this.

Roosevelt comments on the importance of collecting and studying physical specimens but goes beyond, presaging the field of behavioral biology in a brilliant manner. He reflects on the need to observe the behavior of animals in the wild.

Day 1

We were ready to ride before 8 a.m. but had to wait for a telephone conversation with headquarters. The written orders had not arrived yet, but we got on our mules with such interesting names: Passat, Mineira, Taburé, Roxinho, Baiona.

My legs were stiff and I could hardly throw my right one on top of the horse. I have to work on flexibility. The mule attempted to take off but I finally made it. We moved 12.5 kilometers before taking a good break under a tree. The traffic on the dirt roads is somewhat annoying and we had a "horse" incident. A beautiful stallion jumped over the fence and got in the middle of our mules, trying to mount them. Boi finally lassoed the horse and pulled it back while we advanced for a distance. The mules are fine specimens, all healthy and strong. My legs ached after 2.5 hours but our bodies will gradually adjust to the new mode of transportation.

The county was divided into 45 hectare plots and given to needy people by INCRA, the agrarian reform office, but many of the original owners left, selling their plots to more enterprising farmers. The *cerrado* vegetation of short trees, somewhat similar to the African savannah, was removed and pastures were developed by planting special grasses. The temperature is very hot. We advanced in an almost straight line to the bridge on the Sepotuba River, where we would spend the night.

At 4 p.m. we were hit by a storm with heavy rain. The wind made the branches bend and we had to wear our long coats to protect the saddles and our bodies. Within one hour the storm had passed and we were at a one-way bridge which we passed, looking for a place to spend the night. No news from the truck, and we found a place with two wild dogs. The owner, pitch black, was named Lins, an originally French and somewhat aristocratic name. The place had an excellent pasture with water for the mules. We fared a little worse, and the corn shed was the only place left. We cleaned up the place, and three of us slept on corn sacks. I got a tarp that was folded to protect me from the hard soil and a sheep skin dyed red used as a saddle seat to serve as pillow. We had some food left—cheese, manioc, flour with meat, and some bread—and the lady of the house brought us some hot coffee. She wore a dress more appropriate for a whore house, and exposed her old but still lively breasts. At 7:30 p.m. we went to bed and only woke up at sunrise. The property was planted with teak trees which do very well in this region. Angonese was very sick at night, shaking with fever.

Commentary:

While we spent only half a day in Tapirapoan, the expedition spent five. The oxcarts and trucks left one day prior and would not go to Utiariy, but head directly north, seeking the shortest route to the telegraph line. However, Roosevelt and Rondon would proceed north along the east margin of the Verde River, which would take them to the Sacre and Utiarity Falls. That first night they camped by the Sepotuba River, which we also did.

Day 2

We left at 7:10 a.m. after saddling the horses and eating our REI portions. We road was initially filled with large trucks carrying rocks, calcium carbonate, cattle, beer, and other products, but soon we veered right and the traffic decreased. The changes since the Roosevelt-Rondon expedition have been dramatic, but we cannot expect a nation to remain unchanged. Large teak plantations were followed by cattle ranches. The pastures were green and lush, the result of the recent rains. One of the mules started to lie down and roll around and Boi told us that she had eaten some poisoned grass. The situation got worse and worse and at one point she laid down in a track and could no longer get up. Boi had told us horror stories of poisoned mules. He once had punctured the stomach and intestines of one of them but it was to no avail: it died shortly after.

Somehow, Boi grabbed the ears and it was able to get up, but the mule continued to roll around. Other than the little horse with the big gash, the sick mule, my hip hurting as hell, things are looking good.

At 10:30 we stopped by a house and were received by a young woman with two adorable little girls. The husband arrived after a while and they offered to prepare lunch for us. The mules had a good break.

After a delicious lunch, where she prepared a large Brazilian grouse (*perdiz*) and steak, we re-saddled the mules and continued. At 4 p.m. we entered São Jorge and went to the school. We were able to find a place for the mules and the school offered us dinner. We gave a brief presentation to the assembled students. It is gratifying to see the young kids full of interest for our expedition.

We are still waiting for the Marruá. Hopefully, it will arrive tonight so that we can again sleep in our sleeping bags.

I am learning a lot about the trade of horses. Boi has a product that he gives to snake-bitten mules. He claims that it cures the effects and is called *Especifico*. He also recommends it for people. Angonese was bitten by a wasp in the neck and the pain subsided immediately on applying it topically.

The Marruá arrived after sunset, and our expeditionary force is complete.

Commentary:

Our path diverged a little from the original expedition because an extensive cattle ranch with fenced boundaries blocked our path. The 1914 expedition had to cross a terrain which was forested. Since then, the forest has been cleared and we encountered only pastures. Roosevelt comments on the common traveler that never leaves the beaten path and is guided by others. This traveler does not need intelligence or initiative. And he resembles, in a way, a suitcase. Roosevelt contrasts this traveler with the real bushmaster. The latter is both an action and observation person and needs to have both body and soul able to act and to suffer, if necessary and the intelligence to observe and analyze.

Day 3

It is morning in São Jorge and heavy rains started at 5 a.m. waking us up with thunder and clatter on the tin roof. The Marruá arrived at 7 p.m. yesterday and we were offered a classroom, dinner and access to the school computer in the evening. This brings back memories of my childhood, dedicated *professorinhas* (little teachers) working into the night with adult classes. The writings on the wall and school desks on which often these words are being written bring back João Monlevade, the boys with blue pants and white shirts, the girls with pleated blue skirts, and a multitude of feelings since forgotten and buried in the depth of my memory. It is time to recollect and this journey is becoming a journey into my past, the Sundays spent on horseback, listening to the old cowboy *Senhor* Teixeira tell the stories of his life, knife fights, large cattle drives, varied medicines for horses, their ailments.

We gave a second presentation to the assembled grade school kids who demonstrated a touching interest in our lecture, asking a number of questions. At 9:40 we got on our horses since the rain had stopped. We were able to fill our tanks with diesel and the Marruá went ahead. The 17 km to the Jatobá Indian community took us 3.5 hours and it was indeed a pleasant journey since the temperature had dropped. We passed by large farms and some free troops of 200 to 300 steers. They are identical, proving that cloning is a reality in animal husbandry. As soon as we entered the Formosa indigenous area, we were in a different world. Gone are the pastures and the villages have wooden houses and *ocas,* the traditional Pareci longhouses. At Jatobá, Dona Nair received us effusively and described the legend of the rubber ball to us. Manioc plantations surround Jatobá village and a soccer field.

It started like this, she said:

"The ball game was given to the Parecis in the beginning of times, when all were brothers that spread to the world. Then, they arrived at a place where there was a sign.

"What should we leave for our people?

"First, they tried to play with a stone and hurt their head. Then, they took the milk of *mangaba* and fashioned a ball. It worked. They gave this to the Parecis. Wasari and Salua were brothers. There was a third brother that I do not remember. The game is called *raidia.* They ran out of balls, and the fish, the *cará,* played with the heart of a bird, the *pedreiro.*"

She looked at me, a little puzzled. The story was fading from her memory, as her culture inexorably dissolved into that of the powerful 'white' man.

Dona Nair tells me that the conflict arises because the white man uses the land for financial purposes and economic development. Aristóteles, a cherub of three, is standing by me, stark naked, holding proudly his slingshot. Earlier he separated two little dogs in a ferocious fight over a branch, and threw the branch at one of them, the culprit.

We met Carlos Marcio, the twin brother of Marcio Carlos this afternoon. He roams the Pareci and Nambikwara lands on behalf of FUNAI, solving disputes, helping the villages, and keeping order. He committed himself to talk to all the *caciques*, chiefs of the villages along our route, and we will be fine. So, our application to FUNAI worked but in a tortuous way. It enabled us to meet and gain the trust of the twin brothers. Each village will be negotiated with the chief. The twins were raised by Jesuits and are catholic. However, the Jesuits put together different ethnicities and forced them to talk Portuguese. Marcio Carlos told me that there is some resentment, and notably the Chief João Garimpeiro. He does not care for the priests but hates the Protestants much more. The latter are being pushed out.

Marcio Carlos took us on his pickup to a beautiful cave from which a river sprouts out. The water is clear and cool and runs south toward the Paraguay River.

Tonight, I sleep in an old *oca* or Indian longhouse. The Parecis call it *hati*. It is semi-abandoned and only serves for festivities to house large numbers of guests.

The *oca* is preferred by the more traditional Indians because it is quite spacy, can house a small fire in the middle, and is cooler than the tin-roof houses. It can fit two or more families. Wilson told me that the sacred arrow is kept in an *oca* and thus it has a spiritual dimension. It is sad when Indians lose their traditions, language, and embrace the culture of the dominant white. Tonight, I will sleep where countless Indians toiled, when their spirit was alive.

Commentary:

The 1914 expedition climbed the plateau through a steep trail up to an altitude of 610 m. The sun was on Roosevelt's back since it was morning. We were slightly west, approximately 20 km of them and I don't think that they went through the Jatobá Village. It is possible that it did not even exist at the time. Talking to some Indians at the Burnt Village, I gathered that the old trail, which is fairly narrow, still exists, and that it rises in a part of the plateau boundary is very steep. We were able to see a portion of this rocky outcrop, where the Formoso River has its headwaters. Roosevelt mentions the better climate and absence of mosquitos on the plateau. He also mentions the use of trucks by the expedition.

Day 4

We left Jatobá village at 7 a.m. after saying goodbye to Dona Nair and her husband. Soon the road, straight as an arrow and pointing northwest, headed up the gentle slope of the Pareci Plateau. At our right, in the distance, we could see the high walls where the Formoso River is born. The vegetation is a thick *cerrado*, that reaches 7 feet but is difficult to cross on horseback. We veered left at a bifurcation and soon realized that the direction was wrong. This was informed to us by an Indian coming on a motorcycle. We took a shortcut, a narrow trail through the brush, and indeed it was a beautiful sight, the trees leaving only a six-foot opening. The leaves are green and thick and the recent rains have embellished the entire area with a fresh coat of grass. The soft sands eventually gave way to red soil, and we saw jaguar tracks, fairly fresh, following the road for a few hundred yards, as well as tapir tracks. However, other than the band of *queixadas,* a large cousin of the peccaries, that we saw yesterday, no animals were seen. We stopped at km 20 where the Marruá awaited us with a stretched tarp and lunch. On our right the plantations stretch into the horizon, whereas the left is the original *cerrado* that has covered the plateau for eons. Two worlds that are radically different, ruled by different people and serving different purposes. On my right, the booming agribusiness and the new wealth of Mato Grosso. On my left, the land of my dreams, seen by Roosevelt and Rondon, the legendary *sertão* or badlands. My heart rests with the latter.

We arrived at Fazenda Estrela in the afternoon and were well received by the manager. In our earlier scouting trip, we had made contact with him and obtained permission to spend the night there. The farm headquarters is shaped like a star with the arms consisting of eucalyptus trees and can be seen even in google maps. It is well organized and clean. While my colleagues busily organized the camp and then rested, I took the Marruá and drove to the next village, Aldeia Queimada, or Burnt Village. This was 8 km west of the farm. The son of the chief, Armando Mozokai, was close to the *oca* and received me kindly. He asked me in and it was dark inside. A tall shadow walked toward me and greeted me with a smile.

"We were waiting for you."

It was the chief, Nelson Mozokai.

He wore pants but no shirt. Shortly thereafter, two other Indians arrived. They were very friendly and told us that we were expected.

I told Nelson that we would pay him a visit the next morning and give a presentation, and he pleaded for the preservation of the Indian lands. He reported old fights with Fazenda Estrela and their attempts to encroach in the Indian lands. The farmers were eventually pushed back and the Indigenous area of Formoso retains its 19,600 hectares. He promised to show us Rondon's house, behind the village.

Commentary:

Roosevelt does not mention the village but it is probable that he did spend the night there. However, Rondon's house was 1 km from the village and Rondon mentions the Aldeia Queimada Telegraphic Station. This is the place where the trucks were made available to the expedition. This is also consistent with Roosevelt's comments about these trucks that they met on the road. It is possible that the trucks had trouble going up the steep rise up the plateau and that they came from the east to meet the group. There was probably a road to Cuiabá at the time. Father Zahm, who had difficulty riding, joined one of the trucks, that would drive all the way to Utiarity.

Day 5

We slept miserably in a balcony in front of the workers' quarters. They arrived after dark, sweaty and black from dust, driving their monstrous tractors and seeding machines, showered, ate, and went to sleep. We crowded outside but were fortunately protected from the heavy rains that poured for a couple hours. A multitude of beetles congregated on my tent, attracted by the lone light bulb hanging over it. Two of them made it into the tent and were accidentally pushed into my makeshift pillow made with clothes. As I fell asleep, I felt a movement, parts rising. I caught and expelled the first but never located the second. The solution was to lie on my back and rest my head, not my ears, on the pillow. In this fashion, I was spared the constant noise.

The workers started leaving at 4:30 a.m.. The siren was the

waking call. We waited for the workers to leave so that we could have the kitchen and bathroom to ourselves. At 7, we left for Aldeia Queimada. The morning was cool. Nelson and his son Armando already waited for us. We drove to a creek, the headwaters of the Juba River, where we met girls washing clothes and cooking utensils. The *cerrado* surrounded the beautiful creek of crystalline waters, which we crossed on a wood plank. After walking through the bush for 15 minutes, Nelson found the spot where Rondon had built his house, approximately 1 km from the village. All that was left were rectangular rocks neatly put together. Indeed, it was not nature's work and was the floor of the house. Nelson told us in firm terms:

"He passed through here. This house burned down and that is why our village has this name of Burnt Village."

He continued: "While Rondon was away, his people ordered some Indians and beat one of them up. Shortly thereafter, lightning hit the house and it burned down."

I shook my head in agreement but pondered about this last part. Most probably a disgruntled Indian burnt down the place.

After a short lecture to the assembled group, we drove back to Estrela Farm. Later, we heard from other Indians that an old truck from the RR expedition that still remained in the village had been dismantled and taken away. Such trucks belong to a museum and it is a pity that this one was lost.

We proceeded north and stopped at the Verde River that is a little more than a creek. The road was busy, with large trucks ferrying the product of the large farms to the markets. We had transposed the divide between the two basins. The waters are cool and transparent and the recent rains had not muddied them.

Then came three villages: Rio Verde, Kotutiko and Kamai. The first was quite well established, and solid buildings indicated that it served some central purpose. There was a school. These villages are very spacy, with a large yard and a mix of *ocas* and more modern houses. Farther north 5 km, we entered Kotutiko, where we were received by Juvenal, in full Pareci garb. He carried a club, a round stone, and a bow with arrows. I remembered him from our scouting trip. He gave us a lengthy speech about the importance of keeping their lands and traditions. We were surrounded by some twenty Indians. The children played around us with naturality as the adults talked. One Indian brought the barrel of an old Cal 20 shotgun that was completely rusted. Juvenal reminded us that Rondon had given weapons to the Indians, but that FU-NAI discouraged this practice.

We gave our presentation to the assembled group and then watched the 'mule' incident of the day. Hiram's mule backed and jumped when he tried to mount it but he hung on to the bridle and she finally quieted down, after rotating around furiously.

I complimented Hiram on his control of his mule.

"I actually had the bridle wrapped around my hand and could not release it. The mule finally gave up turning me around."

Fortunately, Hiram's mule was the smallest one. Otherwise we would have had injuries. Until now, I have been more fortunate. Perhaps it is the experience from my childhood helping me to guide my mule.

The first incident, much more serious, had been scarier and could have led to serious injuries. As Angonese dismounted his skittish mule the saddle rotated to the belly and it took off, jumping and kicking madly. The saddle loosened and flew behind the mule. Angonese hung on to the mule by the bridle and finally had to let go, with considerable burns in his hands. Boi had a hard time lassoing it, bringing it to the ground, and releasing it from the ropes that constricted its groin.

We arrived at Kamai around 5 p. m. and the chief, named João Garimpeiro, received us. It was a touching display: he wore a coat made of jaguar hide and a headgear of blue macaw feathers. He walked out of his *oca* held by a grandson. Frail but lucid at 84, he welcomed us. We were given a brand new *oca* for the night, which was a pleasant surprise. After settling down we met with João Garimpeiro again and he told us of the many struggles he went through to protect Indian lands against incursions from the farmers.

"I went all the way to Campo Grande and entered into the military barracks. One captain helped us."

The memory of Rondon as a protector of the Indians is still vivid in these villages. It is admirable that the culture is still alive, one hundred years after the first contacts. Brazilians, as a rule, have a very low regard for Indians and consider them lazy and incompetent. The superintendent of the Estrela Farm, who works for Maggi, the mega farmer of Mato Grosso, told us about the 'wasted' lands.

"We could expand our plantations and create two or three counties here," he said, his gray eyes flashing. "Such a waste, this Queimada Village."

I know of current efforts to redistribute the Indian lands, to give them plots that they can then sell. But this will be disastrous for their culture. The gradual and more harmonious evolution that is taking place is the best path. João Garimpeiro has lived among the whites, and was at some point a diamond miner. But he returned to his native land and fought for the preservation of the Pareci language, culture, and lands.

Juvenal and João both mentioned that weapons would be necessary to keep the lands and that Rondon had warned them about the whites trying to take these away from them.

Commentary:

The 1914 expedition advanced east of the Sacre River but

this area is nowadays completely occupied by farms and the region has lost its essential features. Thus, we advanced west of the Sacre River. Roosevelt does not describe Pareci villages before the one at Salto Belo, north of Salto da Mulher. In contrast, we followed a string of villages where we were well received. Roosevelt's naturalist companions had great difficulty to collect specimens during this period because the mule train would invariably arrive after dark and there was little time for their work. The expedition would always camp by a creek so that the beasts of burden could get water, but the same problems encountered by us, lack of food and animals running away, were headaches for them. They must have had a decent road, since the trucks went ahead of them. Roosevelt wrote in the morning and inside his tent, that he shared with Kermit and Cherrie.

Day 6

We left Wakai at 8:30 a. m. after a short presentation. A chief from a neighboring village came to greet us, in his traditional garb. He gave me a rubber ball that they use in their game. It is made from the sap of the *mangaba* tree, whose fruit is edible. The chief told me that there are 3,150 Pareci spread among 70 villages. This makes sense.

The speeches followed as well as pleas to protect their lands. João came out and sang for us. It was a touching moment and we were told that the spirit of Rondon marched with us. Hiram was moved to tears.

Three of the mules had escaped during the night and were finally recaptured. They had walked back 13 km, heading straight home.

After goodbyes, we marched into the *cerrado,* following a road that supposedly would take us to Salto da Mulher Village, two mule days away. A couple hours later, we were informed by two young Indians riding a motorcycle that we were on the road to another village, west of our route. We veered east but the road turned south after a while. Angonese, emboldened by his orienteering skills, decided to take a shortcut. So, we left the road and penetrated into the *cerrado* that grew thicker as the clouds above us became darker. We had already stopped for lunch in the middle of a deluge and did not look forward to a second one. After half an hour under increasingly difficult conditions, our animals running ahead of us, as if in panic, the decision was made to turn back. Another half an hour and we were fortunately back on our original trail. We thought that the road would take us back to Kamai Village, a two to three-hour ride, but suddenly the Marruá appeared. Eder and Yuri had scouted out the place and had found the road, which had been marked with branches by the Indian teens. We advanced 3 km and reached the right road.

As we readied ourselves to camp, the rain returned, coming down from a sky crisscrossed by lightning and thunder. We ate and got into our tents, exhausted. My splitting headache and fatigue made me suspect malaria, not a welcome ailment. The hernia expands on horseback and is becoming quite uncomfortable. I broke off a tree branch, made a pillow with leaves, and inserted it under the belt, on my groin. This did the job which I was previously doing manually. I can feel the intestines as they swell after a meal. Hope the little that is left of the muscles will hold up to the end. We probably advanced a little more than 15 km, although we walked 35 km.

The rain subsided after 9 p.m. but we were already all asleep.

Day 7

Four of the mules escaped! Attempts are being made to retrieve them. They were already difficult yesterday and there is little food in the *cerrado*. We fully realize now the difficulties encountered by the early expeditions. Lévi-Strauss moaning about the interminable searches for mules in the mornings is thus true. If a band of them decides to head back in the night, there is little we can do to stop them. Four of the mules are attached emotionally to the little horse, which we keep tied, and they are still here.

The *cerrado* seems barren of life, except for the occasional chant of the *siriema*. We saw two large partridges lifting, large quail the size of chicken, and a little monkey yesterday, nothing else. The soil is now red and there are tuffs of grass every ten inches, and low trees every few yards. Other than the bees and a few mosquitos, swarms of termites fly out of the mounds after the rain and follow us.

This morning, as we wait for the four wayward mules, bees hound us, and the only respite is the tent, already inhabited by the termites from last night.

I would like to digress a little about the Pareci vision of the world. As João's son told us, there are two worlds, and they have to exist in both. He explained that Indians have a weakness, alcohol, and that wealth from agriculture will only lead to trouble. In essence, he recommends their simple ways with strong family bonds and a gradual adaptation to the white man's ways. The children are especially touching. Beautiful, free, playful, they run around from *oca* to *oca*. I had seen this previously in the Xingu River, and this image is repeated.

However, the diet of the Indians has changed radically and the large consumption of sugar is leading to rotten teeth in the children as well as adults and large-scale diabetes. They do not have our ability to process sugar since the production of insulin does not match ours.

We wait until midday and the Marruá comes back with three exhausted persons and zero mules. Boi had tracked them and found that they headed toward a village called Zanauá. We wait patiently, keeping an eye on the other five.

It was 4 p.m. when they returned, but in an old pick-up driven by an Indian who introduced himself as the chief of the Zanakwa Village. His son, an enterprising teenager, had found the mules miles from the village, and driven them, with his motorcycle, to a corral. These were the good news. The bad news was that the Marruá had lost a wheel... So, we need to call headquarters in Cáceres to get a second Marruá and a repair truck. This will mean a delay of about three days to our trip. So, I will have plenty of time to keep up with my diary writing our experiences and comparing them with Roosevelt's account. I cannot cease to increase my admiration for the 1913-14 expeditioners as we encounter challenges in our journey: rain, mosquitos, and lost mules.

Today, something bit my right leg, which readily swelled up. Bees of two kinds hounded us for the entire day. The small ones do not bite but can be quite an annoyance. Roosevelt mentions them. The bees cover the saddle blankets in a continuous mat and surround us. They seem to be fond of the salt of the skin.

Commentary:

Roosevelt describes the local vegetation in vivid terms: the trees that are rarely higher than a rider, and miniature palms on the ground. He attributes their small size to an enhanced ability to resist the winds, but I have to disagree with him, since we did not encounter strong winds. We saw a couple of *tocandera* ants that have a length of one inch and are highly poisonous. The scarcity of game noticed by Roosevelt was confirmed by us and cannot be attributed to over hunting. I believe that most game is concentrated along the riverine forests.

Day 8

We had again heavy rains in the night, and in the early hours of the morning Mariano, the Indian chief, and his son arrived with their pickup, whose front had been smashed when he hit a tapir.

Although the *cerrado* is green and lush now, it must be barren during the dry season, when the torrid sun bakes the soil for many months.

We have to wait for a decision from headquarters regarding a second truck and will stay here at Zanakwa in the meantime.

We went to the river in the afternoon for a bath and five kids, aged from 4 to 9, were already in the water. What a beautiful sight to watch these dark brown bodies carry out jumps, pirouettes, and dive in the rapid stream, which is shallow in the margins but is deeper and runs fast in the center. In our days of helicopter parents where supervision is 24/7, the scene of free children playing in the nature unsupervised reminds me of my childhood. The little girl was very proud of her diving skills and showed them off repeatedly. They did not speak Portuguese but communicated with wide smiles and laughter. In the late afternoon, I took the bow and arrows given to Eder at the Kamai Village and tried a few shots. The older boy, André, showed me the Indian technique. They don't seem to aim carefully but hit the target fairly well. After a few tries I improved, but my arrows would go systematically to the left, a correction that I could not do.

Mariano showed us the *oca* under construction and the technique used. The *buriti* palms are placed in rows after the stems are folded. Every three rows receive an external strip of wood so that they remain attached to the structure.

The women washed our clothes but the rain hit us in the afternoon and nothing dried. They had worked hard and were able to iron out the moisture of the thinner clothes. In the evening, they arrived with beads, headdresses, and other articles of their manufacture. They gave us a gift each and we thanked them effusively.

At night, as soon as the rain stopped, we were invaded by a

myriad of termites. A bat zoomed in the house and I quickly put up my tent.

Day 9

In the morning, one of the mules had a string of coagulated blood, proving that my decision to set up my tent inside the house was a wise one.

We started at 7 a.m. since Boi had tied the legs of the mules with leather straps and none of them escaped. Four were kept in Mariano's orchard.

I ate a delicious breakfast. The *mangaba* fruit has a sweet-sour taste that is sophisticated and unique. It has the shape and size of a guayaba and is filled with seeds covered by a white and soft matter that provides the flavor. We found a bunch of *mangaba* bushes along the way but they were hard and exuded a milky sap that turned viscous within ten minutes. I believe that they have to be collected in this condition and ripen out of the tree. This would be an excellent 'exotic' natural fruit that could ride on the success of *açai*.

At midday, we stopped and, as I tried to dismount, the entire saddle rotated and I fell hard on the ground, since the mule bucked. Fortunately, I only have a bruised arm. Tightening the saddle periodically is essential, and I had forgotten to do it.

At a distance, on the east, we can see trees from plantations, in the large farms. The entire stretch from Verde and Papagaio Rivers has been occupied by farms, whereas the stretch between Sacre and Verde is a reservation and the vegetation is the original *cerrado*.

At 2 p.m. we entered the boundary between plantations and *cerrado* and the contrast between the two was striking. On our left, the untouched bush. On our right, the immensity of fields that had been harvested for corn and replanted for soy. At a distance, large machinery worked the land. The red soil of the *cerrado* is devoid of stones, making its preparation rather easy.

Two Indians came by in their motorcycles. One of them carried a rifle. The land has been leased to the farmers, and as we entered the Salto da Mulher village, we saw quite a difference from Zanakwai. Solid houses, interspersed with *ocas,* spread over a wide area. The chief, Anselmo, had arranged a comfortable house for us, the most modern in the village. He had built it for his son, who had recently died of a drowning accident in the nearby Sacre River.

As we approached Salto da Mulher, the vegetation became progressively taller. We met a party of Indians in a pickup truck.

"We are going to hunt for deer and emu at the corn fields", said the driver as his kids filmed us with their smart phones. As they did this, Col. Hiram's horse bucked and threw him on the ground. His saddle had loosened and rotated. The same thing that had happened to me earlier and I fell on my left side, bruising my arm. I was lucky that my foot disengaged from the saddle and that the mule did not take off in panic, but jumped up in shock. This is not a country for old men, as I joked in my e-mail!

Boi is very sick and it was decided to take him to the nearest city, Campo dos Parecis, to have him checked by a doctor. He has several abscesses under his left arm and also a persistent cough.

Day 10

Boi came back from town late. He is dehydrated and received an IV, in addition to medication (antibiotics). Let us hope that he returns to his old cheery self. Without him we are lost. The heavy body suffered when he tracked the mules through the bush for four hours. He finally stopped, dizzy and exhausted. The Indian boy, Mariano Filho, had found the mules at Zanakwa.

He looked better this morning, put his mules in form and

saddled them. We hit the road at 10 a.m. with a modest goal: to reach a shed 10 km from Bacaval. The Marruá was sent to town to get fresh supplies. We arrived at the shed at 5 p.m., having spent some time speaking to Parecis on the road. One of them, a handsome fellow 6 foot tall, had completed his Agricultural Engineering studies and gave us a lecture about the new Indian attempt to exploit their lands in conjunction with the farmers. This is a good idea as long as most of the area is left untouched. The Indians want a share of the wealth that is extracted from this plateau, and rightfully so. Brazil is a highly bureaucratic country and this has impeded its progress. The government does not allow this type of arrangement, but the Indians have blocked highways in protest.

In Salto da Mulher, the chief Anselmo told us again that Rondon had armed the Parecis, depositing an immense trust in them.

We proceeded west through a monotonous terrain, but saw some toucans, parrots and hawks. The toucans have a most interesting flight, flopping their wings three times and then resting for the same amount of time.

Boi is feeling better. He has unique way to communicate with mules. They respect him and I have not yet seen one trying to kick him, though they do this to each other all the time. It is especially the case of the paint horse bucking the newcomers, but Boi is treated with respect. He utters some strange loud sounds: eeheeheeh ---shishishisi---viraviravira---. This is said with firmness, and he moves slowly and steadily, his portly body showing intent. If a mule tries to sneak or trick him, she gets a good lash. However, he does not experience rage events, and his strength and consistency is what the mules respect. He delivers punishment methodically.

He was quiet the first day, but his steady composure sweetened when he told me:

"*Doutor*, I went into a village once and the Indian girls had their little breasts exposed." Then, he smiled: "You would love to suck on them, *Doutor.*"

From that moment on, he joked about the Indian girls for the entire day. His life came to us in pieces. He had had five wives or women. "This is common around here, *Doutor.*"

We stopped for lunch along the road, heading straight for the north, after passing the highway with large trucks and stopping at the Bacaval village, one of the largest in the Pareci territory. As we entered the village, we came across a series of ponds which will house fish hatcheries.

Miriam, the *cacique*, received us in a large, open building where a group of women wore white masks and were making soap. Two FUNAI employees instructed them and the goal is to make liquid soap for internal use as well as bar soap and perfumed body soap for sale. Miriam asked repeatedly what our goal was, and we gave our standard lecture. Later, she expressed concern about the loss of land by the Parecis. "We don't have anybody in Congress."

"This government is a disaster", complemented one of the FUNAI ladies. "We deposited so much hope in it."

In any case, she said that Congress had passed a law and now it would be introduced to the Senate to distribute Indian lands. Miriam is a serious and hard-working chief, and I hope that her concerns are not warranted. However, I fear she might be right, since Brazilians look down on Indians as lazy. Deep down, the exploitation and invasion process that started in the 1500s still continues to this day, as the remains of these people are corralled into smaller and smaller plots. If it were not for Rondon they would have been completely obliterated.

The midday stop was an inferno of small black flies and larger ones landing on our skins, on the saddles, and flying everywhere. This curse was already described by Roosevelt; the small, black bees do not bite at us, but the larger ones give painful stings that produced significant swelling in my leg and hand, causing allergic reaction. As I got on the horse and said my good-bye to the soldiers, one of them went right into my mouth. I felt a sting in my throat and prayed that it was not one of the large ones.

"You might have to use your knife for a tracheotomy," I half-joked to Angonese as we departed.

I was lucky that it was one of the small black ones since my throat remained open.

There is no place to camp beside the narrow dirt road and the soldiers macheted a spot for the kitchen and for our own camp. The mules will be tied tonight because there is no pasture. An Indian warned us that we are in jaguar country, and we hope that our mules will be spared. What a pandemonium it would be!

The *cerrado* is now thick and the trees gradually gain height and straighten up. There won't be any food for the mules tomorrow, either.

Commentary:

The slightly different path taken by the 1914 expedition took them to Salto Belo on the Sacre River. Although neither Roosevelt nor Rondon mention it, according to Pareci legend, their people come from a place close to there, where the river comes out of the rocks. We saw a similar and striking cavern close to the Jatobá village: the river goes underground and then reappears, shooting out of a cavern. Out of this cavern the first Pareci came out.

Day 11

The morning light brings clarity to my troubled being. The rains whipped my tent as we got up at 4:30, too early a start for a 50 km stretch to our goal, Utiarity. If we reach it, we will have made significant progress. We had several mule incidents during the night, one of them getting tangled in the rope and jumping around. We had to camp on the road and tie the mules on trees.

Since there is no grass, we fed them corn, which we dispense on the road, in nine piles so that they do not fight.

Coffee helped to warm my body shaken by an insistent cough which lasted for an hour. A couple days ago, I lost my voice completely. At the break of light, we were on our mules, ready for our journey. The morning was cool and the rain died and there was some beauty to be seen above the impenetrable *cerrado*: four macaws flew over us and as soon as they saw us they started their raucous banter and circled around us in reconnaissance before proceeding. I walked for one hour, from 8:30 to 9:30, to break the monotony and pain of riding and to prepare myself for the crossing of the Nambikwara lands.

The temperature gradually rose but was still bearable by the time we stopped at 10:30, having covered 25 km. The break was pure torture, with the bees haunting us as the sun baked us. It was a relief to re-saddle the mules and take off at noon, for an additional five hours to our target. The heat became almost unbearable as the day was sunny and the clouds stayed east of us. The road was a monotonous cut through the *cerrado* that gradually increased to a forest. We passed tapir and jaguar tracks, but saw no animals and only two cars. I got off the mule and walked for another hour.

The sun was already losing its sting when we saw the first roof of Utiarity Village at the end of the interminable stretch. I could hear the hum of the fabled waterfall, which we will visit tomorrow at length. Somehow I still had some reserves left in my tired body and the two-hour walk helped a lot. My companions were sorer than I.

The Indians assembled in front of the house allocated to us and I helped Boi to tie the front feet of the four mules not emotionally attached to the bell horse. This is not such as simple affair, because they do not submit willingly to the restraints. After coercing the group into formation, their front legs are tied. One of them tried to kick Boi and he had to apply a lip-twisting technique to steady it. The upper lip is put in a rope that is severely tightened. Then, with the help of a lever, it is twisted. The animal becomes docile at this point because any reaction is followed by further tightening of the loop. This disciplining and corporal punishment to the mules is necessary because they can be treacherous animals. The village is large but has only one *oca* that needs to be covered with *buriti* leaves.

Day 12

Today we rest at Utiarity in preparation for the crossing of the river and the last two days to the São Miguel farm, where we will say good bye to the mules. It is a welcome rest and we chat with the Indians. They are indeed gentle with their kids and there is no bullying. These Indians bear a striking resemblance to each other and seem to be members of an extended family. Galego, the young man who guided us to the waterfall when we scouted out the place by car and jumped into the river to retrieve the ferry in spite of a bad cough, is sitting outside and will help us again.

Flocks of swallows that nest in the rocks close to the waterfall crisscross the sky, bringing happiness to the morning. The chief, Orivaldo, showed up. He seems to be an energetic fellow and asked pointed questions. Maria Tertuliana also visited us with her husband. We had met her in August and she is an intelligent, talkative, and kind person. She must be in her late seventies or eighties and is the grandmother of Galego and, most probably, of the majority of the local Indians. Skinny as a bean sprout, her face is covered with wrinkles and her little eyes are full of life.

The local teacher came by and talked to us, relaying old stories of Rondon. She told us about the method that he used to attract the Indians.

"He would leave a machete, sugar, and knives by the river, where they would bathe in the morning.

"The Indians looked at the objects, tasted the sugar, and then left everything. At that time, Rondon would come out of the forest, take a machete, and cut a tree with it. When they saw this, they believed him and accepted the gifts."

She and Maria Tertuliana had studied in the Jesuit mission across the river, by the name of Anchieta, in honor of the famous scholar and priest who had written the first Tupi Guarani dictionary and who played a major role in the early colonization of Brazil.

Contrary to the reports of João Garimpeiro, they both were very positive about their experiences in the mission, which brought together kids of many villages and several ethnicities.

"My father was a Nambikwara and mother a Pareci," she said. "Enemies became friends."

The Jesuits took care of the boys and nuns educated the girls. The girls learned sowing, cooking, reading, and writing, and other domestic skills and are proud of their heritage.

"Some kids did not want to subject and ran off to the cities, ranches, or mining camps. But they did not amount to anything."

Thus rang a bell in my mind: wasn't João Garimpeiro a gold and diamond miner before he became chief?

The Jesuit discipline was and is severe but directed people toward both spiritual and temporal elevation. The use of corporal punishment through the *palmatoria* was widely practiced in Brazil, although not in Monlevade, my home town. Ear pulls and skin twists were applied by the teachers, though. In Luxembourg, disciplining by using a ruler was applied sparingly but was often necessary to keep order in the classroom.

"Indians do not punish their kids," said the teacher. "So, we were shocked."

Eventually, the mission closed down. It was an encroach-ment in Indian territory and the development brought by it, a small airstrip to take the severely sick and wounded to the city, a building housing all the workshops, a water turbine for generating electricity all fell apart. I did not ask about the religious aspects of their education.

"Utiarity is the sacred white bird of the Parecis. It would come down from heaven and enlighten celebrations," said Tertu-liana. "But he no longer comes. His spirit is dying."

There is always a twinkle in her eyes. Yesterday she came by carrying a two-month baby, already awake and fully aware of her environment. Today she returned with her husband and told us many stories of the old mission, which we visited in the afternoon.

It was sad to contemplate the tombs of the cemetery where the nuns still have their nameplates. The years of death are 1949, 1954, and 1964. They lived to their fifties. The other tombs were either destroyed or disappeared. The grotto for the Virgin Mary was still there but empty of the statue. The ruins of the church and other buildings are a testament to the hard work of these people. In the heyday, about 300 Indians from many ethnicities lived there. The water provided electrical power to the mission and surrounding village. When the mission closed down, the In-dians from the Sacre Village dismantled the electrical generator and took it. However, they never put it to work in the Sacre Falls and the entire effort was lost.

The Nambikwara chief of Trés Jacus arrived with his entou-rage of about thirteen, including adults and children. He sat down, gave a speech, and proceeded to explain that Indians had financial needs similar to whites, the *Inutis* as the Parecis call them. He mellowed down after a while but his initial stance was quite ag-gressive. Then, he explained to me why they lived so close to the Pareci.

It happened after the measles and smallpox ravaged his tribe. The central-north part of the plateau was left open and this is where Maggi and his cohort entered and opened farms. This was a rapid process with devastating effects for the Indians and their lands. The Pareci chief eventually gave the northern region of his land to the Nambikwara, saying:

"The *Inuti* will take our land anyway. So, you keep it."

Thus, three Nambikwara villages are located north of Utiari-ty. Then, there is a broad swath of land, to the west, about 150 km wide, occupied by farms. It is only west of the Juína River that the major Nambikwara lands start. It is amazing that this process is rather recent, fifty years ago. The danger is that it will continue, if left by itself.

The mission played an important role after disease ravaged the Indians of the region. Entire villages succumbed to measles and smallpox and the priests and nuns gathered the surviving orphans. The Nambikwara, severely reduced in numbers by disease, congregated close to the mission to receive medical help. This led to the emptying of their lands, of which the white man took advantage, advancing and occupying them. At some point the Jesuits asked the Indians to return to their lands in order not to lose them forever, closing the mission.

José Miguel left without a clear resolution but will await us tomorrow. He told me, before we parted:

"We have a truck in Sapezal in need of repairs. The mechanic wants Re 4,000 to fix it."

I balked and answered that it was too much money, thinking that Mané Manduca would ask for at least twice what he demanded. As Angonese puts it so well: 'Meyers, we only have to kill one lion per day.' We will kill this lion tomorrow, when we meet again. My colleagues are afraid that he will arrest us and keep us for ransom, but I am more optimistic.

Commentary:

Although Roosevelt's dream of transforming the area into a Niagara of western Brazil did not materialize, the untouched beauty of the waterfalls is even more precious. It is moving for us to look down into the deep valley adorned by a perennial rainbow and to reminisce about Roosevelt, who sat at this place on a bench constructed by Rondon. Pareci Indians danced into the night for the expedition and the haunting description by Roosevelt brings back to live this ceremony. They also imbibed a fermented mandioc drink. The men celebrated the feats of valiant hunters. They looked healthy and strong, but Roosevelt commented on the smallpox and measles outbreaks that had decimated the Pareci. So, the tragic process of destruction had already started.

Fiala, Lt. Lauriado, and some companions descended the Papagaio River from here. They lost two dugout canoes right away, and then returned to bring the Canadian canoe transported by the expedition and abandoned close to Utiariy because of the excess weight. They successfully completed their river descent and the rowers rapidly adapted to the lighter Canadian canoe. Unfortunately, and tragically for the descent of the River of Doubt by Roosevelt and Rondon, the heavy dugouts caused great suffering.

Since the beasts of burden could not find sufficient fodder, a problem that we also encountered, the equipment had to be severely restricted from that point on. This is the reason for abandoning the Canadian canoe.

The author in 1969 at the Aporinan River, a tributary of the Purus River, not far from the River of Doubt.

Monument inspired by Stanley Kubrick's monolith erected at the entrance of town of Pauiní, on the Purus River. This monument is a homage to the Rondon Project, in which the author participated.

First meeting of co-leaders of 1913-1914 Expedition, Colonels Theodore Roosevelt and Cândido Mariano Rondon.

Cáceres Second Frontier Battalion: start of our journey. From left: Lieutenant Meyers, Colonels Angonese and Hiram, expedition participants, and Colonel Braga, Battalion Commander.

Monument to Auguste Comte in front of Sorbonne, Paris.

Close-up of bust and Church of Positivism, founded by Rondon in Brazil. The frontispiece has the three major principles of the doctrine:
Love as Principle, Order as Foundation, Progress as Goal.

Up the Sepotuba River; Roosevelt's crew hunting in Porto do Carmo ranch.

Our two aluminum boats that were used for the Sepotuba; The Roosevelt-Rondon Expedition also used power boats.

Hunting on Sepotuba River where Roosevelt shot this deer.

Tree at Porto de Carmo ranch where Roosevelt and Rondon took picture.

The long journey on horseback; the Roosevelt-Rondon expedition.

Our journey on mules.

Burnt Village with Chief Nelson Mozokai in front of *oca*.

Chief Nelson Mozokai showing remains of the foundation of Rondon's house, which burned down mysteriously.

Giving presentation to Pareci Indians. They are courteous, hospitable, and keep alive memories of Rondon.

Interior of *oca* where I slept.

Roosevelt, Rondon, and expedition members at lunch.

Our group and mules at lunch break.

Roosevelt watching archer.

Indian boy demonstrating archery technique in our expedition.

Camp in Rondon's days. He loved dogs.

Our typical camp in *cerrado*.

Utiarity Falls: Roosevelt surrounded by Pareci Indians. Note girls holding his leg and shoulder.

On the same spot with our guide Galego.

Crossing of Papagaio River on ferry.

Pareci kids swam across river to give us goodbye gifts.

Telegraph line after Utiarity.
Left: Roosevelt and Rondon on horseback.
Right: Chief José Miguel with the only intact post, probably of the indestructible wood *brauna*. All other posts had rotted away, except a couple we found submerged.

1914 expedition with Nambikwara.

Our team with Nambikwara Chief José Miguel.

The challenge of crossing rivers. Getting mules on ferry at Utiarity, Papagaio River.

Crossing the Juína River with mules swimming across. Boi is 'encouraging' them.

The difficult crossing of the thick bush on foot in Nambikwara land. Fresh troops in the beginning.

On the telegraph line. Angonese holds steel wire.

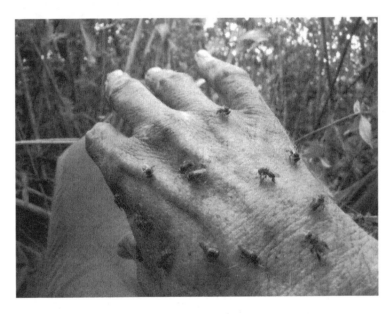

On second day, out of water, trapped by impenetrable vegetation in Nambikwara territory, and assailed by bees. Wild groups of Enawenê Indians still roam these lands. Fortunately, we did not cross paths.

Fallen trees from storm. Nambikwara Ari on the ax.

Opening the road to Kitalu village:Impassable holes that had to be filled before Marruá could pass.

Oca with young girls that have to remain naked and isolated for one month in coming-of-age ceremonial. They are visited by little girls.

Nambikwara group during Lévi-Strauss expedition.

Indian woman and *xiri* at Kitalu Village and carrying our gifts.

Giant armadillo hunted by Nambikwara Indians.

Col. Angonese testing bridge for sturdiness.

Presentation to Nambikwara at Kitalu Village.

Cross in cemetery for Rondon's soldiers and workers. The graves are mentioned by Roosevelt.

Roosevelt River as a small creek on the outskirts of Vilhena. It will grow to a majestic river after 700 km.

Preparation for river descent in Hotel Colorado in Vilhena, our staging place. We are looking at the valuable Google earth maps that will prove to be invaluable, because Col. Hiram marked the paths on each rapid and waterfall.

Meeting at mayor's office in Vilhena. We were able to secure support from the local Fire Department and this proved to be very valuable. Standing: Rita Marta, who is the Ceremonial Chief of the office and a very important person in the community. She proved to be a dynamic and energetic ally and coordinated meetings with the press, which gave us ample coverage.

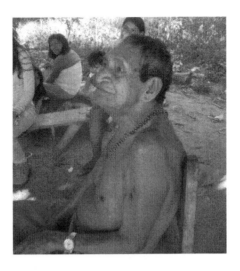

Manuel Sabanê, octogenarian who still remembers Rondon. He has an arrow scar on the left arm and told us stories of the old days when he had to establish contact with the Cinta Larga and was often received by a shower of arrows.

Sabanê girl with peccary. This peccary was left behind when they encountered a school in the forest. Lévi-Strauss describes the doting of the Nambikwara with their pets, treated with the same loving care as humans.

The River of Doubt (still called by this name in maps) at the Sabanê village. This is some 20 km upstream from the launching of the Roosevelt-Rondon expedition. The Sabanê told us that downstream from this point the river becomes a marsh that cannot be navigated. Manuel's wife described to us the immense effort that the tribe had to go through once, when they crossed the marsh.

Exact point on River of Doubt where 1914 expedition launched off. Roosevelt and dugouts ready to descend the river. The level of water reached the beams of the bridge.

Vestiges of same bridge in *Fazenda* Baliza; note the much lower level of water in October.

Roosevelt's dugout canoe loaded to close to waterline.

First day on the river. Col. Hiram holds the canoe while Col. Angonese and Jeffrey get ready to settle in. Once they were seating, stability was good. The weight of the load stabilized canoe.

Leo Miller's photograph of the expedition initiating the descent of the River of Doubt. Miller then proceeded to explore the Gy-Paraná River; Miller was the National Museum's naturalist.

Our first day on the river. We kept the canoe between the two kayaks as a measure of precaution.

Illegal logging in Cinta Larga terrritory. All workers were inside the Cinta Larga territory and we had to portage over the makeshift bridge that blocked the river. The camp housed about ten persons and the cook received us and gave us presents of sardine cans.

Logger truck coming from the Cinta Larga reservation.

Camping in the forest above the Navaité Falls. The chairs enhanced the comfort of our journey.

The Navaité Falls and rapids photographed by the 1914 expedition. The water level was definitely higher.

Narrowing of river to close to 3 meters. Going down these rapids would be certain death.

Portaging kayak through rock formation by the Navaité Falls. This was a relatively easy operation and two persons can walk one kilometer in twenty minutes. However, portaging required about five back-and-forth trips by each member.

The large rock formation at Navaité. We portaged through them with relative ease.

Cherrie showing how river narrowed from one hundred to 2 meters.

Striking classic rifle pose from the early picture of Cherrie. River is a little over 2 meters at this spot.

Col. Angonese in front of rock similar to the one of the famous
Roosevelt-Rondon photograph.

CHAPTER 11

THROUGH THE NAMBIKWARA LANDS: JOURNAL AND COMMENTARY

Day 1

Today was a hard, hard day. We crossed the Papagaio River on the ferry, three mules at a time, without too much trouble. Then, we headed north along the telegraph line, which passed through Utiarity. On a few spots, we saw the remains of rotten posts on the ground. They were barely recognizable from the other fallen trees, and the only distinguishing feature was that they were straighter than the tortuous *cerrado* trees. We did 35 km on a trail that gradually grew narrower. As the mules passed some branches, they awakened hornets and my mule took off. I got three painful stings. The midday stop was pure torture with millions of bees. Roosevelt describes this well and there is a picture of him wearing a net and his thick Western riding gloves while writing. Our destination was not exactly the new Nambikwara village of Três Jacus, but the ruins of an older one in a depression called Buracão that was in exact alignment with the telegraph line.

On our scouting trip, we had gone to Três Jacus, Wakalitem in Nambikwara language, and entered the village, which did not have any *oca*. We headed for the school building and were received by José Flavio, the bus driver. He lives in the village but spends three days in Sapezal, driving the kids to school on the other days. In his naïve way, he explained to us some of the esoteric customs of the Nambikwara:

- They bury their dead with all their possessions and then abandon the house.
- The husband has the right to sleep with the sisters of his wife.
- The old ones still prefer to sleep on the ground by the ashes of the fire.
- They never fight among themselves.
- They are excellent hunters and throw the catch, skin and everything, into the fire.
- The young girls are extremely good looking, with a twinkle in their eyes.

I gathered that a filming crew had been there recently, interviewing some of Lévi-Strauss' last acquaintances. There are some old Indians that still remember him. This was 76 years ago!

We met the Marruá as we approached the depression. The truck could not follow us on the trail and had to make a long drive to avoid the ferry. We were afraid that the ferry could not take its weight and did not want to risk calling headquarters and informing them that the Marruá was at the bottom of the Papagaio River. This would be our last resting place before the mules would cross the Buriti River.

The driver informed us that the Marruá had another flat and we were now reduced to a fourth tire that is on its last leg. Tomorrow this has to be resolved. As we went down, the mules took off ahead of us and lost themselves in the thick brush in search of water. All they found was mud, into which Boi's mule sank. As we searched for the mules, we found fragments of the original insulators.

The Nambikwara visited us in the evening to negotiate the passage through their lands. My Brazilian colleagues resent this attitude by the Indians but I understand them. José Miguel arrived in a big truck with his sidekick. He went down the big hole and showed Angonese the way and then returned and took me to the sole post still standing from Rondon's days. It was a last sentry marking this heroic feat and we photographed it.

We finally agreed on the sum: 1,500 Reais plus 200 Reais for his guiding us tomorrow to the Buriti River. As the sun set, the bees retreated, as if by a touch of magic. However, the pain of their bodies in my eyes still endured. We had a pleasant dinner and got to our tents by 8:30 p.m. as usual. The mules were tied to trees to keep them from escaping.

Day 2

We got up at 5 a.m. and by 6 a.m. were ready to go but no sign of José Miguel. Angonese knows the way through the thick brush and we only have to cover 8 km.

I hear the hum of his truck in the distance and we are ready to follow Roosevelt and Rondon's steps down to the *Buriti*. José Miguel informs us that he cannot come with us.

"My folks collected lots of *piqui* yesterday and we need to take them into town to sell."

These are the duties of the chief, as defined by Claude Lévi-Strauss. He brought a brand new *xiri* but unfortunately, I did not buy it.

We ride down, starting at 6:40, and enter meandering trails that eventually lead to a straight one. It is the telegraph line. At 8 a.m. we arrive at the river, since the ride is easy. It is narrow and swift. And we wait. And wait.

At 10 a.m. Angonese fires a shot, and then heavy rains came. Cold and drenched, I crouched under a Nambikwara shed made with three pieces of zinc. Probably the leftover of a hut and possibly from one of the houses that adjoined the ferry. The rain came in only at certain spots, decreasing my pain and cold. But it also passed, and a new scourge arrived: the bees. Entering our eyes, walking all over us, and occasionally stinging us. We had received the promise by the manager of the farm that he would provide us a boat and engine to ensure the transportation of the mules. In the Roosevelt days, there was a ferry consisting of two canoes tied side-by-side.

Without any alternative, the resourceful Angonese decided to swim across the river and run toward the main farm. After an hour, he appeared and shortly thereafter, a tractor with an aluminum boat. The problem was that it had only one paddle.

We were readying ourselves to turn back on our tracks, up the painful rise to the Nambikwara village, when the Marruá appeared with more news. Ariovaldo, the farm manager, was heading to the next town to get an outboard motor. In the meantime, the rain had stopped and the bees were attacking us without pity. We had not eaten since 6 a.m. and the uncertainty of throwing the mules into the fast current was temerity at best. Boi was especially worried. I pleaded with Angonese. His first decision of pulling the bell horse through the water with the boat on a rope and of throwing all the mules into the water and forcing them to swim freely across the river at the same time would have been a disaster and was fortunately changed. We built a narrow open-faced corral to push the mules into the water. Boi finally looked at us, sorrow in his eyes, and said:

"Each mule has to be driven separately on a long rope. This is the only way."

At 5 p.m. Ariovaldo appeared on the other bank with the motor. He attached it to the boat, tested it, and crossed over. Two people got into the water while Boi and I whipped the bell horse onto the river. After a few tries, the boat pulled out and the rope was successfully thrown to Angonese. Controlling the tension, the boat rode across, and the little horse made it by a hair. If it had passed the beach there was no other place to get off the river since the banks were covered with dense vegetation. The bell horse was able to jump in the last inches of the beach.

Emboldened by this first success, we ferried the mules, one after the other. They heard the bells across the water and we drove them through the corral, from which they could not turn around. Then, we whipped them into the water with loud yells. This forced them to advance until they had to swim. Boi, with his deep understanding of mule psychology, had not taken them to the water to drink all day.

"Once they see the river, they'll get scared and won't jump in."

He was right. All mules were brought over in less than twenty minutes. The operation was swift and efficient, and some of the mules were surprisingly good swimmers, all better than the bell horse. By the time we brought the saddles over, crossed the forest, entered the expansive fields, and rode into the farm, it was already 7 p.m.. The mules ran away once again but we were able to find them behind one of the fields. What a day!

Commentary:

The 1914 expedition crossed the Buriti River on a small ferry. Rondon had established a system of ferries along the rivers, which ran on a south-north trajectory in that region. Thus, the telegraph line, running east-west, intercepted them. None of these barges exist, except for the one at Utiariry Falls. Several have been replaced by bridges, except for the *Buriti* and Juína Rivers. This renders our mule trek more difficult. On the Juruena River a small hydroelectric plant has been constructed at the exact location of the telegraph line. On the Buriti River, we found the location of the house where the ferry operator lived. Ariovaldo also told us that there used to be a cable there, which he threw away. The floor of the kitchen and the place of the stove could still be seen.

Roosevelt crossed the Buriti River on the ferry and camped on the west bank. This ferry was operated by two Pareci Indians working for the Telegraph Commission. He commented that each of them had two wives, as was customary these days. Their houses had been attacked by Nambikwaras earlier and the Parecis defended themselves by firing into the air with their Winchesters, as instructed by Rondon, who wanted to stop the war between these two tribes.

Day 3

The mule truck arrived the previous night, with perfect coordination. By 8 a.m. we had left the large impeccably maintained industrial farm belonging to the Schaeffer group. Ariovaldo, the manager, told us that the group has 320,000 hectares throughout Brazil. Every farm has to adhere to strict ISO rules and not a single piece of trash is allowed in the fields or around the farm. Large modern equipment in spacious sheds demonstrates the level of organization and investment.

"I went to Roraima to look at farmland," he told us. "We have farms even in Maranhão."

Industrial farming on this scale is the way of the future for countries like Brazil, the US, Russia, and Australia.

We also had to hear Ariovaldo's complaints about the Indians. He claims that they spearfish in the river and that his chosen spot is now devoid of *pacu*, his favorite catch. He also implied that they might cross the river at night and hunt on his property. How things have changed since the days in which the nomadic Nambikwara roamed the lands freely. The price of land in the area has skyrocketed to US$3,000 per hectare, making a 1,000-hectare farm quite valuable.

We had to resolve several problems in Sapezal, but were able to visit a small museum built around pieces found by Nivaldo Bertoto, who was one of the first gauchos to come to this area from the south: he arrived in 1978. Like all the people from this area, he had fantastic stories to tell us from these days. This one should be remembered.

"The night I arrived I killed three jaguars. And I'm not a hunter."

He waited for me to ask how.

"Well, I was driving a truck through a dirt road in the forest when the headlights illuminated the carcass of a cow with three jaguars on top. I accelerated the truck and ran over them. That simple!"

After we visited the museum we were touched to witness the invitation by Jair to pray. This was our second such experience, the first being in São Jorge. He read a text from the gospel of John and we prayed a Holy Father and a Holy Mary. He asked divine protection, which we will need for the last, and most difficult part of our expedition.

We finally made contact with Mané Manduca's daughter and he will call us back tonight. So, we hope! He is a Nambikwara chief that we have been trying to contact since the beginning of the expedition.

In the evening, Adriana called us and gave us Jair's number. He is the general chief of the Nambikwara and we talked to him. He seemed very reasonable and we will meet him tomorrow.

Commentary:

In order to arrive in Campos de Julho we had to drive south for 80 km then west for another 80 km, crossing several rivers, the Suia-Unai, Formiga and Juruena being the principal ones. Roosevelt informs us that, after leaving the Buriti, they had to lighten their load again because the oxen of the oxcarts had been weakened to the point where they no longer could pull the load. Nine beasts of burden also had to be left behind. The grass in this thin *cerrado* is very poor and the animals had to be released at night to find something to eat. Apparently, the oxen did not eat at night and therefore were weakened. Thus, they had to spend hours rounding them up every morning. We also had a little taste of this ordeal, but Boi handled it rather well and our supply of corn helped. In the smaller rivers, the loads were removed from the animals and carried on the backs of the men. Again, Roosevelt comments on the tremendous potential of the region for the establishment of industrial activity because of the supply of water and hydro-electric power. According to him, the construction of a railroad connecting the plateau to the great Brazilian centers in the east would lead to rapid development. Alas, one hundred years later a succession of incompetent governments was not able or willing to undertake such a project. It was the visionary impetus given by Juscelino Kubitchek that led to the opening of the highway. The Brazilian Army, through its Construction Battalions, played a pivotal role. But the civilian governments in the past thirty-five years failed miserably.

Day 4

We left the comfortable Hotel Primavera after a nice dinner the previous night. My cough still bothers me but the spit lost the yellow-greenish coloration.

In Comodoro, we met Adriane, who led us to the Indian village of Nova Mutum. Jair was already there. He is a stocky Nambikwara with a pleasant disposition. Mané Manduca arrived shortly later and we presented our plan and declared our intentions, which were found to be reasonable by the assembled Indians. We signed an agreement and I made a payment of Re 2,000 to Jair. A second payment of Re 2,000 to Mané Manduca will be made at the end. Two guides will be provided, at a cost of Re 100 per each and per day. Jair will get Re 2,000 and the other half will be collected by Mané Manduca and will belong the HAIYÔ association.

Mané Manduca accepted to serve as a guide personally and appointed Ari as assistant. We left the village at 11:30 a.m. on a dirt road that grew narrower as we advanced. Our goal: to reach the extreme east of the territory at the telegraph line. The road will take us 30 km from the Juína River. The distance from this point to Vilhena is around 170 km. We passed two villages, the first deserted. A family including the chief, *Capitão* Eulalio, met us at the second. The title of *Capitão* is used by the Indians and derives from the Portuguese. There were two older men and a collection, about eight, women in the village, in addition to the children. Mané Manduca told us that Eulalio is a revered old chief who lived closer to whites before but decided to return to his roots far from progress, since he feared the diseases that came with whites. In the past, these were the infectious diseases. Now, with medical help and vaccinations, the main ones come from the sugar and flower-rich diet. The Nambikwara do not build *ocas* and this is consistent with their nomadic traditions. Mané Manduca also informed us that there is a scarcity of *buriti* on their lands, making this construction difficult. Could this be the reason for the lack of permanent constructions observed by Roosevelt? He mentions cone-shaped houses that he associated with the possible incorporation of African runaway slaves in the colonial period, since he had seen similar structures in his travels through Africa.

The group at the second village questioned Mané Manduca regarding a reward and he promised them Re 500. One of the women, apparently the daughter of Eulalio, was quite vocal and I gathered that he had a previous history of not keeping his promises. We proceeded, and forest, *cerrado*, and thin *cerrado* followed each other, the top of our Marruá breaking branches on the road, a little more than a trail. Neither of the villages had electricity, but a tractor had opened up a wide swath along a portion of the road in preparation for electrical posts.

At 4:30 p.m., five hours after we had started, we crossed the telegraph trail, still visible under the lower trees. Angonese and I walked for one hour and a half in the east direction, toward the Juína River, and we were able to assess the difficulty of our march. It was relatively easy and there was still a semblance of a trail in the bush. We saw several holes dug by the giant Canasta armadillo.

Mané Manduca is an intelligent fellow who has worked for FUNAI for several years. He has only one eye and a few teeth on his lower jaw but the top is perfect-a good upper denture. He told us about the sacred mountain of the Nambikwara and about the Anauanê 50 km north of where we are. These have long hair and a week ago were involved in an incident that resulted in the death of one of them. They were charging toll on a road when the truck driver pulled out a gun and started to shoot. The Indians retaliated with bows and arrows. In the melee one of the Indians was mortally wounded in the chest by an accidental arrow shot from his colleague.

I showed him and Ari the book by Lévi-Strauss and they identified the chief of the Wakletoçu as Capitão Julio, a memorable chief with great capacity for dialogue.

We did not have time to buy food and will have to survive on *carreteiro* rice for the next six days. But this is fine with me. The excitement of covering this hallow ground for the first time in one hundred years is the best meal.

Commentary:

The crossing of the Juruena River by Roosevelt was done on a ferry. This one had three dugout canoes set side-by-side and covered with a platform. These ferries do not require an engine or paddling, and are attached to a steel cable. The position with respect to the current creates the force that pushes it across. It is a simple process that students study in Physics class. The resultant of the forces can be calculated. Thus, the RR expedition arrived at yet another telegraph station. This one was guarded by soldiers commanded by a Brazilian officer from the south, Lieutenant Marinho. Tall, blue eyed, and blond, he resembled an English gentleman. The expedition encountered Captain Amilcar's oxcarts shortly thereafter. His oxen were in better shape.

A group of Nambikwara visited the expedition and Roosevelt comments on their good teeth. He also mentions how they treat their women and children with gentleness, something not common with some African and Australasian tribes. The women were completely nude, while the men had a string around their waist, to the front of which they attach an ornament or a tuft of grass. Confirming the reports by Lévi-Strauss, he stated that they do not use hammocks and sleep in the ashes of the fire and that their sheds barely protect them from the elements.

Day 5

Encouraged by the screams of Hiram hurrying us up, we left the camp at 6:40 a.m., twenty minutes after sunrise. The bees were already present *en masse* and our first couple hours were pleasant since the trail was well marked. We had 20 km of telegraph line to cross before we would meet the next road, where the Marruá would await us.

At 10 a.m. we crossed a creek and at 11 we reached the Camararé River, which we forded by packing our stuff in plastic bags and swimming across. The telegraph wire was visible across the river and some of us hung on to it to cross while I swam. In the bottom of the river ample remains of the wood bridge could be seen in the clear water. I also saw a perfectly preserved post. The water preserves the wood. After the refreshing swim, we ate a pineapple and filled our containers. Progress became gradually slower as we reentered the *cerrado*. The wire was now intact along most of the length and we marched along it, discovering ceramic insulators periodically. This portion of the telegraph line is indeed pristine and had been preserved through isolation.

We stopped at 4 p.m. and extended our tarp as a fortuitous rain arrived. We were successful in refilling our canteens which were completely empty. Strangely, Mané Manduca tells us that he has not brought any water, a major mistake. So, he went around borrowing and taking long sips from our canteens. This is amazing, since I recall the cook filling a large Coca Cola bottle, two liters, and encouraging us to take it.

By 6 p.m., nine hours after we left, we had advanced only 10 km, one half of our target. We had to machete our way through most of the region and there was no semblance of trail. In some parts the *cerrado* was slightly lower along the line.

We set up camp in an inferno of bees. In addition to the medium and large bees, there was now an infestation of the tiny ones that got into our eyes. I had brought the lower portion of the tent with me and so did Hiram. Mané and Angonese laid on the ground, since we set up the tarp as cover. I tried to eat some mandioc flower with dried meat and push it down my throat with controlled sips of water but the flavor was too exotic, since it was mixed with grilled bees, the result of massive attacks on the frying pans last night. At night, the *cortadera* ants attacked the camp and Angonese got into my tent for refuge. Mané stayed out and fought them off as well as he could but Hiram was safe in his tent. I set my tent on top of the telegraph wire!

The only animal marks we saw in this most inhospitable country were the holes and diggings of the giant armadillo. It can weigh up to 70 kg.

Commentary:

Roosevelt reports that after the Juruena the *cerrado* becomes thicker and the terrain more irregular. He mentions the ant holes in the soil and trees. The rains kept hounding the expedition. He spent his waiting hours reading Gibbon. The Juína River was crossed by ferry, no longer available in our days. They were visited by three Nambikwaras, who announced themselves by loud cries and left their weapons behind. I know that this is proper etiquette among the Indians and that sneaking silently in with weapons might result in a less than enthusiastic reception. We experienced this in the Rondon Project, in 1969, when we went up the Aporinan River. On that occasion, we announced our arrival with shots and then loud screams. He also comments on them being a large nation without organization and structure, and that several soldiers had been killed by them. Often, the conflicts arise over women, but in other cases a futile motive might trigger the action. The expedition passed burying mounds from the earlier expeditions along the way. They had a simple wooden cross. This seems to be an inhospitable area and we also experienced the difficulty. In Rondon's day the trail was well kept, but it was completely closed now.

Day 6

As we woke up, the terrain around us crawled with ants. We discovered an anthill ten yards from our camp. Their nocturnal attack was explained. They had cut large holes in my tent during the night. This was our toughest day in the entire expedition. We started at 6:20 a.m. and macheted our way painfully through the thick *cerrado*. We soon lost track of the line and depended on Angonese's compass and Hiram's GPS.

At 9 a.m. Mané heard a shot and answered back. So, the

Marruá and Ari are hopefully at the rendez vous place, a few kilometers ahead of us, on the Mutum River. As the afternoon sun grilled us we grew exhausted. Our water supplies, raided by Mané, dwindled by 3 p.m.. Some clouds passed over and we set up the tarp with no luck. We had to make more and more frequent stops. My left leg hurt but my hernia had disappeared as a result of empty intestines. We chewed on sprouts from a wild pineapple plant. Mané climbed a tree to seek waterholes or evidence of a creek. He indicated a place north of us but we decided to stay on course. We kept pushing through the thick *cerrado* and at 4 p.m. decided to leave the heaviest stuff behind. Angonese and Hiram dropped their backpacks, marking the spot, and I unloaded the heavy insulators and supports that I had been carrying in my back. This was an attempt to reach water, before we were completely exhausted.

At 5:30 p.m. we entered an area with larger trees; our only hope for survival was to reach water before dark. Soon the brush became thinner and we were able to advance faster. Darkness was already falling upon us when the terrain suddenly sloped down. We moved faster, driven by the hope to find water. At the bottom, through the last rays of light, I saw a reflection. We approached it and the view of a tiny stream was a moving sight. The feeling of relief and anticipation as we rushed to it is beyond description.

Hiram is always eager for water and sank into the stream fully dressed with his shoes on. He is clearly of the aquatic kind. A little pudgier than Angonese and I, he heats up more. Water soothes his soul, and he seeks it frequently. I wish it had this effect on me, but my thoughts continue to rattle through my brain. I just stare at the minute creek and thank a Higher Force that guided us to this blessed place. I believe that Col. Hiram, a Mason, is also thanking the Great Architect. We filled our bottles and I drank two full liters of the blessed liquid. Our prayers in Sapezal and São Jorge had been answered.

We set up camp under the tall trees, certain that we would be able to reach the truck the next day. We have only one tent left, which I brought with me. Angonese got into it, but Hiram and Mané had to share a blanket. Nevertheless, we are protected from rain by the tarp that we brought with us at a considerable sacrifice. I finally managed to stick it into my backpack, and this helped us. After sharing two REI meals Angonese and I got into my tent which still offered some protection even after the ants made deep holes into the fabric. I caught one of the super ants which have an overdeveloped head and tweezers for analysis in my lab. I plan to do nanoindentation on the scissors and will try to identify the protein in the cutting instrument: abductin?

Mané told us stories into the night, explaining that he is an apprentice sorcerer and that the spiritual world is opening to him. He is 52 and has health problems. He tells us that he has to rest during the day and was not able to follow us on several occasions. He is the director of the association HAUYÔ and was previously the chief of a village. He confessed to us:

"A bird sang the first day and we know that it has two songs: kukukukuku… and kikikiki….The first is good and the second is a bad omen. Fortunately, it was the first kind. "I hope he is right."

Day 7

This is the day of my class in San Diego, and I trust that Vincent is doing a good job. After this ordeal, I have to face the academic jungle where dangers loom and traps are set by intelligent predators.

We have only 6 km left, and hope that this will happen by noon today. I slept well with Angonese by my side, totally collapsed after a grueling day of macheting. I did it for less than one hour and understand the effort. I wish I did not have the hernia to hamper me and could contribute more effectively.

155

Angonese and Mané returned to retrieve our stuff and Hiram and I wait. The bees are back in full force and they pour through the holes in the tent. I try to clog the holes with leaves and branches but their numbers keep increasing to the point where I have to leave the tent. I hope this ordeal will be over and that I will be able to spend a happy Thanksgiving together with my beloved family.

During the night, a large spider penetrated our tent and climbed up the wall. We are fortunate that it did not bite us.

It is extremely difficult to follow the telegraph line as can be seen form these 16 km in two days. It would take a larger team with porters macheting across 150 km, and it would require around twenty days under these conditions, something suitable for a group bolder than ours. We accomplished enough.

We filled our bottles and continued through the forest, after waiting for Angonese's and Mané's return with the backpacks. It was 9 a.m. when they returned. We proceeded in the west direction through the forest. We moved swiftly, first veering north. After about 200 yards the creek disappeared and we were lucky to have hit it. Had we been slightly off course we would have spent a miserable night without water. Our speed now averaged 1.5 km per hour, almost twice that in the *cerrado*. By noon we have covered 4.5 km and we are, according to the GPS, within one mile of the road. Our screams are answered and we exchange gun shots. We are indeed arriving within a few yards of the Marruá and 200 meters off the telegraph line. Quite impressive.

Our crew had been very worried and was afraid that something, like a snake bite or jaguar attack, had happened. Ari had tried to move towards us but had been impeded by the *cerrado*. The truck took Hiram to the first creek so that he could soak, while we ate and recovered. I moved away from the kitchen because of the bees. However, I would only get ten minutes of respite from the bees each time. We had a small powwow and decided to complete the expedition by truck, since the walk had taken so much out of us and unfortunately, I was pressed for time by virtue of my Luxembourg commitments. Even here, in this isolated territory, our worldly obligations pursue us.

The trip to Kitalu Village through the forest was eventful. We crossed three bridges where we had to go against our judgement since even a small jump on it by a pedestrian produced considerable flexing. We had to cut several fallen trees. In this stretch the road follows the telegraph line and the walk would have been easy.

After four hours of ride along the line we arrived at the village, one of the most remote of the Nambikwara land. Little has changed in one hundred years except for some technical details: everybody but the kids is dressed. The children are playful and get along well. None of the bullying of the US kids. A young man arrived with an armadillo of the *Canasta* species tied to the back of the motorcycle. It was divided equally among the various families. I saw the women carrying their pieces. Tonight, everybody will eat well.

The Indian explained to me the technique used to hunt the armadillo. Once the hole where the armadillo is found, a steel shaft is poked vertically into the ground along the presumed trajectory. If they hit flesh, they can feel the vibration, but the animal does not move and is then traversed several times, something that I saw on the carapace. The next step is to dig up the beast. The Indians also told me that peccaries are a choice game, but that deer are scarce in the region.

There is no electricity or running water in the village and a band of kids took me to a small creek, where I bathed. I was somewhat embarrassed, not knowing how I would keep them from watching me bathe, but they returned, leaving me alone. The cool water soothed my tired muscles and mind, bruised by three days of march. In spite of the exhaustion we gave a presentation to the assembled group.

At night we had our last *carreteiro* rice, surrounded by children and adults. They are very curious about our strange accoutrements.

In the middle of the village there is a round *oca*. Asked what it was, they answered jokingly: "It is a jail for the girls."

I saw girls looking out and they seemed to be naked.

Later, Mané told me that they had their first menstruation and had to stay there for a specified period of time, awaiting a village ceremony.

The village has a few brick buildings built by the government: an old school, a medical post, and a new school. By the creek, an abandoned medical post in ruins. The buildings are poorly taken care of and considered unimportant. I also noticed that many of the children have rotten teeth. The adults have, as a consequence, a profusion of missing teeth.

The family relations are very important and determine the working arrangements. I went to the *oca*. Three girls looked at me with innocent smiles. A bunch of kids chatted with them from the outside and an older lady brought them food. They do not seem unhappy but definitely need a bath. When they leave the *oca*, they will be considered women and are therefore marriageable.

The village has a population of 65. If the population drops below a critical level the culture is lost. This group is struggling but is successful.

The rotten teeth of the children are the direct result of eating candy continuously. I watched this and believe that adults bring it from the city. This will take time to correct, since buccal hygiene is absent among Indians. We know well that if you eat sweets and do not brush, your teeth will rot.

Commentary:

In this region, the terrain becomes irregular and the thick

cerrado and forest give way to grassland, at the higher elevations. The Roosevelt-Rondon expedition camps in a beautiful area by a creek with clear waters and close to a 3-meter waterfall. However, the animals did not like the grass and fled back, along the way. Boi and the Kitalu Indians also described to us the types of grass appropriate for cattle. Apparently, the attempts to raise cattle at Kitalu failed, probably because of the type of grass. The mosquitos continued to hound the expedition, and this is probably due to the rainy season, in which water pooled everywhere and becomes their ideal breeding ground. The expedition then passed through Campos Novos that is located in a vast valley, many kilometers wide, crossed by many creeks that run in deep and narrow cuts and are surrounded by dense forest. Between these creeks are hills covered with grass. Apparently this *fazenda* no longer exists. Roosevelt describes cattle and that they drank milk. There was an ample supply of chicken and they encountered Captain Amilcar and Lieutenant Melo who were waiting for the main body of the expedition. However, Roosevelt warns of the fevers that had been victimizing the inhabitants. This is obviously a 'white' village. The geologist of the expedition, Dr. Oliveira, found fossilized trees in the area, and reported that they are probably from the Cretaceous. From that point on the oxcarts could no longer advance and the materiel had to be carried totally by pack mules and oxen. After Campos Novos the expedition spent the night at the banks of a small river called 12 of October in honor of Columbus' discovery of America. This must have been the date at which one of the earlier expeditions reached it. One of the mountains was baptized Lira, homage to the brave lieutenant that would two years later drown in the Sepotuba River.

Day 8
We got up, packed the truck and walked, led by Mané and

the old *pajé*, spiritual leader, to visit the cemetery where Rondon's soldiers and workers were buried. The terrain and vegetation are quite different from the one we crossed on foot: hills that grow higher toward the south and west and open fields with occasional trees. We stop and eat *mangaba* that is already ripe, and another fruit resembling raisins.

"The village used to be in the valley below, but we moved when people died trying to get up the road," said Mané. He showed us the exact place where he lived as a child.

In the distance, the mountains showed ugly scars from major slides.

"This was a disaster, but we, the spiritual persons, found the reason and stopped it."

He explained that they dug through the earth that had slid until they found a stone that had, according to the spiritual leader, caused it. They crushed the stone and buried it deep into the soil.

"This was the last landslide."

We continued, passing a cassava plantation, and eventually found some mounds on the ground. I was able to put together a cross with two pieces that had orthogonal cuts to fit into each other. Other mounds did not have markers, just stones.

"Later, *seringueiros*, rubber tappers, worked around here. We helped them and they paid us," said Mané. "Some of them are also buried here."

We were able to establish the trajectory of the telegraph line through these mountains, which consist of multiple plateaus. It would be a possible, but challenging expedition to follow the line.

We returned to the village and gave the remaining food to an Indian lady with instructions to share it with the others. She loaded up her *xiri* and left with alacrity. We received news that the road ahead was blocked by fallen trees. There was no gasoline in the village and we took the chainsaw with us with no expectation of using it. Two sharp axes and an extra pair of hands would do the job, and Mané and Ari were overjoyed to come with us all the way to Vilhena.

So, we left the happy village. It was very tight in the back, since Mané rode in front, with the driver. We packed five on the side, sitting on a wood bench, and the two extra fellows just rode on the back gate. Soon we encountered the trees and advance was very slow; it was a painful but safe ride. There had been a strong storm a few days ago, and only motorcycles could get through. Our energetic team of workers did a great job and we were able to clear several trees, until we encountered a major one, with a pickup truck on the other side. It belonged to the Indian Medical Service and was heading to Kitalu to evacuate a woman that was having trouble with childbirth. They had some gasoline which we poured into our chainsaw. In a matter of twenty minutes the tree was cut into pieces and removed from the road. We hit the asphalt a couple of hours later and left the magical Nambikwara lands, entering a modern and dynamic society. The large monoculture farms have replaced the *cerrado* and forests and soon we entered Vilhena, heading directly to Hotel Colorado. That evening, Mané Manduca told us the story of the origin of the Nambikwara.

"There is a mountain beyond the first camping place, before the trek," he said. "If you follow the road, you will encounter another village, called Bacaval or Weig Cayeg Zu in our language. The mountain is just beyond there.

"From this closed mountain, a lot of noise could be heard. People screaming. The Zigzog monkey, that has a red back, moved by curiosity, watched the mountain from a tree. In the beginning of the world, all animals could talk to each other: tapir, armadillo, and others.

"All animals got together to find a way to break the mountain to find what was inside"

He smiled and continued: "The tapir said: 'I will give a huge kick.' But nothing happened. Then came the dear: 'I am the fastest and will hit the mountain at speed.' He tried and nothing. The turtle came and tried to use its shell as a saw, to no avail. One of the birds, the hummingbird, looked at the tapir and said: 'It is not the strength, but the power. I will use it on the mountain.'

"Then the hummingbird flew to a distance and came back, entering the mountain and creating a gash. The Nambikwara, who were trapped inside, saw the light coming in and ran out. The Zigzog monkey had been watching the mountain all this time and burned his back in the sun. This is why it is red."

Mané promised to take us to the Sacred Mountain if we returned to the area.

Commentary:

The expedition crossed an irregular terrain also marked in the modern maps to reach Vilhena. It consisted of deep valleys covered by dense forest and other broad valleys. Dr. Oliveira analyzed the rocks, which seemed to be volcanic. However, he concluded that they were composed of arenite and ferruginous soil, the result of the erosion of rocks. They had bubbles and he explained that they were from a quaternary deposit. Dr. Oliveira mentioned the similarity to South African Cretaceous formations. This is fascinating, because the theory of continental drift was not known at the time. Recent discoveries of diamonds in the area are consistent with the kimberlite deposits. We brought some rocks from the Navaité Falls with us that we plan to analyze.

Roosevelt comments on passing places where Rondon's soldiers and workers were buried. They consisted of simple stone mounds and wooden crosses. We also saw the remains of this cemetery on the telegraph line. There was a piece of wood with a chamfer cut into it.

Day 9

My colleagues drive to the River of Doubt to identify the exact spot where the Roosevelt Rondon expedition launched from. There is a mistake in Roosevelt's book regarding the coordinates and they will set the record straight. My sore throat has returned with a vengeance and I had a sudden dizzy spell. The prospect of spending eight hours in the back of the Marruá does not endear me and I stayed in the hotel and coordinated other important activities. The team returned at 7 p.m., exhausted but content. The manager of the Baliza Farm, Grilo, had taken them on his aluminum boat powered by an outboard up the river. There were several tree trunks and branches in the river, making progress slow. After 40 minutes, they reached the exact place where the 1914 expedition launched. The bridge remains are clear, and there is a beam still crossing the river from side to side. This is an important discovery, since we documented the exact spot. The wrong coordinates in Roosevelt's book led to a slight misunderstanding of the starting point. The river is, in November, much lower than in February. Pictures from 1914 show the water level reaching the beam, whereas the distance is much larger in November. It is also possible that in these one hundred years the level of the river dropped because of deforestation. This could be checked out by visiting the place in January. However, this exact starting place presents a slight problem: it is impossible to unload the kayaks and canoe at that spot, since there is no longer a road or even a trail leading to the bridge.

Commentary:

The 1914 expedition continued north, past Vilhena, through a terrain that alternated *cerrado*, dense forest, and grassland. On the second day, a team from a large *fazenda* named Três *Buritis* came towards them with fresh pack oxen and these were readily incorporated. At that point they had fresh meat from slaughtered animals. Kermit crossed a Nambikwara village that could very well been the Sabanê Village that we visited. The ranch was managed by an uncle of Rondon, the brother of his mother. He was seventy years old but quite dynamic and strong. Almost pure Indian, he wore the usual caboclo outfit: hat, shirt, pants, and no shoes. He had killed three jaguars that year, since they decimated his cattle.

After leaving the farm, they arrived in José Bonifacio, which was a telegraph station. There were about 30 Indians in the village, and Roosevelt comments on their facial hair, which he attributed to early mixing with runaway slaves, something that also happened in the US. At that point they were only 23 km from the River of Doubt, a distance which they traveled in two days. Part of the expedition peeled off from the main body at that point; Amilcar, Melo, and Miller continued towards the Ji-Paraná, a tree-day march. The expedition down the Ji-Paraná would also encounter great difficulty but covered territory already explored and populated by rubber tappers. It is described in Miller's book.

CHAPTER 12

DOWN THE RIVER OF DOUBT: JOURNAL AND COMMENTARY

This chapter, just like the previous three, is presented as a journal, to retain the fresh and informal impressions of the trip. As a commentary, short descriptions of the original 1914 expedition are presented. After the August visit to Vilhena, I returned to the US, where I started in earnest to plan for the expedition, making equipment lists, purchasing the boats that would take us downriver, making weekly runs to the local camping stores and meeting often with Jeffrey, while frantically exchanging emails with Col. Hiram, who had committed himself totally to the project and was looking for the fourth person. Unfortunately, the participation of Corporal Mario had been denied by the Amazon Command, and Col. Hiram attributed this to some old animosity that existed between him and the commanding officer. Our experiences will be compared and contrasted with those of the original expedition.

Day 1

"Alia jacta est," as Julius Caesar said upon crossing the Rubicon. We have had multiple Rubicons and many more to follow. But this part of the expedition is launched and there is no going back. I am in the airplane heading from São Paulo to Cuiabá! We had many changes, adjustments, and a few disillusionments along the way. Nevertheless, the core group is strong and determined: Col. Hiram, Jeffrey Lehmann, Col. Angonese, a last-minute addition to our team, and I. The kayaks have arrived in Vilhena after many delays. The process of ordering started in July, and Opium needed three months to manufacture two kayaks. In the U.S., we would have gotten them in one week at half the price. Based on information gathered on the web, we also purchased a Pak canoe. It performed beautifully in the pool of Marc Meyers at Del Mar's Torrey Pines Lagoon, much better than in the ocean. We managed to tumble it twice and valuable lessons have been learned. It weighs 70 lbs. and can be completely disassembled, fitting in an oversize case. The technology is simple but seems to be sturdy. We will see how much protection from piranhas and *candirus* it will afford us.

We are still struggling with support from the Brazilian Army. We have yeses, then nothing, then an occasional "mission considered too risky." On Friday, we meet the mayor of Vilhena and key people. Vilhena is the staging place for expeditions. It was founded by Rondon in the early 1900s, being only a house along the telegraph line. It stayed like this until the 1970s, when it exploded by virtue of the first road linking the Brazilian northwest to the large centers. Receiving a healthy influx of immigrants, many from the south and from German and Italian blood, it developed rapidly and there is a surreal feeling today: a modern city of 70,000 surrounded by expansive soy, cotton, corn fields. The forest and *cerrado* were burned down and the leftovers bulldozed away to give place to large-scale agriculture on the wide plateau.

The plan could not be simpler: Four of us will go down the river. The rapids and falls (about 12 of them) will require portage. Hence, we carry the boats down, return for the load, and repeat the process until the entire group is transferred beyond the obstacle.

We were informed by the mayor's office that Emmanuel, the historian that we intended to meet in July, had taken his own life. Looking back, it was difficult to predict from his quiet and composed disposition that he would take such a tragic action. But demons tormented him, from which he could not escape. In his case, it was Cupid that fired his poisoned darts. This explains, perhaps, why he did not carry out his promise to take us to the starting point. A sad loss, indeed, since he was an intelligent person. My condolences will be sent to the family.

I also tried numerous times, for the past two months, to establish contact with Tataré, a Cinta Larga Indian who went down with Roosevelt in 1992 or 1993. He was in his 20s then, and should be in his forties. It would be a wonderful addition to our group, since he would ensure safe passage through the two Cinta Larga villages. He lives in Cacoal and works for the local FUNAI office. I will keep trying to establish contact with him.

Day 2

As I enter the modest building that serves as airport in Vilhena, I bend nervously down, peeking through the hole in the wall through which the suitcases are being pushed in. I panicked for a moment. The large cardboard box with the Pak Canoe is not there! This key ingredient to our expedition will, by its absence, derail the entire operation. It finally appears, the cardboard torn in several places, having survived four flights. As the airports grew gradually more modest, from São Paulo to Cuiabá, to finally Vilhena, the box grew gradually weaker. But we are here, and so will hopefully our international team.

The weather is cool, windy and dusty, and there are already rain drops presaging the downpour that is the rain season in the Amazon. This expedition is starting very late. Is it an omen of the water that can pour from the skies in thick sheets and that hounded the R-R expedition even before it reached the headwaters?

But a centennial expedition is much more than musing and dreaming. For me, it has been a constant stream of e-mails, countless details that can derail an effort of two years. Gradually, things are falling into place, detail by detail. The kayaks are in Vilhena, after umpteen exchanges and delays.

How do we get to the river, at the spot that the R-R expedition marked by exact coordinates given in Roosevelt's book? The contacts made in July have been essential. The Head of the Ceremonial at the mayor's office, Rita Marta, agreed to set up a meeting; Naif, who has a fleet of rental vehicles, is committed to driving us to the river. Tomorrow, I will finalize the details aiming for a Tuesday, October 31, start.

Day 3

I check into the Colorado Hotel, where I feel already at home. Dona Angela, the owner, receives me warmly. Col. Hiram had also chosen this place since he was a colleague of the officer that resided in Vilhena during the construction of the highway, in the seventies. There was only one hotel in town at that time, the Colorado. I reserved three additional rooms for the other members of the expedition. I learned that Roosevelt's grandson, who led an expedition down the river in 1992, also lodged there. However, he had a large group and spent two months planning the trip, taking with him an extended crew. Apparently, he made a movie, which I would love to get. We had the meeting at the mayor's office, coordinated by Rita Marta. Naif joined us and confirmed that the kayaks had arrived. We were fortunate that the head of the Vilhena Fire Dept. was there. He is also an ROTC graduate, and a lieutenant like me, and we connected right away. He promised logistic support within the Vilhena County, which extends some 100 km north. He even volunteered to have the Fire Dept. pick-up truck follow us to the river and we will be able to have contact with him through our satellite phone that I brought from the US.

Day 4

Jeffrey Lehmann and Col. Angonese arrive in the same plane, from Cuiabá. There is only one daily flight and they recognized each other on the plane. Jeffrey's rusty Spanish and Angonese's rudiments of English make for a nice conversation. I am excited about the arrivals and Angonese impressed me as a dynamic and enterprising fellow. At 53, he is a retired infantry officer with great Amazon experience.

Day 5

We go on a frantic shopping spree, purchasing food, camping equipment, fishing supplies, and a super BB gun, that has a 5.5 mm caliber and is able, as explained by the salesman, to drop a peccary if hit in the forehead. Just what I need for an emergency. Brazil has very tight gun laws and air guns are the only ones not requiring special permission. Col. Angonese puts my mind to rest, after informing me that he has a 9-mm pistol and plenty of ammunition. We also get a large tarp and rope for the boats.

I am informed by Col. Angonese and Hiram that we need to cook our own food and that the dried rations are only an emergency alternative. Angonese has a local shop manufacture a makeshift stove consisting of two angle irons with perforations for a bar. So, we shop for onions, garlic, rice, and salted beef, and *charque*. I sneak in two bottles of *cachaça*, the Brazilian rum.

After I see Angonese's and Jeffrey's gear and the purchases, my plans for an ultra-light trip are abandoned. We have to remember that everything has to be portaged. Hiram, ever the Spartan, has a minimum of gear.

The husband of Dona Angela knows the owner of Fazenda Baliza, Pablo Altoé, and he gives us permission to enter and to contact Grilo, the ranch manager. Grilo is most certainly a nickname, because it means cricket.

Day 6

This is a day of rest and relaxation, and we eat at the local barbecue place, gorging ourselves for the last time. We do a weigh-in at a local pharmacy and I start taking the anti-malarial pills that I had acquired in the UK. I share them with Jeffrey, since I had purchased sixty of them. In the US purchase is more difficult because a prescription is required. In Brazil, on the other hand, these pills are no longer available, the strategy being to combat malaria at the first signs. Hiram and Angonese do not take anti-malarial pills and I hope that they will be fine.

Day 6

We left Vilhena at 8 a.m. with full support of the local Fire Dept., who provided a pickup truck and crew. On the road, unexpected problems with Naif's pickup truck forced us to transfer the trailer to another pickup truck driven by two young men that volunteered to join us to the river, Guilherme Marquezini and Dariano de Oliveira. After 80 km on Highway 364 we left the asphalt and drove east toward Fazenda Baliza. Grilo already expected us. It is amazing how these contacts can only be made in place and it is almost impossible to plan ahead in detail.

We met two hefty young men in pants and bare chests that explained as best as they could what lay ahead. From the headquarters of Fazenda Baliza to the river the distance was only a couple miles. The farm has electricity and the level of the Brazilian *caboclo* has improved markedly since the times of Rondon and Roosevelt. The two men looked healthy with good teeth. The women stayed in the kitchen and watched us from far, like shy does.

Jeffrey is fascinated with animals and wants to catalogue all the ones seen by Roosevelt and reported in his book. To me they are the normal birds found throughout Brazil: macaws, toucans, kingfishers, and a myriad of smaller ones. Baliza is a cattle ranch with horses and cows and they do not see cars often. They ran away at full speed. Rondonia is cattle country with about 13 million head. Arabs come and slaughter them in Vilhena using a sword and appropriate Muslim practices. Col. Hiram went up-river with his kayak while we assembled the Pak canoe to the admiration of all present. About 200 meters upstream there are vestiges of a bridge. Grilo told us that the original Rondon Bridge was 20 minutes by slow powerboat upstream from the point in which we camped. He confirmed that there were remains of the telegraph poles in that general area. However, the GPS gave readings that were more distant. Roosevelt lists 12°1' South and Col. Hiram went all the way up to 12° 3' 43" South and could not find the vestiges of the bridge.

Commentary:

There must be a slight mistake in the coordinates given by Roosevelt. I discovered a map in Miller's book showing the point at which the telegraph line intersects the River of Doubt. This is at about 12°4' South.

Day 7

We reached the point: 11°54'43" South 60°22'28" West

It was a long day with an advance of 32 km. We started at 8:05 a.m. and the Pak canoe, our mule, was loaded to the top. Angonese in front and Jeffrey in the back were our *camaradas*, as the paddlers were called in the RR expedition. The load was approximately 300 pounds of gear, food, and filming equipment. The river was narrow, not much over 10 meters, and ran fast, forcing us to constant maneuvers to avoid branches and fallen trees. We placed the pack canoe between the two kayaks to protect the load in case of an accident. Twice the canoe faced big logs and twice it almost turned. From behind, I saw Jeffrey bend back completely to avoid a tree, the water pouring into the back of canoe. Jeffrey's rapid reflex and furious paddling by Angonese saved the day.

I wish I could say the same, but my kayak took water as it got stuck on branches. The power of the water is such that it rotates the kayak on its long axis and exposes the hole to the incoming current. I extricated myself and swam, or better hung on the kayak, as my colleagues came to my help. We pulled it to the margin and emptied it. Barely an hour later the occurrence was repeated. This time I was already a veteran and, cold-bloodied, took the rope, keeping the paddle in the other hand, and passed it to Hiram. He towed me to a beach and we repeated the procedure. We had a couple more incidents until I learned to use the steering mechanism. The secret is to look ahead and steer away from the branches. The steering only works if the speed of kayak is higher than the stream and it is difficult to change the direction of the kayak using the paddles only. My kayaks in San Diego do not have a rudder but the Brazilian kayaks have a pronounced keel and are difficult to steer with the paddles.

At noon, we had not yet reached the Festa Bandeira River, but as soon as the added water flowed into the Roosevelt, the river widened and slowed down. From that point on, we saw birds. A royal egret perched high on a tree. Ducks flew ahead of us. A brown heron (*socó*) greeted us from a branch. On top of a high tree, macaws garrulously watched us. At 2 p.m., as we searched for a place to camp, the rain finally came and poured down with energy for one hour. We found a good beach and Angonese and Hiram built a small tent with the plastic tarp.

"The first thing to protect is the fire," said Angonese, a graduate of the Centro de Instrução de Guerra na Selva (Instruction Center for Jungle War), with authority. The energy of Angonese and Hiram, also a graduate of this center, is amazing, as is their teamwork, a quality that I will try to emulate. Similar to Rondon, whom they both admire, they rapidly set up camp. Angonese prepared a delicious *carreteiro* rice meal, while Hiram gathered wood for the shelter. We had a good first day and a lucky one too, because an accident with the canoe would have been disastrous. Tomorrow we will try to double the mileage, to 50-60 km. We sent our coordinates to Sergeant Douglas by satellite and he will be able to follow our progress and meet us at Km 125.

Commentary:

We gather from Roosevelt's book that the telegraph line crossed the river at the starting point. Grilo informed us that there are remains of the original bridge and telegraph posts but we did not find them. Hence, we might have missed the starting point by a few hundred meters. The RR expedition left after mid-day and covered only 9.3 km the first day. Roosevelt describes the numerous fallen trees that they must avoid and the *buritizana*, a tree whose trunk is covered with long spines that is perfectly at ease being partially submersed. We also saw these palm trees whose roots are in the margin but whose trunk often has an s shape and is partially submerged. Roosevelt describes how "… their stems curving upward, and their frond-crowned tops shaken by the rushing water."

The RR expedition reached the Bandeira by mid-afternoon of the second day. They had already crossed it on foot, ten days before, on their way to Bonifacio.

Day 8

Navaité Falls. I sit here in the tent.

Over me, the thundering noise of a storm sends the first thick drops. Below us, the loud hiss of the waterfall. The first night was a happy one, followed by a day in which we advanced rapidly in the river that carries the Roosevelt majesty in greater and greater presence. We saw birds in greater numbers and capybaras, the largest rodent on earth, watched us from some beaches before screaming and jumping into the water. In the morning, we were faced with a surprise obstacle. Illegal loggers had built a makeshift bridge with entire logs whose bottom coincided with the water line. They were camped across the Cinta Larga territory, on the left margin. Nobody was there and the colonels decided to scout out the camp. As Jeffrey and I waited anxiously in our boats, we heard something that resembled a shot. We disembarked in the bridge, expecting the worse, but were relieved to see them returning.

"Just a woman in the camp, a Gaucha," said Angonese, strutting his 9-mm pistol and bush knife.

We portaged our boats and equipment over the bridge and into the rapidly flowing river, using the bed to carry our gear. It was our first portaging experience and was an exhausting but efficient operation. We are in awe of the two officers, that have all the determination, quiet and efficient capability, and affable disposition that Roosevelt described so well 100 years ago.

The lady, Fatima, was blue-eyed and fair-skinned and could have been a German housewife. From her makeshift kitchen, she gave us a convoluted explanation about a deal with the Indians to extract some logs. A big tractor and the four tents set up under a large tarp gave us an idea of the scale of the operation. It is clear that large logs were harvested from the right side of the river and carried across the bridge. She gave us packages of powder milk and cans of sardines. We continued and by 3 p.m. could hear a distant hiss that gradually grew into a roar, as the water ran with increasing rapidity towards the first fall, named Navaité by the RR expedition. We were able to moor just above the rapids. Had we advanced another 100 meters we would have been sucked into the abyss.

The road or path that we expected did not exist. So, the three members went ahead toward the clearing in the forest, while I struggled to tie my kayak, which had fortunately wedged itself between the bank and a tree trunk. With great difficulty, after several attempts, I got down in the deep water and climbed to the margin. Had my kayak loosened itself from the grip of a branch, I would have been dragged into the falls. Using my machete, I whacked a trail. At the clearing, I met the team coming back. What looked on google earth like a plantation, marked by parallel lines, was actually a geological formation of rocks with ridges forming a perpendicular grid. What we interpreted as a house was actually a square of stones. We walked back to the boats while Angonese went ahead to scout out the area. Exhaustion and the beginning of despair took over us when we realized the task ahead: to portage our boats and equipment through a barely visible jungle trail of unknown length.

Col. Hiram assessed the task as a two-day affair, while I hoped that Col. Angonese would return with help from our farmer. The Indian Lino had told us that somebody lived below the falls. We decided to set up camp in the dense forest after we found a ten-yard clearing under the trees. I cleared the floor from the thick coating of leaves while we brought the essentials.

Shortly before dark Angonese walked into the camp. I noticed his unsteady gate but the smile that he always had in his face reassured me that he was alright. He was indeed completely dehydrated. We looked at each other with the realization of the immense task ahead. He had walked downriver for an hour and had not found any house. In the distance, he had seen one in the other side of the river and he could not reach it. So, we would not get any help. Are we up to the task ahead?

After eating the rations that I prepared with hot water, using the kerosene stove, some fortitude came back to us. Our first and second nights had been joyous ones, but this one carries, with the rolling thunder, the realization that our task ahead is greater and more straining than we expected. I walked to the edge of the forest and tried to send a message to Sargent Douglas. The sky was full of flying termites that were attracted to the headlight in large numbers, entering my eyes and mouth.

The thunder rises and rips through the sky as the first drops keep falling, soon to be   followed by the downpour.

Tomorrow will be a difficult day.

Commentary:

The RR expedition arrived at the falls on Day 3. They advanced 16.5 km on Day 2. Roosevelt describes the Navaité falls as a sequence of two six-foot-high drops interspersed with rapids. He also describes "…great naked flats of friable sandstone and conglomerate." This rather geological description matches exactly our observations. He also describes the extremely narrow channel through which the current rushes, mentioning that a mile or so above the river is placid and has approximately 100 yards of width. He mentions the signs marking the presence of Nambikwara Indians. There was a simple bridge, four long poles across the narrowest part. He mentions that the sub-tribe of these Indians are the Navaité and that they baptized the falls accordingly.

Day 8

We woke up to a gray sky, the light barely making it through the forest. Jeffrey had a moment of panic and started screaming that we should start carrying the boats right away, before breakfast. Hiram and I reassured him that this would be an all-day affair and that he needed to first get his tent out of the trail. After breakfast, he relaxed. It was a tight camping spot since we did not have time to seek an open beach and were lucky not to be sucked into the waterfall. We walked down to a perfect spot, crossing the field of black rock interspersed with streaks of bush. This pattern reproduced itself at the sub-meter scale. We found a good course to transport the equipment and kayaks and went to the long portage, approximately 1.2 km. The storm turned into a downpour as we portaged and this was actually good because it kept us cool. The wheels that we had brought for the kayaks came off after 100 meters, but Angonese fixed them with the pliers that he had brought. The pins had to be replaced since the original ones got caught in the grass and came off. The portage proceeded well with intermediate stops so that the muscles would adjust to the different loads without fatigue. It was mid-day by the time we had completed the portage and we felt that it was best to camp at the bottom of the falls and to explore them. The campground could not have been more pleasant, in a little beach surrounded by rocks. Thus, we proceeded to explore the splendid waterfalls. In places the river narrowed to 2 meters and sped as a tremendous jet filled with eddies. The walls were shiny with circular intrusions caused by vorticity. There was a deep crack in the rocky formation, through which the entire water rushed. We think we found the rock where Rondon took a famous picture. It was shaped like a hat and I climbed up while Col Hiram photographed me in a pose that I thought resembled that of Rondon. Later comparisons revealed that I was probably on the wrong rock, since Jeffrey and Angonese photographed another one that resembled the original rock more.

There is an interesting phenomenon, the surface layer of the rock exposed to water being darker and harder. Successive attempts to break off pieces failed while the 'hammer', another rock, comminuted. The rocky formation is sedimentary, since it is friable. I was able to break off a piece and am taking it to analyse it in the SEM. There is a 1 cm layer of darker material, which can be the result of iron or some organic tannin brought by the water, hardening the rock and decreasing erosion. I saw an agouti (*cutia*) during the portage. It had probably gone to check a pile of materiel that we had left to be carried later.

The evening was pleasant and we watched birds perform elaborate maneuvers in the sky, catching dragonflies. Their tail feathers (retrices) fan out and this helps them in the difficult maneuvers where they practically stop midair to catch the insects. We slept well and communicated with Pedro, informing him that our progress was according to plan. The depth at the end of the narrow channel is around 10 m, where the inverse occurs in the river, above the falls. From here we will go 32 km downriver to the Canoa Quebrada (Broken Canoe) Falls.

Commentary:

The RR expedition spent two and one half days portaging and it seems that they spent the first night at the same spot as us in the forest. Roosevelt mentions the difficulty of dragging the canoes across the flats. We completed our portage in five hours. They used small logs that are cut as rollers and placed ahead of the canoes. Then, the *camaradas* harnessed themselves in groups of two and pulled each canoe, while another person pushed in the back with a lever. Block and tackle was used to hoist the canoes out of the river and it must have been a difficult operation, because there was very little space. Roosevelt admires the endurance and strength of the *camaradas* and intelligence of the commanders. There was damage to one of the canoes, the one in which Roosevelt traveled. He mentions the scarcity of animals in this forest, and attributes it to the fact that they are still in the highlands.

Whereas we camped on a beach below the falls, the RR expedition set up camp slightly higher. Roosevelt mentions the stone shaped 'like an inverted beaver hat'. There is a famous picture of Roosevelt and Rondon at its top, proudly looking into the horizon.

Day 9

This was an eventful but tumultuous day. We packed up and hit the water at 7:15 after contemplating one last time the fissure in the rock formation through which the entire river flows. Jeffrey measured the stream velocity by filming a floating branch as it advanced. At 10 m depth and 2 m width, this stream is a rare phenomenon. The glazed walls and semi-spherical intrusions will give us a hint on the geothermal processes to the protective layer. The intrusions are most probably caused by local vorticity and cavitation.

Our idyllic campground behind, with its small beach, we passed the house of the rancher, or caretaker, on the left bank and proceeded down the river. The water velocity was assessed at 5-7 km/h and we made good progress. Plastic trash in a few places was a mark of civilization, an ugly sight. Hiram told me later that these plastic bags are intentionally tied to the branches to identify spots where fishing lines are tied.

At around 10:40 a.m. a motor boat met us. Sargent Douglas and Corporal Iuri, with an Indian at the outboard. Their serious expressions were an omen of worse things to come. They told us that they had not received our last messages, sent from the campground in the forest. And yet I had walked for a few hundred yards into a clearing on the margin of the river. The phone call had reached the message box and I had not, unfortunately, informed him of our progress. I had texted our position to the two phones given by him. In the midst of clouds of flying ants attracted by the light it is possible that I missed the contact. The next day I sent a message at 3 p.m. but they were already on their way. The firemen's boat returned and twenty minutes later another powerboat came up, this one loaded with six Indians. They did not answer our greetings and one of them photographed us. I remember the row of teeth displayed by one of them, like a pit bull's growl.

Sergeant Douglas was supposed to meet us at km 128, but he anticipated it to the first bridge, at km 95. His truck was there when we reached that bridge. His expression was serious and he told me, quietly, that we could expect problems with the Indians. Shortly thereafter a portly fellow, wearing only shorts and a few greenish feathers on his head and beads on his chest came across the bridge, followed by a large group of children and some adults. He intoned a strange song and did not appear friendly. Upon approaching us, Douglas whispered to me: "…this is João Brabo. They killed 120 miners."

He stood straight in front of us and went on a long discourse in his language, sending furious stares at us from his ugly eyes that resembled some kind of jungle bug. After a while, Roberto, the boat pilot that had gone up the river, translated for us. We did not have authorization to enter into his territory and could not proceed.

After completing his harangue, João Brabo hugged Iuri and apologized to him in Portuguese. Iuri looks Indian and actually bears some resemblance to the Cinta Larga, although he told us later on that he has only an Indian grand-mother. But from his appearance Indian blood runs much thicker in his veins and João Brabo felt a brotherhood bond.

He turned to us, in Portuguese this time and said: "I don't go into your lands without permission. How do you dare to go into my lands?"

I tried to negotiate with him, to no avail. Nevertheless, he accepted my gift of a brand-new camera and gradually became friendlier. Col. Hiram was furious and started to unload his stuff without even addressing João Brabo. Col. Angonese tried to talk him into helping us and he became mean again, staring at us with anger and gesticulating as if he were holding a club.

I asked his permission to give candy to the children and he agreed. After opening several bags, surrounded by a crowd of children, I found the packages of little suckers. I grabbed bunches and threw them into the air as the kids frantically grabbed them when they came down. Soon some women joined them and the ice was broken.

I offered the last bag to João Brabo but one of his sidekicks was faster and grabbed it. We packed all our gear into the aluminum boat that was already on the trailer, a feat of science and optimization. Then, we left, relieved that things had not gotten worse. Douglas informed us that the six Indians that had gone upstream in the powerboat had shotguns, which they were fortunate not to use, because Angonese would have mowed them down, after firing a warning shot with his pistol.

It was a happy trip to the Federal Police station of Diamante, a few kilometers away. We were well received by a crafty gentleman, Bandeira. He had a makeshift gym in the back of the station, which he built using old automobile parts, alternators, axles, and the like. He stayed there for periods of six weeks.

"They even threatened to burn down the post," he told us.

Huge trucks loaded with logs having 1-2-meter diameter drove by, coming from the river. I managed to photograph one of them. We are convinced that a good share of the logs is illegally taken from inside the reservation.

We ordered some food from the little restaurant and soon twelve fried eggs, rice, and mandioc flower materialized. A couple of men were roasting pieces of lamb and shared their meal with us. They were rugged jungle types and one of them had two leschimaniasis wounds in the back of his hand. Angonese told us that he had contracted the same disease in the Amazon, during his jungle training. They are the result of the bite of a tan mosquito that has a triangular shape. It is not an easy task to get rid of the ugly wound that spreads and expands, rotting the skin,

A young boy with blue eyes and white hair accompanied by his sister, a beautiful Germanic girl in her teens, was there, unwrapping a basket of eggs. I told her that she could become a New York runway model, such was her grace. She smiled in a shy way, showing her braces.

A haggard-looking man stopped his pickup, struggled to the building, ordered half a glass of *cachaça*, which he downed in one sip. Then, without looking at anybody, he limped back to the car and took off. He obviously had some ailment. I could feel the pain in his eyes.

The policemen gave us 20 liters of diesel, which allowed us to continue to Vilhena. We had two options: to ask Douglas to take us to the ferry, 125 km downriver, and out of Cinta Larga territory, or to return to Vilhena to regroup. We would only have made it to the ferry after dark and Douglas would have had to drive back. Upon Col. Hiram's advice, we chose to return to Vilhena. It was a wise choice. The ride was rough, with the four of us sharing the back seat of the pickup for five hours, most of it dirt. Our legs were stiff when we unloaded at the hotel, after storing the trailer in the fire station.

A nice *churrasco* (Brazilian barbecue) and two bottles of good Brazilian wine later, Miolo Reserva, and we feel much better. My back is sore and my left shoulder is in pain, but I am hopeful that I will have the strength to face the next 550 km. I also confess that the six or seven waterfalls in Cinta Larga territory would have sapped all my strength. The prospect of finishing the journey strapped to the top of the load on the canoe still haunts me, though.

Commentary:

Roosevelt continues his intelligent comments about beehives, comparing the comb to the domestic US bees. His insatiable curiosity and ability to effectively describe what he sees are truly extraordinary. He contrasts the rows of honey-cells and brood-cells in a single row rather than double. In the afternoon, his canoe encountered more rapid current and soon the roar of rapids could be heard. In these days, the Cinta Larga did not live on the river, but on small tributaries, for protection, and thus they were spared our experience. Over the coming days, they had to portage several times, and advanced from rapid to rapid until they had the misfortune of losing two canoes that freed themselves from the moorings during the night. This forced the expedition to stop for five days to build a new canoe. On March 14, they resumed the descent in a torrential downpour. Roosevelt describes whirlpools and rapids. We were spared most of these whirlpools because the river was close to its lowest level. The rapids provided great difficulty and he comments on the superior Canadian canoes, which would have forded them without difficulty. On several occasions the canoes took a lot of water and only stayed afloat because of the *buriti* palm trunks tied to the sides for stability. Bailing had to be performed at every occasion.

Day 10

We rested in Vilhena, after a warm reception by Dona Angela at the Hotel Colorado. I went to mass in the morning, an uplifting experience. Four children were baptized, three babies and a little Indian-looking girl, the latter one probably adopted by the couple. The theme of the mass was the message of the priest that the first commandment was to love God with all our heart, strength, and spirit. This commandment was reinforced by Jesus when questioned by the Pharisees. This love, and the love for our neighbors, is the most important tenet of our religion. The afternoon was spent on shopping for the remaining items. Since it was Election Day, we either voted or justified our absence in the voting booths set up in a school. Within a few hours, we knew that Dilma had, unfortunately, defeated Aecio. Hence, we have to brace ourselves for four more years of incompetent management. But in these far away territories one does not feel the weight of the government. The people are, for the most part, in favor of free enterprise, competition, and economic development, and are tired of the socialistic policies of the Workers Party and of the corruption.

We are extremely fortunate that Sergent Douglas is willing to take us to the ferry downstream from the Cinta Larga territory. We had a nice dinner and hit the sack at 10 p.m.

Day 11

We left at 8 a.m. after a touching good-bye of Sergeant Douglas to his wife and child. He later confided that he is separating from his energetic lady, also a Fireman sergeant. However, the love in her eyes was evident. After crossing Pimenta Bueno, we entered Espigão do Oeste and had lunch. These frontier cities sprung up along BR 364 and are dynamic and progressive centers. The number of motorcycles is quadruple that of cars, and pickups are a necessity and a status symbol. The afternoon was spent on a long dirt road that grew gradually more primitive: 80 km to Pacarana and then 80 km to the river. Before Pacarana we stopped at a *venda* or small country store and met a local fellow, blue-eyed like so many in the region, who showed us his foot that had a deep gash. He had gotten sliced by a sting ray and experienced excruciating pain. Total loss of bowel control was followed by twelve hours of convulsions during which he rolled on the ground. Although the sting had taken place 43 days before, the gash was still swollen and had not yet healed.

We met large trucks loaded with logs and saw several wood mills along the way. Then, we passed three or four Indian villages but nobody bothered us there or asked us for money. Douglas informed us that they are of the Zoró group. The rain hit us, but had already subsided by the time we descended into the river. It was a beautiful sight to be reconnected to our lovely Roosevelt River after two days. Considerably wider, it has the same charm and familiarity. We crossed it in the ferry, which is run by a community of lumberjacks, and stopped at the mill a few kilometers downstream. The crew had gone to vote, thirty men working on three shifts, but Dominguinho (Domingos Braz), the caretaker, received us with a big smile. A dark and skinny fellow, he told us that we could set our tents up in a covered area. We asked him to prepare some food, something he did with alacrity.

With us is also Zé Patroleiro (José Joachim), a tall blue-eyed gaucho that maintains the road with a patrol. He offered us a room with four beds, which we accepted readily. His parents had a piece of land in Paraná and sold it to come to Rondonia. There, his father was swindled, since the land purchased did not have a proper title, and the thirteen children had to struggle. The father's dream, to give each child a piece of land, fell to pieces and they carved a meager subsistence. But these Germans are resilient and hard-working and he told us proudly that his daughter is in Medical School. So is Angonese's daughter, and they exchanged the matte-filled chimarrão and stories about their families. Zé Patroleiro had built a one bedroom trailer in which he lived during his travels. He told us that one day he was working on a roof and fell off, breaking his neck. After several surgeries, it was a miracle that he could walk. The doctor had told him that he would probably end his days as a paraplegic. But here he was, helping us with a kind-hearted attitude and ensuring our well-being. He even offered to share his room with Sergeant Douglas, who accepted. I thought of the high standard of living experienced by the Germans and it is sad that their poor cousins in Brazil have to struggle so hard.

Dominguinho prepared a nice meal and we ate the rice, beans, and chicken stew with great appetite. Dominguinho told us that the mill had pit-bulls that protected the pigs from jaguars. He was proud to state that pit-bulls can actually kill a jaguar. It is wonderful to feel the selfless hospitality in this hinterland of Brazil. So different from João Brabo! But we are the intruders in the Indian lands, and should follow Rondon's philosophy.

Commentary:

The 120 km that we missed due to the prohibition laid by the Cinta Larga are indeed some of the most challenging of the entire river and it is a pity that we could not experience this. I will return to cover this treacherous region the help of the Cinta Larga. Rather than the four days, considering 30 km/day, we would have spent at least three additional days in portaging. This region corresponds to the two tragic incidents in the RR expedition: Simplicio's drowning and Paixão's assassination. Roosevelt's book has a detailed account of these fateful events. The loss of a canoe also required another delay in their descent to construct two additional ones. This is a back-breaking job that involved felling the right tree and digging it with simple utensils. Work had to be carried out into the nights.

Simplicio's drowning occurred first, and there are two versions to the story, Roosevelt's and Rondon's. That accident was, according to Rondon, produced by the bold action of Kermit, ordering Simplicio and João, who were manning a canoe, to cross the river just above a dangerous rapid. Rondon and Lyra were on foot to better assess the danger and there was an island just above the rapids. Kermit proceeded in his canoe to explore the left margin, beyond the island, and seek a passage there. Then, he ordered Simplicio and João who were following him to return to the right margin. Upon doing this, they were caught by a whirlpool and their canoe went down broadside. The exploration by Kermit had been done against Rondon's orders, who knew the danger very well. However, Roosevelt refrains from criticizing his son. Simplicio and João's canoe went down the rapid, taking lots of water. Then, there was a second set of rapids before they could reach the margin. Rushing down, filled with water, the canoe rolled and threw the two rowers in the water. João managed to swim to the shore after trying to pull the canoe with a rope, but Simplicio disappeared forever, never to be found again. Roosevelt describes the heroic effort of Kermit to salvage the canoe, almost losing his life in the process. But the conclusion is that the boldness of Kermit led to the accident. I was also caught a few times by whirlpools and they can completely change the course of the boat. This was in the dry season. In the rainy season, these whirlpools are of much greater danger, as was reported to me by Pelado in Vila do Carmo, at the end of our journey. He reported entire canoes being drawn to the center of the whirls.

A second incident as tragic of the first, but caused by one of the *camaradas* was the assassination of Corporal Paixão by Julio. This incident carries a racist tint in that Julio was the whitest of the *camaradas* and Paixão was a black man with a disciplinarian nature that had served in Rondon's army earlier as a sergeant. He was in charge of supplies, had caught Julio steeling the sugar and had punched him in the face. Roosevelt describes Julio with uncanny vigor as "...a fellow of powerful frame, utterly useless, an inborn lazy shirk with a heart of a ferocious cur in the body of a bullock." It is amazing what these difficult conditions do to people; some grow stronger while others simply fall apart. Upon being reprimanded by Paixão for stealing some dried meat, Julio took the rifle and shot him through the heart, killing him instantly. Then, his rage gave way to fear and he ran away into the forest, leaving the rifle behind. This shows how crazy he had become, under the conditions of duress imposed by the expedition.

At this point a dispute over how to dispose with the assassin arose between Rondon and Roosevelt. Roosevelt, the American cowboy still alive and well in him, strongly argued in favor of shooting him, while Rondon, always following the law, argued that he should be captured and taken prisoner for the courts to decide. This difference remained unresolved because the party sent after Julio came back empty-handed. The most probable end to this man was in the hands of the Cinta Larga, who enjoyed roasting their enemies and eating them. The shots fired by the expedition were most probably attention gatherers in the deep jungle, and the persistent cries for help by Julio at the end of the first day, when he was trapped in the margin opposite to the camp, must have been heard by the Indians. The jungle has swallowed numerous people throughout history, and a lone man without fire does not last long.

The expedition continued, the most treacherous part of the river having been crossed.

Day 12

I woke up before daybreak and watched the sky gradually shed its shades and acquire a blue tint. I walked through the mill and inspected the monstrous logs, harvested from the Amazonian forest and, according to Joachim, all legally. This system is called *manejo* or management. Only big trees are targeted after identification, and the forest is then left to rest for a number of years. Apparently new large trunks form, in this Darwinian competition among trees. The Brazilian Government tags individual trees and only those can be removed through roads built in the forest. But there are lots of opportunities for corruption.

After coffee, we had to start the Mitsubishi from the Vilhena Fire Dept. The battery was completely discharged but we were fortunate to have the help of José Joachim who came up with a front-end loader and cables. After trying several approaches, we exchanged the batteries, and got the truck to start. Then, we disconnected the cables and reversed the change. As long as Douglas would not have to kill the engine he would be fine.

We drove off through the forest and soon came to the river. At 8:37 we launched off two miles north of the mill after crossing a dense forest. The river is indeed splendid, with rocky formations mixed with a few sandy beaches. The altitude at our entry is 120 meters, quite a drop from the 450 meters at the beginning. Rapids interspersed with quiet stretches kept us on our toes. But, after a while, we got a hang of it: avoid the spots where the river boils up and paddle forcefully through the vortices that populate the rapids.

The Pak Canoe got stuck on a shallow stone forcing Angonese and Jeffrey to dismount in the water to lighten the load. By 1:30 we reached an impressive wood bridge and decided to camp, having advanced 32 km. I felt very tired and the two days of rest did not seem to increase my stamina too much. In the coming days, we expect to start earlier and gradually increase our distance to 45 km. But this will be tough!

Angonese made good *carreteiro* rice and we feasted on it. Fishing was poor. We heard some cars crossing the bridge during the night.

Our expedition was reinitiated downstream of the Cardoso River. Thus, we missed the terrible rapids and falls that considerably weakened the RR expedition. These 120 km are the most treacherous in the river, excluding the last portion. I would like to return to help erect a decent burial site for Paixão and Simplicio, heroes and martyrs of this first expedition. The ease with which we can go down the rapids using our kayaks and canoes is wonderful. Nevertheless, we also dealt with moments of great danger and one of us could have easily left his life on this river.

Today our expedition passed the point at which the RR expedition encountered the first signs of white man, through the carved initials J.A. on a post. The first hut encountered was empty, but showed signs of having been abandoned recently. Apparently, the woman was home at the time and ran away in panic, thinking that an Indian attack was imminent. Shortly thereafter the expedition found a second hut inhabited by a black man. While we covered 32 km, the RR expedition covered 22 km that day. The second house that they encountered had coordinates of $10°$ 24' S. Each 5' correspond to approximately 10 km.

Commentary:

Roosevelt describes large piranhas that were caught and eaten. These must be our black piranhas that are indeed delicate but have quite a few bones. Other than that, the forest is silent and very few animals are seen. An occasional curassow and parrots flying overhead are the birds most sighted. The expedition meets the first signs of civilized life, a post with the initials J. A., and shortly thereafter, a thatch-covered hut that been recently abandoned. They found an old black man in a second hut and continued on to a third house. The family had abandoned it, afraid of Indian attacks, but returned after they realized that it was an expedition. It had taken the expedition approximately forty-five days to reach this point at which rubber tappers had come up. They informed them that the river was known as Castanho, because of the ubiquity of Brazil nuts in the area. It is only then that the RR expedition was informed that the Castanho was an affluent of the Aripuanã River and that the journey downriver from that point would take approximately two weeks.

Day 13

We did about 30 km, from the bridge to a little fishing camp. Behind a 100-meter strip of forest there was a large property. Col.

Hiram walked a mile to it and soon the manager, Lourival and his side-kick came to check us out. We asked and were granted permission to camp there. Lourival had a strong Minas Gerais accent and indeed he confirmed that he was a *Mineiro*, having lived on this ranch for 18 years. The ranch has 14,000 alqueires (100,000 acres) and 40,000 head of cattle. It is owned by four brothers in São Paulo and goes from the bridge to the Branco River, 30 km downstream. He bragged that jaguars abound in this area, eating his cattle, and that he had killed one hundred already. Although pit-bulls are being used with success against jaguars, he hunts them the old-fashioned way, also described by Roosevelt, tracking them with dogs until they climb up a tree. At this point it is an easy job to shoot them, even with a 22 LR on the head. Not a glorious sport by any measure. The old *zagaia* way, using a spear, was sportier. Lourival picked Jeffrey up at night to charge up his batteries and they returned half-drunk a few hours later.

The river intersperses slow stretches with rapids. Since the Pak canoe was taking lots of water, we unloaded it and turned it over to inspect it. One has to be careful all the time because rapids have rocks that can tear the fabric of the canoe and crack the fiberglass of the kayaks.

It is interesting to note that we did not see a single soul all day. The right side of the river is a national reserve.

I saw two curassows (*mutums*) crossing the river and a few macaws high up. We also came across a couple bands of the garrulous hoatzil, *jacu-cigana*. The whistles of the *paquerador* bird, fiu-fiu, followed us all day and broke the silence. Our end point is Km 345 in our map (10° S).

Commentary:

Roosevelt's book carries no further mention of these regions other than a statement about the significance of their geographic discovery of a 700-km river whose course the expedition established. One has to go to Dr. Cajazeira's, Cherrie's and Candice Millard' s accounts to understand this silence for the last 300 km of the expedition. Roosevelt became seriously ill at the crossing of Paixão's canyon. In addition to an infection in the leg, he developed a weakness in the heart which made walking extremely difficult. His situation deteriorated with high fevers that would not abate. He had undoubtedly contracted malaria, which in his case was much more serious than the one developed by his son Kermit. Cherrie reports that he had serious problems walking from one camp to the next along the river, as the dugout canoes were lowered with ropes along the stream.

Problems developed between Cherrie and Rondon at this point of the expedition, the former bitterly criticizing the latter for the constant delays in the descent. Kermit's dog Trigueiro had jumped off the boat and disappeared in the forest, probably pursuing some animal. The entire party stopped and Rondon sent two men back, while he and his crew documented the mouth of a sizeable river that they had encountered. From the map, it is either the Cardoso or Branco River. Cherrie accused Rondon of deliberately delaying the expedition for his measurements and was highly concerned with the well-being of Roosevelt, who spent one night in a delirious state and almost succumbed to the fevers. It is possible that Roosevelt already exhibited the symptoms of angina pectoris, excruciating chest pains that are the result of clogged heart arteries.

Day 14

After getting up at 5:20 a.m., we finally started at 7:30. It seems hard to beat this time. Jeffrey is never ready and today we waited for a good 30 minutes. He lacks the military training and discipline, whereas mine is coming back, under the influence of the colonels. There was no great change in the scenery. The river bed contains rocks that in places reach the surface, causing a tremulation in the water that serves as a warning. There was a spot where the Pak canoe had to be pushed through after Angonese and Jeffrey stepped out. We passed a shack where the occupant, probably a fisherman, greeted us with loud yells. We told him that we were going all the way down and he acted surprised. At 1p.m. we found a nice spot to camp, having covered 32 km, ten less than our goal. I was relieved, since my arms and back ached and I was close to collapse. But this is the third day of our second round on the road and I feel that I might hold up. These are old bicycle injuries that bother me a lot. My left shoulder has major problems. However, the fact that Hiram was the victim of a terrible accident, having been run over by a car during the September 7 parade in Rio, serves as encouragement. He broke a leg, the back, multiple ribs, and it is a miracle that he is so agile and strong. He tells me that pain also bothers him and gave me some *guaraná* pills to push me through the most difficult moments.

I think of my father, who took us to the Araguaia River several times. He was probably my age on his last trip and we spent one night on a beach, away from the noise of the boat, where some fat Brazilians drank and bragged all day long and into the night, being served by a uniformed waiter.

We finish at 9° 57' S.

Commentary:

One would expect the population of the river to have increased significantly in 100 years. Such is not the case. Roosevelt describes the night spent at a third house and that the rubber tapper Antonio Correia informed Kermit that the journey to the Aripuanã would take a further fifteen days. At this point the diary goes blank and we have to use other sources to reconstitute the remainder of the journey. The extraction of rubber, started in the 19th century, supplied this product to the entire world that was undergoing rapid change with the process of industrialization. Tires consumed vast quantities and the only supply was the Amazon. The 1914 expedition occurred shortly after the crash of the rubber market, caused by competition from Asia, where it was planted and produced in large quantities. The price of rubber dropped precipitously in the years following 1912 and the fortunes of the entire Amazon basin were thrown into a descending spiral. An Englishman, Henry Wickham, took thousands of seeds and planted them in the Royal Botanic Gardens, Kew, London. After the technique was developed, the seeds were taken to Ceylon and Malaysia and planted on a large scale. Far from the pests of the Amazon, the trees grew in tight rows. The combination of more efficient harvesting and cheap labor from Malaysia resulted in a dramatic increase in production and, consequently, drop in price. In 1914, the rivers of the Amazon were still inhabited by rubber tappers, *seringueiros*, and the RR expedition found a larger population than we, 100 years later.

Day 15
We started earlier today, at 7 a.m., and the scenery was pretty much the same. The river was extremely slow and we discovered that this is a characteristic in the lower course. The waterfalls and rapids dam the water. We stopped at beautiful rock formations, which appear to be basaltic and not sedimentary as in Navaité.

We are starting to see more dwellings and at noon we passed a ranch with a ferry for cattle. There were two islands covered with sand and pebbles. I feel stronger and use alternate positions to relieve the back, shoulder, and leg pains. Although the Pak canoe fellows have to paddle harder, the position in the kayak is extremely uncomfortable. The ease with which Hiram paddles is due to thirty years of experience. Upon touching his shoulder, I realized the source of his stamina. It feels like steel and is broad and strong, double the thickness of mine. He can cover twice the territory that we pain through. I work hard to keep up with the canoe.

At 1 p.m. we came to a significant waterfall. We had to walk the canal at three spots and in one of them Angonese could no longer hold the rope, as he slipped down a shallow rapid. The canoe got stuck on a rock and we almost tipped it. Fortunately, nobody was injured. This would have been a major problem since help is far away. We will be more careful in the future using two ropes upstream and one downstream to control the canoe. I have always been an advocate of this method but being a mere lieutenant have to follow the orders of the colonels. The kayaks are considerably more maneuverable in the rapids. They are also safer, since only a direct hit will crack the hull. Nevertheless, I felt rocks hitting the bottom hard as I went down through rapids. Jeffrey is a powerful paddler and we would have been in trouble without him.

This is a beautiful river, which is growing daily as we descend it. The number of animals is discreet, capybaras, macaws, kingfishers, brown herons, but we have a chance to glance at them every now and then. I suspect that seasonal lakes have a greater concentration of birds because the trapped fish are a much easier prey. So, it is for alligators of which we only saw a few small ones. But we are starting to catch some fish. We have three piranhas for dinner, and Angonese caught them at spots where we usually would not expect them, fast running water. Tonight, we will try to catch some catfish to supplement our Spartan diet of *carreteiro* rice.

Day 16

Having been able to get Jeffrey ready earlier, we left at 7:00 a.m.. We have developed the following routine: I make the fire and prepare breakfast every morning. We ate the watery oats and milk and I got some coffee ready just before we left. They are all so worried about the quality of water, using chlorine pills but often the porridge does not even reach a boiling point! I told them that it wasn't water, but food. Oh well, nobody got the runs. At around 11 a.m. we reached Fazenda *Buriti*, where two 'fishermen' informed us that a German group had bought the 14,000 alqueires (140,000 acres) ranch and had reserved it for reforestation. I checked the houses and they were neat, but the fruit trees were empty. Local fishermen use the place and the two fellows we met at the water are probably disassembling parts of the farm and carting them away. They had two good pickup trucks and told us rather vaguely that they were fishing.

In the morning, we saw a tapir on a clay lick. It allowed us to approach to within 40 meters prior to running up and into the forest. Two kilometers downstream from *Buriti* we met the Branco River. From there, the Roosevelt acquires considerable width and it now is about 400 meters vs. 170 meters at the bridge where we camped (measured by Hiram). The first airplane in many days flew over our heads, a monoplane with one motor. We stopped at noon a couple kilometers below Rio Branco, at a farm. We need to go down another 8 km if we want to keep the pace of 30 km per day.

It is amazing to see how the river that we followed since its birth in Vilhena becomes a majestic stream of a size comparable to the large European rivers, such as the Rhine. We are now at km 429 and in two days will have completed two thirds of the journey. I waited by the river guarding the equipment while the other fellows walked up to the ranch house. Within an hour, they returned with oranges and coconuts. The rancher had told them that a few Indians had camped by the river some time ago and claimed to be the original inhabitants. I don't know how, but they must have been flushed out by the owner. Roosevelt does not report any Indians in these regions, only rubber tappers.

We had one major waterfall before the end of the afternoon. A storm also hit us with strong upstream winds. I had to stop and hide the kayak under some branches in the bank to wait out the heaviest. We are now moving independently, regrouping periodically. Col. Hiram is faster and goes ahead, scouting out the river, and I am usually the straggler. After the rain subsided I was able to continue and join the other boats. After some debate, we decided that it was wiser to rope the canoe down through the right bank, which was more accessible. Col. Hiram macheted a path through the stream and we used two ropes this time, with Jeffrey at the front, downstream. But at some point Angonese slipped on a rock and disaster was imminent, being avoided by Hiram. The use of two ropes was our salvation. After we got the canoe through, Angonese took my kayak down the center of the rapids that were steep but straight. I could not garner courage and he walked up, took my kayak, and rode it down, banging it hard on a rock. Fortunately, the kayak did not suffer anything more than a deep gash. It is very solidly built and has withstood severe impacts.

After the fun at the river, we found the most idyllic place to camp: a beach interspersed with rocks. We had already exceeded 30 km and decided to stop. To simplify dinner, we prepared our rations, which Angonese calls *ração operacional* from his Army days, fortified by a bean soup.

Day 17

Today, the Day of the Dead, was a dangerous one, with two waterfalls after some currents. We ran down the first one after Hiram found a spot where our boats could rush through. Hiram's kayak hit a rock and the canoe went down without problems. I was perfect, for a change. We found a house where we were wonderfully received by Ailton Estelita, originally from Cuiabá. He lives there since 2004, all alone, and is completely self-sufficient. He is of medium height and dark complexion with straight hair. The Indian blood runs deep in this former miner who worked close to the Cinta Larga lands. He told us that he developed leschimaniasis on the leg and sought treatment instead of continuing to mine blindly for diamonds. An interesting and wonderfully hospitable character, he gave us a dozen eggs, pineapples, and some guavas. He has two pigs and two dogs and seems perfectly happy growing mandioc and pineapples. He explained to me his philosophy of life, being in harmony with nature. He did not need money and traded his goods for some tobacco, coffee, and an occasional bottle of *cachaça* (Brazilian rum). An interesting chap with, most probably, a troubled past. But the important is that he found a place in communion with nature. The tapir almost greets him in the morning and his chicken lay their beautiful bluish eggs with regularity. He has only one enemy, *cachaça* that drives him crazy when fishermen offer it to him. He and his wife abandoned each other a long time ago. He informed us that we had 13 km to the next waterfall, at Fazenda *Buritiz*al. We made it painfully, through rain and against a strong headwind that wrinkled the surface of the river with wavelet and slowed down the advance.

When we arrived at the waterfalls we received good news from Hiram. He had arranged for the manager of *Buritiz*al ranch to help us cross the falls. More importantly, the kind gentleman, Jair Schiabi, had offered us dinner and a roof above our heads. He said that the falls were easy and sometimes he went down them on his aluminum boat with only the help of paddles. We followed him in his boat powered by a 25 HP outboard. However, it was not as easy as his description, and I had a scary experience. I went down the first and second runs but then the kayak got caught in a whirlpool and turned 90 degrees, hitting some rocks. I was suddenly going down backwards, all my companions yelling orders at me. Paddling desperately, as the kayak took water and almost tipped, I was able to, somehow, redress the situation. From that point on, the heart in my throat, I continued the downward rush until the end. The important technique to remember is to paddle with all the energy down, because the steering mechanism only works if the velocity of the kayak is higher than the current. This is scary but necessary. Any hesitation and the current takes over. I felt a deep relief but worry about bigger falls to come; will I be able to handle them?

We got a wonderful reception from Jair, his wife Edna, and son Jackson. We were offered one of the comfortable houses of the ranch (which had about eight and even a chapel) and settled in, after a shower.

Jair told us that the ranch has 20,000 hectares and 3,000 head of cattle. It belongs to a São Paulo man, A. J. Barros, who is also an author of quality, which I gathered after leafing through his two books, one on the internationalization of the Amazon, the other on the Compostela trail: two voluminous suspense novels inspired on Dan Brown.

O Enigma de Compostela-The Compostella Enigma
O Conceito Zero (history of the region), The Zero Concept
The email of the ranch is: fazenda*buriti*zal@gmail.com

We looked at the map for the route to follow and evaluated the coming obstacles. I, or better, we, will be lucky to get out of this. There is a series of waterfalls with a length of 13 km! But our strategy is to face one waterfall at a time. The conversation with Jair was also very helpful and he indicated a more appropriate route for the pick up after the completion of the journey. Everything has to be well planned in such an expedition. The road that we had chosen existed on the map only, and had not yet been cut into the jungle! Hence, we sent an email to Douglas informing him of the longer road: Vilhena-Jaru-direction Machadinho do Oeste until Guatá, also called 180. From there, continue on HI 230 until the Aripuanã River, in the direction of Apuí.

We also sent an update to our most supportive reporter in San Diego, Gary Robbins.

Commentary:

Since Roosevelt's diary has only a few lines of description at this point, we must surmise that he was indeed very ill. They were received by a local merchant, Barbosa, who provided them with a boat in exchange of which he received one of the heavy dugout canoes as well as food. Replenished, the expedition continued, passing the Branco River.

Day 18

After a good breakfast of home-made cheese and bread, we started our descent. Hiram went to the orchard and filled a sack with oranges and mangoes. The pigs followed him and one of them ran off pulling the sack. However, for our luck he tripped spectacularly, doing a summersault. This gave Hiram the chance to recover our bounty. The other pigs rapidly grabbed whatever oranges had fallen from the sack during the escapade of their mate. The previous evening Jair had given us some valuable advice about the Panela waterfalls, our next challenge. He also told us that a group of paddlers had come by a few months ago. Through the identification of their Pak canoe, identical to ours, we concluded that it was the David Freeman/Paul Shurke expedition.

We arrived at the ferry at around noon. Following Jair's instructions, we shadowed the right margin, but steered left after the ferry and entered a narrow canal, which ended a few hundred yards down. Had we gone more to the center, we would have been sucked into the falls, a disaster. We scouted out the place and, indeed, there was a trail that led to a clearing below the fall, after 300 meters. The Panela Falls also mark the location of a small village which we did not visit.

I had spent the morning thinking about my family, having bad feelings. Hopefully this is the result of my state of mind and of my own worries. I hope that Alaide and Jacques, the most vulnerable of them, are fine. Linda was curt on the phone yesterday. I hate this coldness.

The main changes observed in the river today were a gradual increase in human activity. Every few kilometers we now see a house. We are in the state of Mato Grosso and will enter the Amazon before the end of the journey.

After this expedition is completed I need to thank Jair and Edna. They refused to be paid for their wonderful hospitality. Jair is an athletic and energetic fellow, with a combination of White features and Indiatic eyes. He clearly displays the qualities of leadership and determination required in these tough regions.

We portaged our gear, which took us two hours. Exhausted, we climbed on our boats to face another series of rapids. At one point, I could not advance my kayak and almost went down the wrong side. There was an island downstream and the current bifurcated, the right towards a waterfall and the left towards a more sinuous and less steep path. Using the last strings of my tired muscles, I paddled for life. The kayak stalled in the current, then slowly advanced, inch by inch, until I was out of the main current. These rapids are terrifying for this neophyte. They probably are simple, but exacting stretches for an experienced young kayaker.

We paddled down for a good hour, seeing houses every few hundred meters. It was time to find a spot to camp but the margins of the river were becoming higher, ten meters or more. The prospect of lugging our load up a steep bank and of cutting a clearing in the forest was resolved by a house that we found. There was a ramp cut into the bank. Upon inquiring with the caretaker, a fellow about four feet tall, we learned that it belonged to a rich fellow that had died in an airplane accident. He used it as a fishing lodge. The caretaker allowed us to use the abandoned place and we promptly set up tents in the spacious veranda. There was even a long table for our meals. The tin roof radiated the intense heat of the afternoon as I laid down and fell asleep, exhausted by the long day. I never had great stamina and this has not changed with the impending old age.

I was initially concerned, since I saw a kid and dog running away and into the forest. I warned everybody about possible theft and we kept an eye on our possessions.

Arão Macedo Santos is indeed an interesting fellow. He does not grow anything and survives solely on fish and manioc flour. Barely taller than a child, he is hard of hearing. His face is clearly Indian, but he has a thin beard. He told us with pride that he used to be a rubber tapper in the many *igarapés*, side rivers and creeks, that disimboc into the Roosevelt. He was proud of his new gas stove and we boiled two liters of water for our rations. His little eyes shining, he told me about wild Indians that used to kill rubber tappers and eat them, only sparing the calves, which they considered too 'tough and sour.' We served him one of the rations but he only took a couple bites into it, obviously not liking the taste. He showed us his mouth with a lonely tooth and said, politely, that it was not the taste, but the difficulty of masticating the rice-and-chicken concoction. We also boiled the eggs from Cuiabá for breakfast.

This homunculus found his mission in the difficult and solitary task of walking through the jungle every day, cutting the tree bark at an angle, and placing a cup at the bottom, into which the white rubbery sap would flow. I thought he was a member of some forlorn tribe but he informed me that his parents came from the *Nordeste*, probably part of the Rubber Army in the 1940s. He also told me that he had sisters that were quite taller than him. Watching him bathe, Angonese detected an enormous growth in his gonads, perhaps a hernia.

The longing and nostalgia that Arão expressed for the old days when rubber tappers entered the most recondite streams and carved out an existence in the jungle are only partly justified. After the loss of monopoly by Brazil in 1912, the fortunes of the Amazonian rubber barons shrank but the toil of the *seringueiros* - rubber tappers - continued, albeit in a more difficult manner. When I visited the Purus River in 1969 I still encountered this culture and was amazed by how these men could survive, alone and without any outside help, in the forest. Each stream was owned by a merchant that traveled up a couple times a year and exchanged goods for rubber balls that weighed between 80 and 150 pounds. These balls were made by slowly pouring the white viscous liquid collected from the trees onto a wooden pole that was rotated over a slow fire. Thus, the liquid stiffened under the influence of heat and smoke, and adhered to the pole that rotated horizontally, held by two forks like a primitive barbecue spit. The balls gradually grew and when they reached a certain size, they were separated from the pole and the process started again. I remember seeing boats laden with these balls coming by. During WW2, there was a large government-initiated migration from the Brazilian Northeast, in response to the havoc raised in Asia by the Japanese and consequent disruption of the rubber supplies. Thousands of 'Soldiers of Rubber' were transposed to the Amazon from the poor Brazilian Northeast. About half of them died, and Arão is a descendent of them.

Commentary:

Panela is mentioned in Roosevelt's book but not by Candice Millard's specifically; it is probably one of the places where they had to portage. The expedition camped in a roomy house at that latitude where they encountered a number of rubber tappers. Roosevelt also mentions that there were, in addition to tappers, permanent settlers. There were also a number of abandoned houses that exceeded the inhabited houses. Roosevelt's condition deteriorated to the point where he had to have his wound lanceted and cleaned by Dr. Cajazeira. There was danger of infection spreading through the body. Roosevelt stoically watched as the incisions were made without anesthetic. The doctor cut the abscess and inserted a drainage tube. However, the fevers did not subside and there was a night, related in Dr. Cajazeira's report and Millard's book, in which he was delirious and they were afraid that he might not make it through the night. Roosevelt's account of his illnesses is much more stoic, since it was not in his nature to commiserate himself.

Day 19

We left at 7 a.m. with the plan of meeting at Cotovelo Island. I felt strong and the river had no obstacles. We paddled energetically until noon and stopped in a good spot. Hiram abhors afternoon paddling and he is right that the winds pick up. We also have the problem of feeding because we get weakened at about this time. I stopped periodically to peel and eat an orange. An early dinner is a necessity.

The google earth map did not show any decent camping spot downstream within striking distance. During the morning, we passed isolated houses every few kilometers and I noted progress in the mode of transportation of the *ribeirinhos* as the riverine dwellers are called. Whereas they had dugout canoes and heart-shaped paddles in the Purus River, fifty years ago, they now use wood plank canoes and small engines with a long shaft.

We are at 9° South, 70 km from the Roosevelt Lodge. Our spirits are high and we have a good stock of oranges, coconuts, and pineapples. Today we will have *carreteiro* rice, a dish that Angonese makes so well. It takes about one hour of preparation and half an hour cooking time and he uses generous quantities of onions and garlic together with the *charque* which is salted beef. We wash it three times after cutting it into tiny morsels and this removes most of the salt. I usually assist the cook. I am getting ready to perform my piranha-biting experiment. All we need a few good hard-biting piranhas.

The rains have spared us one more day. Tomorrow we have to make more than 30 km, if we want to reach the lodge by the 6th of November. The river is now straight with high banks and travel is monotonous. I saw only birds in small numbers and this confirms Roosevelt's observation that they were scarcer on the River of Doubt than in the *Pantanal*. At his point, Roosevelt was already sick with malaria and his leg was already infected. The first contact of the 1914 expedition with rubber tappers was at $10^O24'$ S. I can only admire the determination of these explorers that did not have our modern technology to advance through the jungle. However, we are performing the feat of both *camaradas* and leaders, paddling, setting up camp, cooking, writing, and discussing science.

Commentary:

The expedition encountered the first store close to this region and Roosevelt describes the local inhabitants with great accuracy. Having visited many rivers in the Amazon basin, I can vouch for the ethnic mix of these people that have southern European, Negro, and Indian blood. Although one finds pure representatives, the majority are of mixed origin, in different degrees. Roosevelt mentions the wonderful hospitality displayed by these people, something that we also encountered. They were "friendly, courteous, and hospitable. Often they refused payment...." Roosevelt feels sorry for their lot, because they are simple squatters and have no legal right to the land. He felt that "...the land laws should be shaped so as to give each of these pioneer settlers the land he actually takes up and cultivates and upon which he builds his home." He continues by stating that small landowners are the greatest element of strength in any country. These are American ideals that were implemented in the West with the settlers that received each a plot of land.

Day 20

Col Hiram left before us to scout out our camping place for the evening. Last night, for the first time, fishing was productive and Angonese caught four piranhas and a smallish *pirarara*. I performed a biting experiment on them and the second one took a couple of energetic bites on our gage/sensor.

The food continues to be excellent with Angonese preparing his *carreteiro* rice. We have a fresh supply of oranges which are most welcome and that we devour with gulps of coconut water. We are again in uninhabited territory. What kept this river so pristine is the sequence of waterfalls which impede larger boats from coming up. These necklaces of dark stones which embellish the Roosevelt are, at the same time, its protection. Enough environmental damage is being done throughout the Amazon, and hopefully this entire river will be, one day, a World Heritage Site. Its beauty should be preserved for future generations, in the same manner as the national parks created by Roosevelt.

We have totaled 32 km today and will have to paddle 40 km tomorrow if we are to reach the Roosevelt Lodge at our scheduled day, November 6.

As I travel down this monotonous route, I put my mind to work on a project: the book. Structure:

- Reading Candice Millard
- Backflash to Purus River
- Paris-Auguste Comte and advertisement: the complex Gallic psyche
- Manaus: emotion and disappointment
- Visit to Vilhena
- More contacts with Army; Col Hiram confirms participation
- The team is formed
- Delays and headaches
- We hit the water
- Comparison of Roosevelt's and our journey
- The Cinta Larga
- Legal vs. illegal logging-sustainable development?
- Large *fazendas* vs. riverine populations

We stopped at 1 p.m. to explore an *igarapé* and Angonese caught two large *tucunaré*, peacock bass. The river descent is smooth and uneventful, and I saw some black geese, *biguás*, and brown herons. What was going to be a calm day ended with a piranha biting Angonese's finger. He was straightening the line and cast into the river. Upon reeling in he caught a small white piranha by hooking it on its back. As he held it up, it came loose, falling down. In the process, it touched Angonese's hand and delivered the bite. A second later, his hand bled profusely. We bandaged the gash that described a helical trajectory around the index finger, at the height of the knuckle. I hope that the wound, being closed right away, will heal without stitches. We proceeded to join Hiram who had gone ahead to scout out a camping spot, and braved fierce winds.

We met him an hour later, having covered 32 km in little

over 4 hours. As I was struggling against the wind, staying close to the bank, something hit me hard on the head, just under the ear. I believe that it was a fish, and its impact stunned me temporarily. It was a freak event and I was lucky it was not a piranha.

Col Hiram picked a beautiful spot at the encounter with an *igarapé* but warned us that he had seen a large alligator (~4 meters) by the beach. So, tonight we do not take the usual bath, since these large alligators (*jacaré açu*) are known to attack humans.

Day 21
I fished last night and missed four *pirarara* (red-tailed catfish) runs. Roosevelt describes one of these fish in his book giving the proper classification: Siluriformes. I confess that in two of these runs I made basic mistakes: I had made a knot in the nylon line and it slipped on the first run. On the second, the *pirarara* went under some branches, something they usually do. After some pulling the branch broke but it appears that the fish was only grabbing the bait and was not hooked. Two runs later and the loss of another hook, and biting stopped. I would not be surprised if this was the same fish, such is the voracity of this species. However, I caught a black piranha of about 2-3 kg. We caught two and tried, with limited success, to measure the bite force. The critters would not bite the gage sandwiched between two wood strips inserted into their mouth. Later, one of them bit Angonese's machete until its teeth broke, but it had a knife inserted into its head which might have helped. I noticed an important fact: the biting is invariably associated with trashing, which makes the measurement difficult. These two joint actions, however, are responsible for removing morsels of flesh. It is also possible that the piranha recognizes the hard wooden surface and does not dig into it, because this would damage its teeth.

This morning we started slower because of Angonese's condition. Jeffrey and I loaded the Pak canoe. The plan is to do three 1.5 hour runs and then a shorter one.

I saw a colony of otters which are recognizable by their white markings on the chest. They emit a characteristic warning shriek, and then jump into the water. I am sure that Jeffrey is filming them, because I warned him of their presence.

We have the following hurdles ahead: Gloria, Inferninho, and Piranhas waterfalls. We will hopefully get local help in the last one. For the others, we will use ropes (*sirga*).

We arrived at the encounter with the Madeirinha river at around 3:30 p.m. and stopped at a beach to catch our breath. The scenery is fantastic and the encounter with this river brings greater beauty to the Roosevelt.

When we arrived at the lodge Hiram was waiting for us with several fellows and a tractor with trailer! This was a surprise and Jeffrey immediately felt better, since we were spared a tiring portage. The trail was approximately one km long and we could have, with some difficulty, had made the transition on our feet. We loaded up the stuff and walked down the trail, cut into the forest. There is an airstrip by the lodge, which is splendid. The manager called Rondonia and asked for the price for an overnight stay. The answer came: 400 Reais per person. We declined and were allowed to set our tents on the beach. We also arranged for dinner with the crew. We are fortunate that this was an off week at the lodge. No fishermen were there and we had the place for ourselves. The manager opened a room and we used the toilet. Hiram and Angonese enjoyed the ice-cold drinks and I was starved. In the morning, we had breakfast with the crew that consisted of eight young fellows. In the evening, Angonese fished a little and caught a *bicuda* close to the waterfalls. The scenery and design of the lodge are spectacular.

We have four waterfalls before the end, and will have to rope down our boats a few times. We expect the remainder of the trip to take between five and six days.

Commentary:

Roosevelt mentions the Madeirinha River and the falls with a drop of over ten meters below the confluence. This corresponds to the present-day Roosevelt Lodge. A guide helped them get across the falls. The baggage was carried about 750 meters and the canoes were run down through channels known to the locals. At the bottom of the falls there was a big house and store. They met a number of rubber tappers that were waiting for the *batelões*—the big boats—to come up with supplies.

Day 22

I am writing in my drenched tent under a torrential rain that came to us suddenly at 3 p.m. of a torrid day. We left the lodge shortly after 7 a.m. and soon were in a challenging rapid, at the end of which we averted disaster. Jeffrey fell off the canoe and hung onto my kayak until we brought him ashore. Unfortunately, his camera took water, but Angonese fabricated a desiccator with one kilo of rice and several bags.

We are facing tougher rapids with increasing assurance. Three kilometers later we hit the real waterfall. I believe it is called Gloria. We roped the canoe in some stretches and this was the safe decision, rather than risking an overturn by running it. I went down the rapid on the kayak but hit two stones. I felt the bottom warping and it almost cracked. If the canoe had gone down the same path, its bottom would most certainly have been ripped.

Ten kilometers later we hit a second waterfall. Like in previous occasions Col. Hiram went ahead of us and scouted the place out. We went down segment by segment through some treacherous rapids. Then, we roped the canoe and had a second close call. As it was being pulled down a rapid, Hiram could no longer hold it, lost the rope, and floated down the violent current which swerved around dangerous stones. Our guardian angels were looking after us and he escaped with barely a scratch! This could very well have been the end of the expedition.

We proceeded to the third waterfall and camped above it, after negotiating some rapids. From the tent, I hear the intense rush of water reminding me that we have another tough day tomorrow. These waterfalls are the greatest danger of our expedition, and each one that we go down represents considerable risk. The important thing is for us to stay united as a team.

This portion of the river is pristine and identical to the one seen by the original RR expedition: no houses, no boats, and no human presence except for the beautiful lodge which is a gem.

This afternoon I feel more fatigued and somewhat weak. I believe that I should have eaten more yesterday. The working crew at the lodge consists of about eight young fellows, mostly from the Panelas Falls upriver. They are a nice bunch and know Arão and Jair well. Their help in portaging us through the Inferno falls is greatly appreciated. I paid the manager 400 Reais, which I asked him to distribute among them.

We saw a large alligator floating by, of the *açu* kind. Today we did 33 km, helped by the swift currents. We will try to rope our way through the falls tomorrow morning and reach an advanced post of the Roosevelt Lodge. We are at km 660 of our 760-km journey.

The coordinate is 8° 22' S

Our *piranhaingamberi* (piranha leftover in Guarani) is doing better in spite of the water that the bite has taken yesterday. Angonese has amazing stamina for a blue-eyed blond Italian-Austrian under these difficult conditions. Jeffrey overheats and drinks enormous quantities of water. In contrast, Angonese is slim and fast. The military training of Hiram and Angonese has been essential to the success of this enterprise. Yesterday I arrived at the final destination exhausted and somewhat dazed. I tried to point the kayak to a little spot left by the canoe on a sand bank but it turned 90°, the tip stuck at the front. There were stones, against which the kayak went, putting me perpendicular to the current. The body started to gradually rotate and take water. If it were not for Hiram I would have made it down the rapid hanging on to the kayak, risking hitting two big stony afflorations in the whitewater. These dangerous moments happen suddenly and unpredictably, and we have been blessed until now. Hiram jumped into the water and held the kayak with his two arms in an embrace. He then pulled me to the beach. I got out and roped my way down, a safe action, while Jeffrey and Angonese canoed down, avoiding the boulders in two swift maneuvers; it was an impressive run. They are mastering the technique of controlling the canoe. We spent the night just downstream from the falls after a torrential rain drenched my tent in this wonderful location. Alas, fishing was poor because it was a shallow sandy bottom. The full moon came out and the night was clear as dawn. The sky was blue with orange streaks that lingered until late and the purr of the waterfalls nursed us.

Commentary:

The RR expedition continued down after the canoes were reloaded. In one of the rapids they had to unload the canoes, but nevertheless made good progress. They slept in an abandoned house, probably close to where we spent the night on the beach. Whereas they met six *batelões* coming up the river, we did not see anyone. This shows, again, that the population on the lower Roosevelt was larger one century ago.

Day 23

Today was a lazy morning and we left at 7:40. It will be a short day with less than 30 km to the advanced site of the Roosevelt lodge, where we plan to camp. There is an *igarapé* downriver from the camp and Angonese is eager to fish for peacock bass. They like to congregate at the entrance of these creeks.

I saw a small alligator or, better, heard it as it rushed into the water with a big splash. The most interesting sight was a curassow (*mutum*) with its white-tipped tail feathers. I found a few of them and we plan to study them in San Diego. At our campsite, we saw an interesting rock formation. The rocks exhibit clear cracks that are perpendicular to the surface and have almost plane surfaces. They are due, in my opinion, to thermal stresses. The rock is gradually fractured and then wind and water erosion take over, rounding the edges. When the hot rock, warmed by the sun, is cooled at night, the surface temperature drops and it wants to contract, while the interior is still hot. The surface, due to the difference in the thermal expansion, is set under tension, and over the years microcracks grow into macrocracks. This is a thermal fatigue process that is fascinating to watch and that comminutes the rock. This process might take hundreds of thousands of years but is inexorable.

We reached the advanced camp of the Roosevelt Lodge, a pleasant location under the trees. The houses, on stilts, are locked except for one, which we readily occupied, setting up two tents per room. We discovered that the water reservoir was not empty, which enables us to get a supply of fresh water.

The tall trees establish the canopy and several have buttresses in the bottom to stabilize the trunk and attach it to a broad root system. These buttresses can be enormous in the largest trees, the *sanauma*. They are known as *sapopema* by the locals. I have a picture of such a monstrous tree taken in Manu Park with my daughter Cristina. They are another interesting example of how nature uses strengthening /structures similar to the ones developed by humans, especially in the medieval cathedrals, that were built to 'reach the skies.'

Today was, as predicted, a rather easy paddling day: five hours. Nevertheless, I was a little dizzy when I arrived, due to the combined effects of heat and exhaustion and, perhaps, hunger. As I sit here and write, I realize that we have been very fortunate up to now. I only hope that we can survive the last waterfall, 13 km long, without an accident.

I think of my father often, and his image hauling wood the night we spent on the beach keeps coming back. It is sad that he left us so soon, in such an unfortunate and preventable manner. I hope that my brothers Pedro and Carlos take care of their health. Our body is a fragile but complex array of organs and performs beautifully. However, we cannot abuse it and we need to heed the warnings.

The heavy rains hit us again in the afternoon but we were well protected inside the unlocked hut. By the time I had prepared the *carreteiro* rice, Angonese came back with three large *tucunarés*, peacock bass. He told us that he had caught a dozen and only stopped when his equipment broke. So, tonight we will have both meat and fish, if the rain does not kill the fire. The thunder rips through the sky and the rain brings a welcome cooling. The tarp on top of the fire is holding up and I proceed to cook, while Angonese and Hiram clean the fish. One of them was already half eaten by piranha.

Commentary:

The RR expedition made 50 km on this stretch, twenty more than we did. They had stronger paddlers and they were, after 50 days on the river and a few days of a good diet, in top condition. They reached the Carapanã Falls, while we spent the night in the small house 60 km south of the Inferno Falls.

Day 24

We were met by a fellow in a motorboat at around 10 a.m., three hours after we departed. He was tall and had the features of a German serial killer. He informed us that his name was Marcos and that Hiram had passed at his place and invited us in. We crossed the river and arrived at a neatly arranged fishing lodge. He co-owned it with a doctor from 180 (yes, this is the name of the city), Dr. Rogerio. We were received by Dr. Rogerio's family. The entire crew was there under a large tarp, and Angonese took a long look at some *pasteis* – meat pasties - sitting on the table. The lady told him that they were old but nevertheless he accepted one. She took a good look at us and offered to fry us one each. This was a wonderful experience, since she and the doctor are from Minas Gerais and *pasteis* are one of my favorite foods. Hence, we feasted on them and beer.

The lodge is the preserve of Dr. Rogerio and Marcos. They bring their friends and family on weekends. Dr. Rogerio, his wife, three kids, sister and mother-in-law were there and he told me how he got to this distant parages from his native city of Uberaba, in western Minas Gerais. He is the doctor in a town 80 km from the river and bought some land, approximately 550 hectares that he is trying to exploit for cattle, sustainable logging, and tourism. They have approximately five boats and a nice lodge. We got detailed explanations about the 13 km waterfalls awaiting us downstream, that can be divided into four, the most dangerous being Apuí Grande:

Carapanã
Apuí Grande (two large falls)
Senauma
Galinha.

These falls are interspersed with rapids. Hiram had already studied them in his maps and had drawn, for each, the best possible route and approach. Marcos told us that a few months ago, a group of paddlers had come by and that one of them was in bad shape. This was the Shurke expedition, and they stopped at the same places we did. The doctor told me that four years ago he saw an Indian bathing in the river. Upon approaching in his powerboat, the Indian ran away. There are rumors of a tribe in the region that avoids contact with white man, and for a good reason. Contagious diseases usually wipe half of the tribe and these Indians probably have seen neighboring tribes being destroyed. The modern FUNAI philosophy is much more lenient, and forcible contact with tribes is avoided. It is left for the Indians to approach FUNAI, when and where they want.

The descent has become rather boring, with the river now 400-500 meters wide and flowing lazily. We have to use all our muscle power to advance. I believe that this will change later today, as on the left bank there is a high red cut of approximately 20 meters. Hopefully the river will become narrower and help us tired paddlers.

I am sitting in front of a complex that seems to be a modern farm. Behind it, verdant fields that can be pastures or some type of plantation. This is the first such farm that we encounter in six days. A hundred yards of the forest were cleared along the river and a generator hums and breaks the silence.

We faced a difficult afternoon. At 2 p.m. a fierce wind was blowing against us making advance impossible because of the energy expended. We waited until 3 p.m. and the winds decreased somewhat. The canoe went ahead, propelled by two paddlers and I struggled behind. They did not wait for me at the established meeting at 4:30 p.m. and I proceeded, watching the darkness in the sky surround me. Fortunately, the river had turned glazy again. The thick clouds amassing above me and the late hour combined to decrease the light. The last glimpse of the canoe was at around

4 p.m., when they crossed from one side of the river to the other, in a curve. I passed some sandy beaches and a place that looked like an island, the place designated for camping by Hiram. It was now almost completely dark and I was afraid that I had passed the spot, although I did not see anybody. I yelled and listened. Nothing. There were some rapids ahead, and I decided to run through them, since the sky was now almost black. My assessment of 13 km in two hours must be correct, I thought. I had my tent, sleeping bag, and some oranges. So, I decided to stop at the next beach and spend the night.

It was then that I saw a large rock in the middle of the river. Yes. This is where I would camp, away from an unwanted animal. As I approached it, two lights flashed in the darkness that now completely surrounded me. A voice. Col Hiram! I was saved. I paddled downstream from the rock, as he waived me to my left, and beached my kayak. Then, I let my companions know that I did not have a map, since it was with them. They had paddled straight through the last meeting place, eager to arrive before night, forgetting the straggler. Angonese told me that he had turned back several times and could see my yellow kayak and the paddles lifting rhythmically. I, on the other hand, did not have glasses and could not see the green canoe that blended with the background. All is well that ends well!

A few minutes after my arrival a fierce wind picked up as we rushed to protect the fire with the blue tarp. We struggled to assemble the tents. We had not finished when the sky came down in the strongest rain we ever experienced. We huddled under the tarp and had to push it up every few minutes to drain the pooled water. After a good hour, the rain and wind subsided and we were invaded by flocks of termite-looking insects flying into our food, cups, etc. The water that we were collecting from the tarp to drink was full of wings.

Had I been on the river twenty minutes later I do not know whether I would have found the camp. It is important to stay together because small problems can become irreparable accidents.

Day 25

This is a world of water and vegetation molding the sand and occasional rock. The fish in the water and birds on the trees are a mere consequence of this encounter, as is the rare mammal. The high temperature and humidity are a paradise for insects. Euclydes da Cunha referred to this universe in constant change, discharging enormous loads-a constant freight train loaded with soil-into the Atlantic, as: "This is nature portentous but at the same time incomplete. It is a stupendous construct lacking internal coherence."

This constitutes the most majestic ecological system on the earth. And yet monotony is extreme, kilometer after kilometer of water framed by the verdant forest. The land is not built on the human scale that delights in change, surprise, slope, and movement. Everything here is static and the occasional trashing of a fish, scream of a bird, or sting of a mosquito are reminders that we are intruders. For centuries, the Amazon posed this challenge and explorers and workers alike suffered under the oppressing conditions.

The slow advance propitiated by the manual paddling enables us to absorb this vastness in all its grandeur. The Roosevelt River is exceptionally well preserved by its guardians, the massive falls. It is only with difficulty that the rubber tappers crossed them, and the *batelões* (merchant boats) did not go beyond the confluence of the Aripuanã River.

Today we descend 20 km until the start of the 13 km waterfalls. Col Hiram is ahead of us to make the arrangements. There is supposed to be a house in the left bank just before the falls and supposedly there are people there specialized in helping boats get across. We will see. Another big ranch on the left bank. I stopped at a lodge and the caretaker informed me that it has 30 km of waterfront and has 5000 head of cattle. These are staggering numbers but I believe that the heavy rainfall in the Amazon helps the grass to grow all year. There are now severe restrictions on burning the forests and we did not see any fire. But perhaps we are late in the season. The situation is very different from the one witnessed by me ten years ago, when all of Mato Grosso seemed to be on fire, and smoke clouds made air travel difficult. Owners who burned increased the value of their lands. The ones who did not do it then can no longer can do it. Therefore, the persons use two numbers: the total acreage and the acreage that is cleared.

I did not want to be left behind the canoe after yesterday's experience and will forge ahead whenever I have the chance. Saw a snake crossing the river, its harmonic motions propelling it forward. I followed it for some time. It is amazing that this little animal has the courage to cross the wide expanse.

The river is now much straighter, with long islands. I am a few kilometers from the first waterfall, Carapanã. We arrived at the falls at around 2 p.m. and went down the left bank, looking for Hiram. He had an exhausted expression when he greeted us from the trail in the jungle. He had just completed an 8-km trek taking him to the point below the fall. A portage of such a magnitude would take at least a day, probably two. Thus, Angonese got ready to depart to try to find Vitor's house. This was our only hope to be spared the portage. If this is not possible we will have to tackle the falls one at a time.

In the forest, I saw several rubber trees carrying the distinctive scars and rising up to a height of 3 meters on the trunk, in some cases. These old trees witnessed the glorious days when the Amazon was rich and the sole supplier of rubber in the world.

Rubber fed the industrial automobile production but had been used by Indians for thousands of years. These trees have, through their healed wounds, a particular dignity and could very well have been there when the R-R expedition came through this last set of rapids one hundred years ago. Roosevelt was already sick and his book does not carry a significant amount of description for this last stage. In the late 1800s Brazilians penetrated deeply into Bolivia and Acre was conquered through the boldness of Placido de Castro. Rubber tapping as a profession is almost dead in the Amazon, replaced by synthetic rubber and by the vast plantations in Asia. When I was on the Purus, in 1969, the Pauiní River was still being exploited. However, this was already the end of an era of sacrifice, riches, and lots of suffering. During WW2, the occupation of many countries by Japan required Amazonian rubber again. Thus, a new wave of rubber tappers, the 'soldiers of rubber' as the government euphemistically called them in the 1940s. Transposed from the northeast and left in these immense parages some progressed and many died.

I cut into a tree with my machete and soon tiny bubbles form from several veins. They coalesce into drops and a white liquid that is viscous at the touch gradually dries. Although the Indians found applications for it after it is stiffened in fire, it was the industrial society, starting with the breakthrough discovery of the Quixotic Goodyear, which brought rubber to its heyday. This natural elastomer found numerous applications and until the seeds were taken to London and then to the Far East, the Amazon had the monopoly of its production. But the rubber tappers of Roosevelt's days are gone, only the trees serving as witnesses to the past.

Commentary:

Before facing the Carapanã falls, they met José Caripe at the top of the rapids. He was the head of the area, controlling the rubber tappers. In the traditional pattern of the Amazon, he provided goods and services in exchange for rubber. In exchange for the last dugout canoe, he provided them with a light-weight boat, guided them through the rapids, and showed them where trails had been cut into the forest to portage through the falls. This crossing took the expedition only one and one half days.

Day 26

Angonese and Jeffrey returned late and exhausted, but with good news. They had found the house, which they described as an oasis of peace and quiet in the middle of the forest. They were given the promise that Cleber would get us out of our wedged position by means of a pickup truck. If this his hope was unrealized, we would have 8 km of portage ahead of us. They said that the house was about a two-hour walk through the forest and described the multitude of sounds that they heard. They encountered peccaries and were concerned that they were being followed by a jaguar, since they carried some 5 kilos of ribs in a burlap bag, something to catch the attention of the sleepiest feline. Angonese fired a couple shots into the forest when the fear overtook them and then they were able to make it back.

We spent the day waiting for the pickup and I took the canoe to the middle of the river, from where I could observe the various channels. In fact, I suggested a passage but Hiram told me to be patient, since the pickup option was infinitely better. It was past 4 p.m. and we were getting ready to spend one more night at our camp when we heard the distant hum. Indeed, Cleber appeared with his buddy and they had a trailer onto we quickly loaded our gear. We drove to past the house and unloaded it by the river. We were saved, having been able to avoid the dangerous Carapanã Falls.

Day 27

I woke up in this paradise, complete with a gazebo and a deck over the gorgeous creek and small waterfalls, by the insistent crows of a rooster. The dogs, two puppies among them, greeted us. One of them had bit into a hook a couple of days ago, and had his tongue operated on by Angonese and Jeffrey. The hook had been extracted by pushing it through.

Cleber (Cleber Mariano de Almeida) has a collection of about 50 pigs, which are mixed with wild boar. He tells me that his biggest boar has faced a jaguar, who finally gave up, looking for easier prey. We checked the hybrid pigs but they looked peaceful. Skinnier and longer snouted than domestic pigs, they were heavier. Angonese went with Cleber to milk some cows and we will take our time this morning. The boats and load wait for us below the Apuí-Grande Falls. The Senauma Falls, which follow it, are named after a girl who drowned there, according to Cleber. There is a chapel, and people pray there and pay their promises.

We have 45 km left in our journey, and have to follow some swift currents but no major falls. We should be arriving at the Aripuanã River tomorrow afternoon. The return trip will be a challenge since there are few roads in the Amazon, and the famous Trans-Amazon Highway (BR 230) is still a dirt road. We are all more relaxed and considerably slimmer. Hiram, who was somewhat pudgy, looks like a cadet. I feel like my love handles are gone. Angonese has the appearance of an overactive skeleton. Jeffrey lost his pouch, the reminder that his boyish face belongs to a fifty-year-old man. He looks again like a 35-year-old athlete.

However, the pounds will return, and fast, since our diet is rich in meat, eggs, and rice. Yesterday, we had a big barbecue and eggs to top it.

The days have been lovely and the tranquil nature enveloping creates the illusion that everything is peace. However, the jungle looms around us with wild peccaries, jaguars, and all the other species of the Amazon.

We walked to the river, packed our boats, and hit the water. The deep hum of a big waterfall came soon and we went along the left bank as much as possible, running down some rapids. But the ominous Senauma waterfall was too high and too wild for any boat. We found a trail in the forest, which I followed until a chapel, a modest building with a few crosses in front indicating that it was also a cemetery. As I stepped in, a band of bats flew out and almost hit me. These are bad omens, I thought, as my eyes gradually adjusted to the darkness. She stood there, her peaceful features carved in dark wood, wearing a white lace dress. I took my rosary from the right pocket and deposited it in her hands, adding it to several already there. Around me were reminders of miracles, of wishes fulfilled. Crutches and wooden feet littered the corners, and shirts hung from the ceiling. Angonese arrived and we lighted two candles for the spirit of the lady that had drowned in these waters. After a little prayer, I left with the certitude that our journey would come to an end without mishap. She would be there, the drowned lady, looking after us.

After a 300-meter portage through the trail in the forest, we launched again after Col. Hiram conducted a reconnaissance on the right bank. Fortunately, he came back with good news. We crossed with care, aware of the rapid water that could, if inattentive, drag us into the main waterfall to certain death. We did this by paddling upstream and close to the bank and then, by crossing at an angle, always pointing up. The narrow passage led through rocks where a forgotten portion of the stream meandered. We had to run through a narrow channel between the rocks. At the end, Hiram tipped his kayak, at a tricky spot under a rapid where the current changed direction by 90°. I tried to help him from the rock but eventually the tipped kayak, Hiram hanging on to it, freed itself and ran downstream to a quiet spot.

Once we crossed that waterfall, we still had challenges left. Emboldened by our own experiences, we ran down sizable rapids, avoiding dangerous whitewater spots, marking rocks. In one of the runs, the canoe could not avoid a stone in the rapids after I had squeezed by it, and Jeffrey fell off with a fracas. He swam to shore and we continued after emptying the canoe of the large quantity of water it had taken.

At 3 p.m. we arrived at the site where we would spend our last night. The place is sunny and pleasant, and we have been spared the rains for four days. The view is splendid in its beauty of stone and sand.

As Angonese cooks his last *carreteiro* rice, I reflect about us, about the return to the routine of our lives, chores, and families. For three weeks, we shared this unique experience. Happy but tired, we have accomplished the dream of reliving the epic journey of Roosevelt and Rondon, we experienced the same difficulties, overcame similar challenges. We come out of this experience with images of this magnificent body of water that will always remain with us.

The hum of the waterfalls is behind us, and I hope that they will continue to protect the river and be its guardians, so that future generations, Brazilians, North Americans, or from anywhere else, can experience the vast beauty of this land.

Commentary:

Roosevelt thanks *Senhor* Caripe for guiding the expedition through the Carapanã falls and therefore shortening the time considerably. This would have taken the expedition a 'fortnight' as Roosevelt mentions, and was reduced to one and a half days. He mentions one short portage, which could have been the same as ours. We did not have the help of rubber tappers and therefore would have encountered much greater difficulty if we did not have the pickup truck of Cleber's buddy. He mentions the graves of four men that had succumbed in the falls and this is probably the location of our chapel in Senauma. They camped in a place just below the portage and there were three graves at that spot. He also reports clear trails at the critical points were the boats had to be unloaded. There seemed to be much more traffic through the falls in his days than in our modern times. There is not much reason to cross these falls nowadays because of available road access.

Day 28

I am sitting here on a beach, my back on the kayak, writing. We have 8 km to go before we see the Aripuanã. On this last day of our expedition, the river reserved a last surprise for us: a stiff wind, upstream, of course, that hounded us from the beginning from about 7:30 to 10:30. My right side no longer pains, but my shoulder still bothers me a lot. The river widens and narrows with the rocks that periodically spring up. Our campsite was pleasant and Angonese made his last pot of *carreteiro* rice which we devoured, with three cans of sardines given to us by Dona Fatima.

As we traveled down, the river revealed us its secrets and showed us its strength. It also tested us with the long, boring, but painful stretches in which all muscles in our body begged us to stop.

This homage to Roosevelt and Rondon also strengthened us, and provided us an understanding of our limits. We are fortunate to have experienced this river since its beginning, all the way to its end. It carries some of Roosevelt's qualities: determination, power, beauty. We hope that through this journey we will be able to protect it. It is exceptionally-well preserved for these 100 years and we should put our minds together to create a national park, which could be named Roosevelt-Rondon.

We arrived at the encounter with the Aripuanã at 2 p.m. exhausted but exhilarated with the accomplishments. Indeed, the team held together in spite of the difficulties, and each member contributed within his capabilities. Col. Hiram was an enthusiastic supporter from Day 1. His experience on the river and currents was essential and he guided us through difficult falls and currents. He is quiet, focused and disciplined, qualities that Rondon also had. He also has some *Charrua* Indian blood, from the south. Col. Angonese has great jungle experience and is extremely-well conditioned. He had the arduous task of paddling the canoe with Jeffrey. Jeffrey, the powerful paddler, documented the entire journey by filming it.

Last night we started hearing the periodic hum of distant trucks, and today, as we approached the lodge, we passed two boats with fishermen who kindly offered us some soft drinks and boiled eggs. The manager [of the lodge] could not accommodate us and allowed us, though, to camp in the lawn and to use the pier.

We had a nice lunch and proceeded to the next stage, going to the ferry, this time with a powerboat. We need to plan the next stage, our return to Vilhena. The enchantment of our solitude is broken and, as we return to the normalcy of life, I already miss the isolation, silence, and Spartan living. A happy band of pot-bellied fishermen asked us lots of questions. Pelado, an enterprising young man, is helping us and will build a rack for the pickup.

Commentary:

At this point, Roosevelt describes meeting Pyrineus and his nice camp. From that point on, they were taken care of. They also received news that Amilcar and Miller had run down the Gy-Paraná and Lauriado and Fiala the Papagaio River. The two other parallel expeditions had considerable less difficulty than his. Roosevelt reports that Cherrie was bitten by a piranha. Rondon organized a ceremony in the morning and that, by order of the Brazilian Government, the river, the largest tributary of the Madeira, with its source near 13° S and its mouth a little south of 5° S would be from that moment on named Rio Roosevelt. It is interesting to note that this promise was only partially kept. The Roosevelt is now considered a tributary of the Aripuanã. And the first part of the river is still recorded in the maps as Rio da Duvida, River of Doubt.

Day 29

We left the lodge early in the morning and by 7:40 a.m. we were on our way. I paid Vadinho, the lodge manager, Re 500 for the four meals and transport. By the time two dozen overweight fishermen hit the boats, painfully descending the long stairs, we had embarked our load and were on the way down the rapids, to Vila de Carmo, also called "Mata-mata".

The Mitsubishi truck was loaded with two kayaks. Pelado had built a wooden contraption to elevate them and we had everything ready to go. The pick-up equipped with its new rack fit us all and we drove east, after giving Pelado's our left-over food. Soon, we advanced at about 100 km/hour along a good dirt road.

On the way, we passed a string of Indian villages along the highway. There has been trouble recently, and the death of a chief on the road led to a terrible vengeance. Apparently, the *pagé* (spiritual leader) had a dream of a black car with three persons, and an unfortunate teacher from Apuí that drove by shortly thereafter was massacred together with two of his people. This led to an immediate reaction from the population of Vila do Carmo and Apuí. Eighteen pickup trucks with eight armed men each went to Marmelo and broke the barriers. Then, they proceeded to invade a village, the Indians running away. In retaliation, the Indians tried to burn down the bridge to trap the punitive expedition and it barely made it back. The Federal Police and Special Forces were sent to the place and found the burial places of the victims, as well as a number of additional bodies buried. Apparently, they had killed truck drivers, robbing their load. However, they are quiet now. The road was built through their land and they see progress and wealth increasing, while their living conditions have not changed. So, they started charging Re25 per car and Re75 per truck and this worked well for a couple of years until the tragic event. This source of income is gone.

At noon, we arrived at the ferry over the Madeira River and had a nice lunch consisting of fish, tomatoes and rice, while waiting for the ferry to come. In Humaitá we will meet Sergeant Douglas at Hotel Norte and hit the road to Vilhena. We will probably arrive tomorrow by noon. We met prospectors on the ferry. They carried samples of ores that they claimed were rich in tantalum and gave me a piece, in hopes that I would enter into a partnership.

We left Pelado after crossing into the town. The Madeira River is several times the width of the Roosevelt, much murkier and more populated. Sergeant Douglas awaited us on the other side. We transferred the load to his trailer and left readily. At 6 p.m. we were in Porto Velho after crossing a modern bridge over the same Madeira. It has become a modern city, quite changed from the days of 1969 when it was a provincial capital at the end of an interminable trip up the Amazon and Madeira Rivers. We stopped at the Madeira-Mamoré Historical site and admired the narrow gage (1 m!) wheels. Then, we headed south on HI 364. We still have 700 km to go, having already done 500 km. We drove until 10 p.m. and found a good hotel in the city of Ji-Paraná, Hotel Comercio. A two-meter tall guy received us in the hotel lobby. Taller than Jeffrey, he is a descendant of Germans, like so many we saw. This reinforces the idea that massive immigration of Rondonia from the south created an entrepreneurial environment.

I sit in the hotel room on November 14, and inspect my feet that are swollen due to 14 hours of cramped travel in the back of the pickup and full of tiny wounds from mosquito bites. Cracks are forming in the heel and are deeper and more painful than yesterday. My chin has scars from the kayak, and I am still mentally in the nebulous region between the river and civilization. The Gideon Bible by my side reminds me that I am back. Tomorrow we will be fully integrated into the modern society and in a few days, we will have regained our strength. There are other challenges ahead, and many tasks connected with this expedition. We are fortunate to have shared this experience and overcome a great many obstacles. The backs of my hands are charred from the sun. Only the extremities of the fingers are white since they were under the tube that held the paddles.

I consider myself very fortunate to have had the company of this wonderful group. General Montesano is my next target. This will probably have to wait till next August, but a plan is already being formalized in our minds—take an Army boat as far up as possible the Paraguay River, starting from Porto Murtinho. Visit the *fazenda* (ranch) where Roosevelt stayed.

Commentary:

At this point, Roosevelt proceeds down, leaving Rondon, Lyra, and Pyrineus behind and continues on the new boats, running down the last rapids that we also encountered until a little hamlet of São João, owned by the rubber tapper *Senhor* Caripe. In São João, they are regally received by *Senhor* Caripe and his wife before boarding a river steamer commissioned by Pyrineus. In twelve hours, they are on the majestic Madeira River, the largest tributary of the Amazon. Eighteen more hours and they reach Manaus, which at the time was a 'remarkable city' as Roosevelt comments. He says good-bye to the *camaradas* with friendship and regret, giving each a gold sovereign. The travel agency Booth books him a steamer to Belem and a regular cargo-and-passenger boat to the Barbados and thence to New York.

It is an admirable quality of Roosevelt that he does not lose his cheerful disposition and optimism, even under the most difficult of circumstances. This is a man that had charged up a hill in the battle of San Juan on a horse and had been shot at during a speech. He had lost loved ones under the most difficult circumstances. Nothing could faze him: disease, wounds or any hardship. He does not mention the surgery on his leg in Manaus or the fevers acquired in the expedition. His fascination is with the land, the people, and the proud exploration of a river that he claims to have 1,500 km in length. Later revisions have put the Roosevelt River as tributary of the Aripuanã, shortening it to 800 km.

CHAPTER 13

THE BURNING OF THE AMAZON

The numbers are staggering (source: Wikipedia: Deforestation in Brazil):

PERIOD	Estimated remaining forest cover in the Brazilian Amazon (km2)	Annual forest loss (km^2)	Percent of 1970 cover remaining	Total forest loss since 1970 (km^2)
PRE-1970	4,100,000	-	-	-
1977	3,955,870	21,130	96.5%	144,130
1988	3,723,520	21,050	90.8%	376,480
1997	3,576,965	13,227	87.2%	523,035
2007	3,387,381	11,651	82.6%	713,837
2008	3,375,413	12,911	82.3%	726,748
2009	3,365,788	7,464	82.1%	734,212
2013	3,341,908	5,891	81.5%	758,092

Twenty percent of the Brazilian Amazon forest has been lost since the massive occupation started in the 1970s. The rate has decreased from 0.5 to less than 0.1% per year but this still represents a yearly loss of 5,000 square kilometers. Thus, the burning is slowing down and the more rigorous government control imposed by IBAMA (National Institute for the Environment) is having a positive effect.

Google maps show wide swaths of land cleared in the forest. The process has a pattern. First, long highways are built to penetrate the Amazon, designated with the acronyms BR364, 214 and others; then, narrower roads emanate from these main arteries. These narrower roads give rise, themselves, to tertiary roads, along which the vegetation colors change from dark to light green. This process has been most intensive in the northwestern states of Rondonia and Acre, along BR364, along the east, the Belem-Brasilia artery, and the famous Trans-Amazon High-way. Thus, this large-scale clearing of the forest has been enabled to these astronomic proportions by the construction of roads, an effort initiated under the president, Juscelino Kubitchek. In the 1960s, Juscelino came to Vilhena, Rondonia State, and symboli-cally fell a tree to commemorate the advance of the highway to Vilhena. Today, a president could no longer commit such an ac-tion without incurring in the wrath of the nation. Brazil has the 'Day of the Tree' and millions of them are planted every year to commemorate this occasion. Reforestation programs have cov-ered large areas with eucalyptus and there were tax incentives for such investments.

The military regime that was implanted in 1964 in response to strong pressure from the left and takeover attempts by com-munists stimulated and accelerated the construction of highways in Amazonia. The Fifth Battalion of Construction Engineering, 5º BEC, as it is known in Portuguese, took the lead in construct-ing BR 364, which incidentally followed, *grosso modo*, the trail opened by Rondon's Telegraph Commission during the first part of the century.

The construction of the road opened the doors to massive immigration. Some of my colleagues worked on the construction as officers in the Fifth BEC. Col. Carlos Elias told me that he could only count on two thirds of the troops, since one third of them would be down with malaria or other ailments. They had to clear a wide circle in the forest and set up camp (about 500-me-ter radius) in the middle, to avoid mosquitoes. He never left the camp at dawn or dusk, and told me that people that would go to the waterfalls to take a bath invariably caught malaria.

In 1969, I spent ten days in Porto Velho, the capital of Rondo-nia. It was at the time a sleepy town, but the excitement of change could already been felt. We spent one night at the Fifth BEC

Headquarters, sleeping in a large dormitory. I remember that the top portion of the building was open; only a chicken-mesh fence separated it from the outside to keep the bats out. This allowed for some freshness during the night. In 2014, I revisited Porto Velho, this time by car. A monumental bridge crossed the Madeira River. Modern buildings abounded and the city is a dynamic center. Two dams provide electricity to the region and additional large projects are under way or in the planning stages.

The distance from Cuiabá to Porto Velho, close to one thousand miles, can now be covered in a 24-hour bus ride. I traveled the entire road, and attest to the fact that only small pieces of forest are left. The countryside consists, for the most part, of large pastures. The forest was cleared and special grasses (*coronhão*) planted in its place. Is this process inexorable, and will the occupation of the Amazon basin (Amazonia) result in the destruction of the forest? There seems to be a global worry these days, but Brazilians stubbornly adhere to their mantra: the Europeans and North Americans cleared their forests in order to promote their economies and now it is our turn. The counter-argument by the ecologists is that the Amazon is the lung of the earth.

Thus, there is a national paranoia, born from some unknown feeling, that the U.S. or the United Nations intend to occupy the Amazon, under the excuse of internationalization and environmental protection. In this mayhem, ranchers accelerate rather than decrease the process of deforestation because they feel that the pressure is increasing. It is a simple economic fact that a forested area has less value than one that is covered with pasture and fenced. The ranchers that we visited quoted two numbers: total area and cleared area. In defense of the environment, the demarcation of large areas for the indigenous populations is creating protected areas, in addition to the national parks and forests. A number of national parks were created by the Brazilian Government in the Amazon.

Recent archeological discoveries are changing the picture of pre-Columbian Amazon in a significant manner. The lively and sometimes acrimonious debate between two separate anthropologists has added fire to the fuel: Betty Meggers and Anna Roosevelt.

Meggers, a Smithsonian Institute archeologist and author of the book "Amazonia: Man and Culture in a Counterfeit Paradise" (1971), analyzed agriculture in the Amazon, reaching the conclusion that the only possible manner that it can be practiced is through small (a few acres) of slash-and-burn plots. This is how the indigenous people and riverine populations practice it. After the trees are cut, fire completes the process. Manioc, corn, beans, and other crops are planted among the leftover stumps, and the land is productive for a few (up to ten) years. Then the process is repeated while the forest vegetation recovers the original plot. This, in her view, sets the limit for villages at approximately one thousand. She expressed her law as:

"The level to which a culture can develop is dependent upon the agriculture's potentiality of the environment it occupies."

Thus, she simply discounted Carvajal's (1541) description of dense populations along the Amazon River as a figment of his imagination. More ominously, it has been suggested that Orellana needed a good justification for having left Pizarro behind and continuing his downriver trip in the Napo River, all the way to the mouth of the Amazon. He had to exaggerate his suffering. Large-scale Indian attacks were invented to justify this action.

Meggers' nemesis Anne Roosevelt, at that time of the Field Museum, excavated the Marajó Island, an enormous expanse on the Amazon delta. With a surface of 40,100 square kilometers (15,500 sq. mi.), Marajó is roughly the size of Switzerland. Surprisingly, she found evidence of large settlements and suggested a population of well above 100,000. This was contrary to Meggers' law and stirred a heated debate. According to Anna Roosevelt, who is the great-granddaughter of our hero, Teddy, the inhabitants resolved the dilemma by creating artificial platforms, through earthworks, on top of which villages were built and intensive agriculture was possible. This large population, she claims, was able to construct major earth works.

It is now thought that large populations, such as those described by Frey Carvajal, were possible in the Amazon by clever manipulation of the environment. In certain regions, *terra preta* (black earth) and *terra mulata* (brown earth) are found. These rich and fertile pieces of land are believed to be man-made. Through controlled burning, and without allowing the process of carbonization to be completed, large areas are covered with charcoal, which is then mixed with the earth and blended again with additional organic matter. This fertilizes the poor soil of the Amazon. Most patches are five to fifteen acres and at the edge of the flood plain. In the mouth of the Tapajós River such an area was found, three miles long and one mile wide. This is evidence of a large pre-Columbian population. Indeed, Mané Manduca told me that such plots exist in the Nambikwara lands. But I perceived that he is anthropologist-savvy, and that somebody passed him this information.

One possibility is the following: if the burning is carried out just before the rainy season, the flow of water can interrupt the process and leave entire carbonized tree trunks intact. These can, with some work, be disintegrated and mixed into the soil. Thus, the soil can be enriched as the land is cleared.

Another piece of evidence points to a large population in the Amazon. In 1977, a Brazilian student, Alceu Ranzi, worked at PRONAPABA - Projeto Nacional de Pesquisa da Bacia Amazonica (National Amazon Basin Research Project). Flying over deforested land in the state of Acre, northwest but adjoining Rondonia, he identified geometric patterns on the soil, which he named geoglyphs. These circles had supposedly been constructed by carving ditches; they had become visible because the forest had been cleared.

Additional geoglyphs have been identified and the number is approximately two hundred. The purpose of these geoglyphs is not yet understood, but it is possible that they are connected to the Beni culture. The province of Beni in Bolivia contains a flood plain that is grassy in the dry season. One finds in it periodic circles covered with forest. These are about sixty feet above the level of the plain and are connected by straight causeways. This is still a cause of debate, but it is possible that the raised circles are formed by a natural process that the local indigenous population utilized them for agriculture. They subsequently built the causeways to control the flow of water, trap fish and manipulate the environment to their advantage.

Another area where archeological studies are revealing evidence for much greater populations is the upper Xingu River. There, an archeologist named Michael Heckenberger has discovered the remains of large villages, having moats with an original depth between 12 and 14 feet, and a width of approximately 30 feet. The diameter is approximately one mile, indicating that a fairly large population was housed inside. These moats contained a stockade, in a way similar to the ones encountered by early settlers in the coast. There were roads, causeways, and bridges connecting the villages. All this points to a large pre-Columbian settlement in the Xingu River. If one reads about the conquest of the land by the Portuguese, one can understand how these settlements were destroyed, first by disease, then by war, and finally by displacing the original inhabitants, whose survivors escaped into the forests and reassumed a much simpler lifestyle as nomadic hunter-gatherers, to escape the 'civilizing' pressure.

The debate about the pre-Columbian population of Amazonia rages on and it is quite possible that the forest had been explored before and that the landscape had been modified by a large population—estimated at 7 to 8 million—in need of food. We know today that successive measles, flu, and smallpox outbreaks decimated the indigenous populations of the Americas, which was, at the time of the 'discovery' (1492) equal or even larger than that of Europe. The Amazon does not have large quantities of stone and, in any case, the work required for stone constructions was not advantageous. Thus, the archeological evidence is less solid and pottery is one of the few pieces of evidence. Nevertheless, there are solid indications that pottery had been developed in the Amazon 6,000 B.C.; this is the oldest in the Americas. This evidence was obtained by Anna Roosevelt in the Painted Rock Cave, on the left bank of the Amazon, close to the mouth of the Tapajós River. But whatever "terra forming" or environmental changes were exerted in pre-Columbian times, they pale in comparison to the massive deforestation taking place today. The large ranches, up to 100,000 acres, conduct this transformation in a systematic manner. I cannot help but ponder whether this change has also beneficial effects. Certainly, the mosquito population decreases, and some animal species, such as capybaras, undergo a population explosion after the jaguars are eliminated by cattle ranchers. Economies are thriving, and it is possible, even probable, that the growth of special cattle grasses on the soil will enable it to retain its fertility. Abundant rainfall keeps this artificial savannah green for a good part of the year. If these areas can be interspersed with forested swaths, reserves, Indian territories, perhaps a satisfactory solution will be found for this conundrum. If not, the much-feared desertification process will inexorably progress. I documented the thin topsoil at the banks of the Roosevelt River. These banks expose the sides during the rainy season through erosion. The water eats away the margins and all the vegetation in the outside of the curve, while the inside is filled with sand. In many places, the complex root system was the only retention of the sand.

In any case, these are important issues where research can provide answers. We should avoid indiscriminate burning of the forest at all costs. The example of Europe, that has managed its forests for centuries, comes to mind. Luxembourg, the country of my parents, has 30 percent of its area covered by forests. We can envisage a future with 60-70% forest cover keeping the rainfall and the ecological variety intact while being economically viable. Tree planting and harvesting of wood would be an integral part of this system, and cattle grazing would be controlled. The sports fishing and hunting industry could provide significant resources to the region, if properly managed. At present, the rivers are rapidly being depleted of fish by commercial exploitation while the forest animals provide food for a rapidly growing population.

The level of water in the bridge constructed by Rondon on the River of Doubt is a gage of the changes that occurred in the one hundred years. We visited it in October, just before the rainy season, while Roosevelt entered it in January. Nevertheless, the difference, approximately three meters, is striking.

CHAPTER 14

LÉVI-STRAUSS

When Claude Lévi-Strauss, the French lawyer-turned philosopher-turned anthropologist started his expedition from the staging town of Cuiabá in 1939, he had been in Brazil since 1935 as a professor at the University of São Paulo, with the French mission that helped to found it. This expedition represented for him a journey of vast ambition, and he followed the tracks of Rondon along the telegraph line, up to and beyond Vilhena. He continued on, to some of the most remote regions of Brazil. Twenty-five years, a quarter of a century, had passed, and yet little had changed on the Parecis plateau and Amazon jungle north of there.

Lévi-Strauss' seminal anthropological work in Brazil started by accident. As a student of philosophy in Paris, he took a class in psychology taught by Georges Dumas. This class took place at the Sainte Anne Hospital in a room with walls covered by art from the 'lunatics' as the patients were called in those days. After the exposition, Dumas would bring in the patients and interview them in front of the students. Apparently, the well-trained patients responded as expected and confirmed Dumas' theories. Lévi-Strauss talks kindly about this towering intellectual figure of France and describes him as a descendant of the sixteenth century humanists, merging medicine and philosophy. He had only one intellectual shortcoming: he was a positivist. This philosophical school had fallen out of fashion in the Parisian salons, replaced by more aggressive Marxism-Leninism, with whom France has toyed for three quarters of a century. The only thing that can heal this wonderful nation from this fascination would be a good few years of a communist regime.

After completing his class, Lévi-Strauss was, one day, approached by another professor at the École Normale Supérieure, Celestin Bouglé, asking him if he wanted to study anthropology. Lévi-Strauss must have shown some interest in this discipline, since the professor asked him. It so happened that Georges Dumas had spent his youth in Brazil and had helped to found the University of São Paulo, which became and still is the leading higher education institution in Latin America.

This fortuitous encounter with Bouglé would change not only Lévi-Strauss' life but also lead to the collection of important anthropological information on Brazilian Indians. The fate of the Nambikwara was already sealed and successive epidemics would decimate their population to the brink of extinction. Lévi-Strauss' discourse on the written word is essential in this respect. Although he does not believe that writing in itself can lead to civilization, his opinion is that it is a powerful mechanism of centralized control by the government: you learn to read and write and I can command you, tax you, send you to war. In essence, I can control you. But were it not for writing, the culture of the Nambikwara would have disappeared forever with their dwindling numbers. The old Sabanê Indian that I met by the Roosevelt River was a link to the past, which ranged some seventy years. But his son, Lino, is already totally ignorant of these days. Thus, Lévi-Strauss preserved a precious treasure that he brought with him to France and polished, using his finely tuned mind, into a powerful construct: structural anthropology.

The cataclysm that followed the first contacts was drastic: Rondon estimated the population of Nambikwara at 20,000, considered by Lévi-Strauss an exaggerated number. Nevertheless, the flu epidemics of 1918 and 1928, in conjunction with internecine wars, decimated the population. When Lévi-Strauss studied them in 1939, they numbered approximately 2,000. There have been subsequent outbreaks of measles in 1945 and in the 1970s, further reducing the population to less than 800.

Lévi-Strauss' expedition was organized in much the same way as that of his predecessor Rondon, a quarter of a century earlier. He found reliable men chosen by Fulgencio, an honest person living in the outskirts of Cuiabá. He was poor, wise, and virtuous, as described by Lévi-Strauss, and had a natural dignity. The men belonged to an old Portuguese family and adhered to their austere tradition. Other than a protégé of the Bishop of Cuiabá, that he took along, this formed his expeditionary group of thirteen men. Riding their mules and using pack oxen, each carrying between 60 and 120 kg, they followed the telegraph line until the Utiarity Falls. The road to that point was rideable by truck, on which Lévi-Strauss rode with his wife. The expedition left Cuiabá in June 1939, in the middle of the dry season. Thus, they were spared the tribulations of the RR expedition.

The region used to be called 'Serra do Norte' because it was thought that a mountain range existed in the divide between the Amazon and Prata basins. Such did not exist as Rondon found out in the expeditions, each longer than the previous one, starting in Cuiabá, close to his hometown of Mimoso. Lévi-Strauss soon discovered that progress was exceedingly slow; the daily tasks of unloading the beasts, setting up camp, and cooking were also repeated in the mornings. The scattered animals had to be reassembled and have their backs checked for sores. Then, they had to be harnessed and loaded. Roosevelt witnessed and described the same daily routine that took several hours. Our experience confirms these tribulations.

Lévi-Strauss moved ahead of this troop in his truck waiting for it at the Utiarity Falls. This was at the Papagaio River, which was close to the Sacre River.   He describes the trail, *picada* in Portuguese, running along the telegraph line. This line had been poorly maintained after its completion, since the telegraph was superseded by the wireless radio. Nevertheless, Rondon's mission had a much broader goal than the construction of a trail from the center, Cuiabá, to the northwest, Porto Velho. It was an attempt to connect two regions of a vast nation. His humane treatment of the native inhabitants was manifested in the training of Pareci Indians to operate the stations along the line, approximately 70 km apart.

Lévi-Strauss describes the state of disrepair of the telegraph line and the near abandonment of the stations in his usual melancholic tone. The line sagged between rotten posts in many places and some of the stations had not received supplies for years. The operator of the Vilhena station obtained his meat from a herd of deer. He carefully managed to keep the population at a healthy level. A few years prior to his expedition, in 1935, one of the posts had been attacked by the Nambikwara that periodically visited them.

It is interesting that Roosevelt's descriptions cover the geography, flora, fauna, and climate, whereas Lévi-Strauss concentrates on his task at hand. He makes only cursory comments about the environment and is totally indifferent to animals, fishes, and plants. His primary preoccupation is Man. Therein lies the sign of the passionate anthropologist. He affirms that there is only a limited number of ways in which cultures can organize themselves to survive. He makes some outstanding discoveries in his visit to the Nambikwara, which compose, as he calls it, a moribund society. His pride has no bounds, as he takes us through his florid Gallic writing deeper into the social structure of this society. This will be revealed in the coming pages.

The Nambikwara spend six to seven months, the dry season, traveling in small groups. I was fortunate to see one of them, some ten individuals, from the car in HI 364. Their characteristic shelter of palm leaves was there, and they sat placidly under it, close to a stream. At the stop, two children, their broad faces, wide mouths, and almond-shaped eyes undeniably Indian, watched us, smiling occasionally. These groups assemble and separate depending on the availability of food.

Lévi-Strauss asked a chief to take him to a village and this was done, for the sake of gift distribution. So, four oxen laden with gifts were readied and they proceeded, guided by the chief of one of the groups. This was a somewhat risky journey, for twelve years earlier seven telegraph workers had been killed by the Nambikwara. The village consisted of several semi-permanent huts used during the rainy season, when the smaller groups congregate and the nomadic life takes a rest. Lévi-Strauss had the opportunity to observe the interactions among the groups, several of whom had gathered in the village to receive the gifts. Some of the Indians had no previous contact with whites and were therefore somewhat skittish. There was also danger. The trip and contacts with different chiefs gave Lévi-Strauss the opportunity to evaluate the selection of and leadership among Nambikwara chiefs, two of which he observed closely. The chief is referred to as *Uilikandé* which is translated as 'the one who unites.' The two chiefs that Lévi-Strauss analyzed were Wakltoçu, from the Utiarity village, and a Taranduré. Although both had quite different personalities, they had common traits, quite distinct from the other men and that set them apart. I shall go in some detail, since the generality of Lévi-Strauss' conclusions carries an important message.

First, political power among the Nambikwara is not hereditary. When a chief is old or feels incapacitated, he appoints his successor. This is not done blindly, but after consultation with the members of the group. The appointed man can simply refuse or may accept the responsibility. And indeed, the responsibilities are many, because, during the dry season in which the Nambikwara are nomadic, he has to determine the travel route, work at finding fruit trees, roots, and game, as well as tend to the demands by the members of the group, who constantly ask him for food and favors. Lévi-Strauss puts it as: "…a capacity for logical thinking and a continuity of purpose which were quite exceptional in a Nambikwara, since these Indians are changeable and capricious."

The chief also fixes the time and place for the semi-permanent camp during the rainy season and decides which plants will be grown. The Indians expect more than just a good chief. He has to be better than the other chiefs, in the competition for food and territory. Thus, the burdens are multiple.

In order to compensate for the extraordinary burden imposed on the chief, he is allowed to take multiple wives. This also has the beneficial effect of ensuring that the positive traits of the chief have a greater probability of being propagated. Polygamy among other members is the exception. In smaller groups, especially, this will cause a sexual imbalance which leads, according to Lévi-Strauss, to homosexuality. This is tolerated among young males, but is treated with some humor. Indeed, the entire Brazilian society has inherited this duality toward homosexuality: it accepts it but at a price. The homosexuals are not openly discriminated but are often the "source of jokes, which remain discreet."

These homosexual relationships are allowed between cross-cousins as opposed to straight cousins. However, there is no resentment in the group about the number of wives of the chief. It is possible that many of the wars between groups, which often involve the stealing of women, are at the root of this scarcity.

The relations between the different wives are harmonious.

The first wife retains her status and dignity, even when the chief takes a younger wife and favors her amorously. The daughters of the first wife are often of a comparable age to the other wives, and they become close friends. In this way, the women form a close-knit community, working and playing together, while the little boys lead a more solitary life.

Lévi-Strauss states that power among the Nambikwara originates from consent and is bound by it. These observations from a society stripped of all material trappings, possessing one of the most rudimentary social and political organizations, led Lévi-Strauss to make a universal statement: "Chiefs exist because, in every human group, there are men who differ from their fellow-beings in that they like prestige for its own sake, are attracted to responsibility and for whom the burden of public affairs brings its own reward."

Lévi-Strauss followed the trail of Rondon's telegraph, which was also trekked by the Roosevelt-Rondon expedition in 1914, crossing the Juruena, passing through Campos Novos and Vilhena and reaching Três Buritis. Roosevelt describes the valleys as densely wooded while the higher grounds had open pastures. Três Buritis was, in Roosevelt's day, a government-owned ranch managed by Rondon's uncle, Miguel Evangelista. He was almost pure Indian and reported to the expedition that he had killed three jaguars that year because they were attacking his mules and preferred them to cattle.

Lévi-Strauss' description focuses mostly on the Nambikwara and on his philosophical musings. After passing Três *Buritis*, his expedition reaches Barão do Melgaço, on the edge of the Parecis plateau. From there the valley of the Machado River could be seen. This is probably a couple days past the point where the RR expedition embarked on the river. But Lévi-Strauss also had plans to go down the Machado River, in search of Indians of the Tupi-Kawahib group. These Indians were quite different from the Nambikwara, stemming from the large Tupi family that in the 1500s inhabited the northeast Brazilian coast, all the way to the Tapajós and beyond. They obtained two plank boats and descended the Machado River until its encounter with the Pimenta Bueno, where there was a small outpost. We passed this place in our way back from our expedition and it was a progressive city along Highway 364, about 80 km north of Vilhena. In 1939, it was inhabited by about twenty people, a few whites and Indians of various tribes from the Guaporé and Machado Rivers. Lévi-Strauss was fascinated with the prospect of meeting remnants of Tupi Indians in their natural state, although not too hopeful, because it was thought that they had dissolved and melded with the local population.

Receiving information that he was misinformed, he proceeded up the Pimenta Bueno by canoe, with some of his crew, the other members staying with the animals in Barão do Melgaço. From the 31 oxen that they had originally, 17 were left, the others having perished. This is similar to Roosevelt's experience, where they lost a considerable number of animals and had to leave their loads behind. There is a legend about this place that needs some telling. The gold mine of Urucumaçuã. This name derives from a Mayan prince and supposedly a gold mine was discovered by Rondon in one of his expeditions. Apparently, the rights to this mine had been recorded by Rondon in 1934 in Guajará-Mirim and Cuiabá. According to Julio Olivar, author of "Caminhos de Rondon," this mine was situated between the 60th and 61st meridians (West) and the 12th and 13th parallels (South). We started our journey on the River of Doubt at Baliza Ranch at 60° W and $12^{\circ}1'$ S. Since each degree is roughly 100 km, this is the approximate distance to the mine. It has been rumored that it is located either in the valley of the Barão do Melgaço or Pimenta Bueno.

And since legends grow with time, it seems that Rondon killed the witnesses who discovered the mine with him and deviated the telegraph line from its location so that it could not be discovered. Indeed, this is a sad story, and is reported by Rondon's grandson, Colonel Rondon. But this is totally out of character for Rondon, and is the result of imagination.

But Lévi-Strauss' quest was for a different kind of gold: a society reduced to its simplest expression. He found it with the Nambikwara, then again with the Mundé that he encountered after going upriver on the Pimenta Bueno for four days, braving rapids similar to ours, portaging the boats or unloading them, carrying the load on their backs, and then reloading up to five times per day. He describes how the river travelled between rock formations that split up the current into several fingers. On the fifth day, they saw a slim canoe and a trail leading to a plantation and village, in which approximately 25 Indians lived. Quite different from the Nambikwara, they were lighter, and had features the Lévi-Strauss describes as 'faintly Mongolian which gave them a Caucasian look.' I look at the Mundé pictures in the book "Saudades do Brasil" and am struck by how similar they look. This is caused by endogamy, and indeed the features are vaguely Caucasian. Lévi-Strauss does not seem to be overly attracted to the women, since he abstains from compliments to their beauty. On the other hand, he was quite impressed with the Nambikwara girls. And indeed, some of the Mundé women are almost identical to the men, with the exception of the breasts. These Indians lived in three circular houses about four meters high. They were artfully built and covered in palm straw, which was flattened to offer protection from the rain.

After the Mundé, supposedly members of a group coming from the Guaporé Valley, he had still one visit to make. His canoes went down the river, this time facing the rapids without portages and reaching Pimenta Bueno in two days.

Upon returning, back in Pimenta Bueno, he was informed that there was indeed a Tupi-Kawahib village in the forest, three days downstream. These Indians had been pushed west, away from the coast, by other tribes. Rondon had encountered them and noticed their large plantations. Their chief, Abaitara, commanded a village of approximately 600 people. These were decimated to 60 by the influenza of 1918 and further reduced by the time Lévi-Strauss visited them in Pimenta Bueno. A Tupi chief had been brought to France in the sixteenth century and Montaigne reports on his interactions with him. Other French intellectuals mentioned them also. So, Lévi-Strauss was intent on setting foot on a 'virgin' Tupi village. In Pimenta Bueno he met somebody, the son of the chief Abaitara, who took him down two days by canoe and then along a trail to the village. On the road, they encountered two Indians that informed them that they were going to Pimenta Bueno, a promise they had made one year earlier.

It was there that Lévi-Strauss witnessed an episode of great symbolic significance. One of the Indians carried on his back a harpy eagle. The Tupi were known to keep this animal in a cage, and it was a prized possession. They used the feathers in their ceremonial costumes and plucked them off the caged animal. These are among the largest eagles, preying on monkeys and sloths. They have massive claws, intended to grasp and lift mammals of considerable size. After some argumentation — the Indians wanted to continue their trek toward Pimenta Bueno, where a few Tupi also lived — Abaitara's son was able to convince them to return to their village of origin. The Indians summarily dropped the eagle, leaving it on the ground to be most probably eaten by predators, since it lacked a good portion of its larger feathers and could not fly. This callousness with an animal that represented a prized possession and was meant as a gift to the Indians in Pimenta Bueno can perhaps be understood as a first step in the decision they had already made: to abandon their ways and join the society of the white man. Hence, Lévi-Strauss witnessed a key moment in the process of acculturation of the Indian.

He visited the village, composed of approximately 25 people. The huts were rectangular, like those of the *caboclos* but their construction was somewhat different. This suggested that the structure was not adapted from the white man, but a genuine Tupi architecture. One can see these houses in the photographs in 'Saudades do Brasil,' as well as the empty eagle cage. The language spoken by this group contained many words familiar to Brazilians, taken from the Tupi language: *takwatip*, the name of the tribe of Pimenta Bueno, derives from *taquara*, a type of bamboo. *Cunhatsin*, white woman, derives from *cunhã*, a well-known Tupi word for 'woman.'

In their trek from the riverbank, they crossed a large swath of rock with little vegetation, similar to the one we saw at Navaité Falls. Lévi-Strauss' diet was also similar to ours; *charque,* salted and dried beef, rice, and beans. The visit to the group marks the end of his exploration of native tribes in the region. After that, they descended the Machado River until Jurupa where they embarked on a larger vessel whereby they reached the Madeira River. The settlements along the river included rubber-tapper posts and the diet as well as human interactions became more varied as they returned to 'civilization.' Reaching Manaus, Lévi-Strauss descended the Amazon until Belem using commercial river boats.

This was an extraordinary journey for a person who said, in the first line of 'Tristes Tropiques': "I hate travelling and explorers." His observations of these remains of the Native American, of societies reduced to their most basic expression, as he puts it, led to the development of structural anthropology, a highly acclaimed theoretical framework for the understanding of humans.

CHAPTER 15

SCIENTIFIC OBSERVATIONS AND EXPERIMENTS

The 1913-1914 exploration was somewhat ambitiously named the Roosevelt-Rondon Scientific Expedition. Nevertheless, there is a wide trajectory between science, as it was conceived in the 19th century, and its current practice. Amateur science was a well-respected endeavor, and many discoveries were made by 'weekend researchers' in those days. The professional scientist, focusing in a minute slice of a highly-specialized field, and commanding an army of graduate students and technicians, is born of necessity and of the explosion of funding. The stimulus for this broad expansion of specialization has come from the cornucopia of technological instruments that have poured out from the augmentation of our knowledge. This can be manifested in all scientific fronts. Even mathematics, long considered a solitary pursuit left to marginally schizophrenic geniuses, is more and more a collective undertaking, where a 'point person' is backed by a well-trained group of experts.

In the nineteenth and early part of the 20th century science was a labor of love. Major discoveries were made by people that had a true passion for the subject and pursued it in their spare time. Thus, the Australopithecus was discovered in South Africa by an orthopedist, Dr. Raymond Dart. The great-and controversial- discovery of the Java man was made by Eugène Dubois, a Dutchman fascinated by the origin of man who chose to work in Indonesia as a civil servant in order to pursue his dream of finding 'the missing link.' His diggings by a river bank in Java unearthed a most important skull, about one million years old. In my home city of Belo Horizonte, the British consul, a certain Mr. Walker, used to sell cases of Scotch to my father carrying, coincidentally, his name. This whiskey was sent to him from the UK for official functions and he made a little business out of it. The profits, he invested in diggings around Lagoa Santa, where Lund, the Swedish naturalist, had discovered old skeletons. So, Mr. Walker spent many years searching for an ancient American 'missing link' that we now know does not exist, since migration of humans to the Americas is a rather recent event: 15,000 years at most. This pales in comparison with the Peking man, Java man, and ancient fossils found in Georgia (the Tbilisi man). Nevertheless, it illustrates the pursuit by passionate individuals moved by the thirst of knowledge and the adventure of quest.

Prior to 1914, the Amazon had been crisscrossed by a number of scientific expeditions, such as von Humboldt, Langsdorf, La Condamine, and others.

It is between the two World Wars that modern science came to birth. Its discoveries had tremendous impact on the conduct of military affairs. The powerful new explosives, stronger steels and aluminum alloys, radar, the emergence of the computer, together with technological advances changed the course of war forever and, as a corollary, the pursuit of knowledge. At the end of WW2, the US and Soviet Union established large research institutes and even science cities. Knowledge was pursued in a systematic manner on many fronts. Sciences were divided into disciplines, teams replaced individuals, new characterization methods emerged, and the powerful program manager replaced personal curiosity. The results of these concentrated efforts were multiple, society being impacted in an irreversible manner.

A single piece of equipment, the transmission electron microscope, costs millions of dollars and needs trained engineers and technicians to be operated and maintained, enabling observation at the nanometer level. This is just one piece of equipment in a battery of powerful instruments that can probe nature at an increasing level of detail. Scanning electron, scanning tunneling, atomic force microscopes are other instruments of equal power. They are essential to advance our knowledge and are required to make meaningful progress. This is a scientific world radically different from the one in which Roosevelt lived. Both he and Rondon could have been considered as contributors to science in their day. Rondon collected important anthropological information on the Indian tribes that he met. Roosevelt tirelessly collected information on animals throughout his life and can be considered an accomplished naturalist. Accompanying the expedition were the North Americans Cherrie and Miller, a respected ornithologist and mammologist, respectively, and a Brazilian geologist and naturalist. Rondon always brought with him experts to document the land, vegetation, animals, and humans encountered in his voyages. The Brazilian scientists were part of the Miller group led by Captain Amilcar that descended the Gy-Paraná River. They were Euzebio Paulo de Oliveira, a geologist, and Henrique Heinisch, a taxidermist and belonged to the Brazilian Telegraph Commission.

"Our trip was not intended as a hunting-trip but as a scientific expedition." It is the fascination that Roosevelt had, from childhood, with animals and nature that led him to pursue this interest all his life. And it was at his instigation that the expedition became a 'scientific' one, and not just a touristic fling. Roosevelt developed a lively interest in the social behavior of animals while, in his days, most naturalists were mostly preoccupied in describing their physical characteristics. And to classify them, documenting their ranges. Foreshadowing later studies on the social behavior of animals such as Konrad Lorentz with geese, E.O. Wilson with ants and Jane Goodall with chimpanzees, Roosevelt comments, after observing a bird on a branch near a nest: "A naturalist could with the utmost advantage spend six months on such a ranch so as that we visited." This refers to the observation of the behavior of animals. He continues: "The books most needed are those dealing with the life-histories of wild creatures."

So, Roosevelt visited some friends at the American Museum of Natural History, in New York, prior to the expedition and asked them if they were interested in sending a couple naturalists to collect specimens. Two were chosen by the curator of ornithology of the museum: George K. Cherry, in his late forties, and Leo Miller, a young man. Cherry was already a legendary explorer, gun runner, and ornithologist and had spent half his life in South America. In the tradition of 19th century adventurers, he had faced a squad of galloping lancers in Venezuela, shooting down several of them until the survivors ran away. He had spent time in South American jails and participated in liberation fights. At the time, he was living in his apple farm with his wife and six children, and reluctantly took the job, under the assumption that it would be a 'walk in the park.' The idea was for Roosevelt to complete speaking engagements in Argentina and Chile first. Then, the team would leave Buenos Aires, navigate north along the Paraguay River, and then cross over to the Amazon basin along well known rivers. Time allowing, the team would navigate up the Negro River, famous for its black waters, traverse the Casiquiare canal, and cross to the Orinoco River, which they would descend, crossing Venezuela. It was a fascinating trip, with many challenges, but only covering known territory.

This was all changed by Minister Lauro Müller's fateful suggestion, to explore an unknown river.

The second person, Miller, was at the time collecting specimens in Guyana. He joined the expedition with considerable
more enthusiasm than Cherrie, who had been in Latin America
25 times, at his count.

The established technique at the time was to shoot down the
birds with a 16-gage shotgun and to preserve the bodies. The animals would have their stomachs checked out to establish their diet
and they were preserved using field techniques. Indeed, thousands
of birds were sent to the American Museum of Natural History.

My introduction to this 'adventurous' aspect of science was
fortuitous and occurred in my adolescence, as I followed my father on a hunting trip in the north of Minas Gerais, in a region
dominated by *cerrado* vegetation, interspersed with small forests.
As I lay in a wood, escaping the afternoon sun, I observed toucans
flying above me, in the tree canopy. I took a few steps and discovered, to my amazement, the skeleton of a bird. I picked up the
bright yellow beak and was amazed by its light weight. Yet it was
strong, and resisted my energetic twisting and bending actions.
This image stayed in my memory for half a century, resurfacing
every now and then. It was at that time that I started to conduct
my research on biological materials in an effort to seek inspiration
for novel synthetic designs. One of my students, Matt Schneider,
finally accepted my challenge and one day purchased a beak from
a breeder in Fallbrook, Jerry Jennings of Emerald Forest. He sold
live toucans for approximately $8,000 and we convinced him to
sell us a dead one for $250! We proceeded to analyze it using mod-
ern techniques of materials science and were astounded to discover an ingenious structure which maximized torsion and bending
strength while minimizing weight. The study demonstrated how
this large beak, about one third of the size of the bird, can perform
all the necessary functions by weighing only one thirtieth of the

toucan. We proposed that this ultralight weight structure could serve as inspiration for man-made designs, and our research was featured in National Geographic and Nova's Materials sequence, hosted by David Pogue. It was a source of pride for our group and marked a new direction for our research.

But I had other tricks in my hat and my fishing expeditions to the Amazon basin confronted me with other superb research specimens. The *arapaima* (*pirarucu*) is one of the largest fresh water fish on this planet and its preferred habitat are seasonal lakes that form when the Amazon Basin Rivers overflow and flood the forest during the rainy season. As the river levels drop during the dry season lakes form on the margins. These lakes fester with life and provide ample food supply for the *arapaima*. But they are also inhabited by another predatory species: the piranha. As the dry season advances, piranha and *arapaima* eat whatever they can catch.

This provided me the idea for my research. The Indians use bows and special arrows and wait for the fish to rise and breathe. This living fossil has lungs and has to come to the surface every twenty minutes. There are two ways to fish the *arapaima* using a line. The bait, one entire fish called *traíra* is attached to a hook and thrown ahead of the point where the *arapaima* has surfaced. In a few minutes, voracious piranha devour the bait, which is most of the times. But, if the *arapaima* finds the bait in its trajectory, it takes it in its mouth and runs with it, eventually swallowing it. I was lucky to catch such a monumental fish and to observe in detail its morphology. The scales are large, about 10 cm in length, and tough. After being dried, they are commonly used by Amazonian women as nail files. Inside the mouth, the tongue is heavily mineralized. It is used as a wood file, after being dried. Thus, the fish is perfectly armored. And this has to be the case, because otherwise it could not survive piranha attacks that occur in packs.

I took some scales and subjected them to rigorous study using all techniques available to the modern materials scientist. Two top scientists became interested in the scales, Rob Ritchie at Berkeley and Markus Buehler at MIT. Rob has access to unique facilities within Lawrence Berkeley National Laboratory and subjected the scale to a battery of tests in the scanning electron microscope and the light source, performing small angle X ray scattering experiments in the latter. Markus Buehler's team is one of the top computational groups on the earth and developed novel techniques to simulate organic components of biological materials, collagen prominent among them. We teamed up and demonstrated that the layered structure of these scales is an outstanding biological material that can withstand the biting force of the piranha. But one question remained unanswered: what is the biting force of the piranha? We conducted calculations based on the thickness of the muscles connecting the skull to the maxilla and including the various angles that define the bite geometry. The results were surprising: we got a very modest number, about 4 pounds of force. What renders the piranha especially dangerous is the sharpness of the teeth, comparable to that of a razor. The cutting edge has a radius of 40 micrometers. An added effect is the geometry of the teeth, which contain minute serrations. The muscle is sliced by the action of the teeth, which capture the collagen and muscle fibers in a guillotine-type action.

But the ultimate answer had to wait for our trip to the Amazon basin and measurements on live piranha. My student Vincent Sherman built a wooden contraption by inserting a pressure gage between two wood strips. We did not have time to pre-test it prior to the trip and therefore it was a high-risk experiment. On the tenth day Angonese caught a large black piranha and we proceeded to test it. It had an impressive set of teeth but we had considerable difficulty getting it to bite. Even after inserting the gage into its mouth it would not bite. This procedure was repeated with a second black piranha, with greater success.

Unfortunately, Angonese did not have the same luck with a much smaller silver piranha that bit his finger while it was falling from the hook, free in the air. Back in the laboratory in San Diego, we extracted the data from the instrument and were surprised with the results; our calculations were confirmed. We got a maximum bite force of 25 N, or 5 lb. What makes up for it is the rapidity at which the bite is applied, the extreme sharpness of the teeth, and the trashing that automatically accompanies every bite. So, we surmise that the triangular teeth can sever the collagen of skin in mammals and scales in bass and other fish with small scales. Roosevelt tells the story, passed to him by a member of Rondon's team, of a fully dressed man that fell, accidentally, in the water. When he was found, his clothes were intact but all that was left of him was his skeleton. Piranhas had gotten inside his pants and shirt without damaging the cloth. Tapirs, capybaras, and alligators seem also to be impervious to piranha attacks and this can be due to the fact that they cannot penetrate, by biting, though their hide. But our delicate skin is no match for the piranha. However, any cut that damages the epidermis is immediately attacked. There are also reports of *arapaima* that lost a scale. The exposed area is immediately attacked and the animal is devoured, since the piranha can get at the underlying tissue and can readily cut it, trashing to rip it off completely.

The Jarina seed has mechanical properties and appearance that was utilized in the manufacture of buttons up to WW2. Since then synthetic polymers-plastics-have replaced it. Nevertheless, in spite of its strength, its interesting microstructure had never been investigated. Instigated by a colleague of mine, Carlos Coimbra, we proceeded to study it in a joint project. This seed has a resistance to crack propagation, a property that we call toughness-and a white appearance that gave it the name of 'vegetable ivory.' This plant grows in the Amazon basin and our study concluded that we can possibly grow bigger seeds through selective breeding. The seed has the size of a small lemon. If it could be grown to the size of an orange, many new applications could be developed. It is commonly used in Indian decoration, and the white beads in bracelets and necklaces are made from this seed. Easy to be processed, it is nevertheless limited in size.

This brings me to INPA, the National Institute for Amazonian Research. I visited it in preparation of our expedition and in the hope that INPA would designate a member of its staff to accompany us. The Director of the institute, Dr. Vals, was unavailable. I had met him previously at the Brazilian Academy of Sciences, where he gave a presentation on Amazon research. His Associate Director, Dr. Galvão, received me, first with considerable suspicion that gradually gave way to a customary Brazilian affability. My gringo appearance and name indicated to him that I could be a member of one of the much-maligned NGOs, intent of robbing the Amazon from Brazil, or of stealing some hidden biological treasure. After my introductory remarks, he became more relaxed and opened up. He was in deep conversation with a local person of some political importance and gave him most of his attention. His mind was somewhere between puzzled, amused, and annoyed. "What is this Portuguese-speaking gringo doing here?"

He concluded by saying that one of the members of INPA had gone down the Roosevelt River a few years before and gave me his phone. My numerous attempts to contact him failed. So, my attempts to have a member of INPA join our expedition failed and the four of us had to carry out our experiments and observations in a much more limited capacity.

One morning, as I inspected the island where we camped, I found a pile of black feathers. Immediately I was puzzled by them and collected the larger ones for subsequent research. From the white tips on the longest feathers, called retrices in scientific jargon, my colleagues deduced that they belonged to the tail of a curassow. Back at home, I gave them to one of my graduate students, Tarah Sullivan. She proceeded to study them with the detail and attention that we give to materials: first photographing one of them, then looking at it at a high magnification in the scanning electron microscope. The complex features came alive, and our scientific curiosity was wetted by the ultra-light weight features. Although feathers are well known and have been studied and used in many ways, there are still outstanding questions that we, as researchers, identify and resolve. In my case and that of my students, this is by a combination of observation, mechanical testing, analysis, and computational modeling. Tarah is applying these four pillars of Materials Science to elucidate the functions of the feather. If we look at a feather, we see a central shaft from which vanes radiate. These vanes, called barbs, are thin shafts with a platform each. These platforms are connected by tiny hooks, so that the entire surface is flat. The little hooks, called barbules, can unhook and the linked barbs thus separate. But birds have an ingenious way to re-hook the barbules and recompose the structure of the feather, making it airworthy. We call this activity 'preening.' For us Materials Scientists the feathers pose a challenge of considerable magnitude, because our ultimate goal is to copy their structure using synthetic materials.

This component of our field of endeavor is called "Bioinspiration." There exist already successful examples of bioinspired devices, the most common being the Velcro with which we are all so familiar. A Swiss engineer, Georges de Mistral, was hunting when he noticed that burrs would get stuck to his dog's fur. Upon closer observation, he discovered that the burrs contained tiny hooks. He then had a eureka moment and started his ten-year work that would eventually lead to the production of *Velours Cro-ché*, consisting of tiny hooks, on one side, and loops on the other. The hooks catch the loops and upon being pulled apart, bend and separate. So, we hope to do the same for feathers, creating structures that are light, stiff, and can best current synthetic ones. We are supported by a large grant from the Air Force Office of Scientific Research and will hopefully generate new advanced materials for airplanes. In any case, we are adding to the understanding of nature using the plethora of methodologies developed in the past fifty years.

Two other findings triggered my thinking process. As we were crossing the difficult *cerrado* on foot, macheting our way through bushes, I came across a vine that had an almost square cross section. In spite of the fatigue and thirst, I took a couple pictures, aided by Angonese, and cut off a sample. Unfortunately, desperate that evening, we emptied our loads, and I accidentally threw away the vine. Upon my return to San Diego, I continued my thought process, inspired by a paper on the square tail of the seahorse that we published in Science. The first author and intellectual force behind that paper was Mike Porter, who is currently in the faculty of Clemson University. Our paper explains why the seahorse tail is square. Indeed, square shapes are a rare find in nature, that favors round shapes. At the cellular level, they are present in plants (cork), and the original name for a cell was given in the seventeenth century by Robert Hooke upon observing them in a microscope. They resembled the cells of monks and Robert Hooke used this word to describe them. This is the origin for the name, although the cells in other animal kingdoms are closer to spheres. Upon closer inspection of the curassow fathers, we observed that they change from round, at the stem, to rectangular, from the center on. These observations were made by my graduate student Bin Wang. We used our knowledge of mechanics and explained in an elegant manner why this was so. Interestingly, in non-flying birds the square shape is virtually absent. These results were published in a prestigious journal, Advanced Science, and the photograph of the square vine, obtained under duress, is prominently displayed.

The scientific component of our exploration consisted of identifying and collecting specimens with unique structures and functionalities. Amazonia presents an amazing diversity of organisms. This biodiversity has been quantified and approximately 10% of species on the earth are in the Amazon. By tapping into this biological reservoir, we can advance knowledge and, importantly, obtain new technological materials and devices inspired on nature. In our case, the findings followed a serendipitous pattern and the observations we made, transported into a laboratory setting, yielded fascinating results. I cannot claim that the characteristics of the fauna and flora of the Amazon are unique, and it can be argued that some of these discoveries did not require such an expedition. However, the long hours spent riding, walking, and kayaking forced me to reflect on my surroundings. Had I been in the office answering a deluge of emails and juggling committee meetings, classes, brief visits to the laboratory, and student advising sessions, these thoughts and 'discoveries' would not have occurred. This recreation of an earlier Victorian science which melded with exploration was particularly enriching. This inquisitive questioning of the nature also permeates Roosevelt's account and led to a number of important scientific discoveries.

ACKNOWLEDGEMENT

This expedition would never have been possible if it were not for the help provided by numerous persons who, along our path, selflessly donated their time and effort. First and foremost, the members of this expedition should be acknowledged: Col. Hiram Reis e Silva, a legendary kayaker with 10,000 km of experience in the Amazon; Col. Ivan Carlos Angonese, a brave and energetic Infantry officer who commanded many missions deep in the Amazon, Jeffrey Lehmann, a UCSD graduate and cinematographer. They accepted the challenge of this expedition and were invaluable members. Two institutions were essential to the success of the expedition: the Brazilian Army and FUNAI, the Brazilian Indian Support Foundation. The Army provided logistic support for the land portion of the expedition, from Cáceres to the Roosevelt River. Through Cristina Meneses, from the FUNAI Headquarters in Brasilia, we obtained permission to cross the Pareci and Nambikwara Indigenous Areas, comprised of many villages. In Cáceres, Col. Braga, Commander of the Frontier Battalion, was a generous host. The Cáceres attorney Eduardo Sortica got us in touch with one of the last cattle drivers on this earth, Manoel Ramos. This enabled us to hire the mules and cowhand Eduardo (Boi) Ramos, who saved us from difficult moments. The twin brothers Carlos Marcio and Marcio Carlos from the FUNAI in Cuiabá established contact with the different Pareci villages, where we were well received. The Technical Coordinator of the FUNAI Comodoro Office, Adriane Vicentini, was instrumental in negotiating with the Nambikwara, and Mané Manduca was our loyal and capable guide through this perilous part of the journey. The river portion of the expedition was significantly aided by the City of Vilhena through Rita Marta and by the local Fire Department through Sergeant Douglas. We also received, at critical moments, assistance from local persons. Dave Freeman and Paul Shurke completed the river portion a couple months before we embarked and gave us excellent advice regarding the Pak Canoe that we used successfully.

In Rio de Janeiro, our support team consisted of my brother Pedro who generously supported the expedition financially. My loyal friends Cols. Carlos Elias and Luis Leme Louro, and Gen. Umberto Andrade from the Military Institute of Engineering provided contacts and the needed moral support. Dr. Albert Lin encouraged me along the many uncertain moments and connected me to the Explorers Club. Dr. Vincent Sherman helped me out with the manuscript and prepared maps and cover. To all of you, and to the many other persons that we encountered along the way, our most sincere thanks.

SELECTED BIBLIOGRAPHY

Cajazeira, José, Medical Report of Roosevelt-Rondon Expedition, 1914.

Caspar, Franz, Tupari, G. Bell and Sons, 1956.

Chagnon, Napoleon, Yanomamö: The fierce people. Third Ed., Holt, Rinehart, and Winston,1983.

Cherrie, George K., Dark Trails: Adventures of a Naturalist, Putnam's Sons, 1930.

Comte, Auguste, Introduction to Positive Philosophy, Hackett Publishing Co., Indianapolis/Cambridge, 1988.

Da Cunha, Euclides, The Amazon: Land Without History, Oxford U. Press, 2006.

Gomes, Emmanuel, Rondonia:História e Geografia, Grafica e Editora Express, Vilhena, Rondonia, 2012.

Grandin, Greg, Fordlandia, Picador, 2009.

Grann, David, The Lost City of Z, Vintage Books, 2010.

Lévi-Strauss, Claude, Tristes Tropiques, Penguin Books, 1992.

Lévi-Strauss, Claude, Antropologie Structurale, Plon, 1974.

Lévi-Strauss, Claude, Saudades do Brasil, Companhia das Letras, São Paulo, 1994.

Mann, Charles C., 1491, Vintage Books, 2005.

Meggers, Betty, Amazonia: Man and Culture in a Counterfeit Paradise, 1971.

Meyers, Marc A., and Chen, Po-Yu, Biological Materials Science, Cambridge U. Press, 2014.

Millard, Candice, The River of Doubt, Anchor Books, 2005.

Miller, Leo E., In the Wilds of South America: Six Years of Exploration in Colombia, Venezuela, British Guyana, Peru, Bolivia, Argentina, Paraguay, and Brazil, Charles Scribner's Sons, 1918.

Eliot John L., Toucan, National Geographic, Dec 2006 vol. 210 issue 6, p.14

Olivar, Julio, Caminhos de Rondon, Grafica Imediata, Porto Velho, 2014.

Ornig, Joseph R., My Last Chance to be a Boy, Louisiana State U.Press, Baton Rouge, 1994.

Porter, Michael, Adriaens, Dominique, Hatton, Ross L. Meyers, Marc A. McKittrick, Joanna, Why the seahorse tail is square, Science, July 2015: vol. 349, Issue 6243

Roosevelt, Theodore, Through the Brazilian Wilderness, Seven Treasures Publications, 2009.

Wang, Bin, and Meyers, Marc, Light as a Feather: A Fibrous Natural Composite with a Shape Changing from Round to Square, Advanced Science, Dec. 2016.

Photos taken by the four members of the expedition, Ivan Angonese, Jeffrey Lehmann, Marc André Meyers, Hiram Reis, and from various other sources and archives

Cover map: Valley of the Amazon accompanyng Lt. Herndon's Report, by: H. C. Elliot, 1853.

Back cover portrait: photograph by Jeffrey Lehmann

Heroic pose of Cols. Rondon and Col Roosevelt on a curious rock formation close to Navaité Falls.

Author striking pose on similar rock.

Lieutenant Lyra and the portaging heavy canoes. This was an immense ordeal for the 1914 expedition. Photo by Kermit Roosevelt.

Laying wood rollers and pulling canoe during portage.

Getting ready to run empty canoe through some rapids.

Struggling in a rapid. Angonese is fighting the current while Jeffrey and Hiram hold the canoe. Kayaks would just 'gun' down.

Two Brazilians of contrasting backgrounds: João Brabo is the fierce Cinta Larga chief that has raises havoc in the region; Col. Hiram, who also has some Indian blood (Charrua), is an exemplary officer of the Brazilian Army, a graduate of the Elite Agulhas Negras Academy, and veteran of the Amazon.

Candy distribution for the Indians, which helped to clear the air. There were very few males in the group, and we suspect that they were hiding somewhere ready to pounce on us if we tried to go penetrate deeper into Cinta Larga territory.

Cracks in rock produced by successive contraction and expansion cycles following day to night temperature fluctuations. Then, wind and water erosion complete the job of separating and rounding off the pieces.

Fully loaded canoe ready to be run through rapids.

Walking the kayak through channel in the river.

Walking kayaks through rapids. This was always the safest choice.

Island in the middle of the river. This island becomes submerged in the rainy season, since the level of the river is several meters above the current one.

Peacock basses caught at the mouth of small tributary, an *igarapé* as called by locals.

Waiting for catfish (*pirarara*) to strike at night. We lost several runs due to my poor reflexes and rusty knot-tying skills.

Giant otters basking on fallen tree. We saw several schools along the river, and they can be quite aggressive, swimming toward us and screaming.

Nice break at the Roosevelt lodge, below the Inferno Falls. In Roosevelt's day, there was a large building at this site and a considerable number of rubber tappers were camped there, waiting for fresh supplies brought by the *batelões* (larger transport boats). We met an intrepid group of guides whose food we shared. We camped on the beach. They also helped us with the short portage, a welcome break from our travails.

Cols. Rondon and Roosevelt at lunch break on an island where very tall trees grew. The weary expressions denote their uncertainty. The dog could be Trigueiro, Roosevelt and Kermit's favorite. It disappeared in the forest shortly before the end.

A relaxing morning at camp. Each evening we would lay a tarp over the fire to ensure a supply of hot water.

Running a rapid. The kayaks had an easier time than the canoe but Jeffrey and Angonese got better as we gained experience.

Kayak running down a rapid. It looks easy but it is important to have an exact knowledge of the area beforehand to avoid rocks. An impact against a rock-they are usually marked by white water- can rip up the bottom. Our kayaks survived several hits.

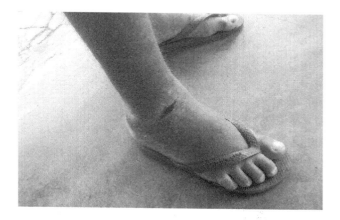

Wound on foot produced by ray sting; the pain that follows is one of the worst ever recorded. This was 42 days after accident.

Former rubber tapper Arão. We spent the night in an abandoned house in front of his hut. He lived exclusively off the few fish he caught and reminisced about his rubber tapping days, when he lived alone in a small tributary. His stories about companions being killed and eaten by the Cinta Larga were fascinating. With a sly smile exposing his one remaining tooth, he said: "They don't eat the calves. Taste too sour." How would he know?

Jeffrey's face showing the damage from mosquito bites.

River bank showing section entirely made of sand, with minimal layer of organic topsoil. The roots are exposed by erosion in the banks and show that the topsoil layer is very thin.

Large black piranha caught and later barbecued. This is a solitary fish and we did not catch any red piranha on the upper ranges of the river.

Establishing bite force of piranha with pressure transducer built by Vincent Sherman.

Roosevelt at his writing desk during expedition. He wears his Western gloves (which he calls 'gauntlets') and net as protection against mosquito bites.

My version of writing. A pensive moment with impressions recorded daily in diary.

As we descended, the river widened and, often, the banks became higher, making camping more painful because we had to drag everything up.

Jeffrey shaving in nature.

Nasty piranha bite.

Col. Angonese endured constant pain during paddling. We were very worried about an infection, but daily care, changing of the dressings, and, importantly, antibiotic cream prevented a major problem.

A rubber tree, *Hevea brasiliensis*, testament to intense extraction activity many years ago. Each day a cut would be made on tree and a tiny cup placed at the bottom. In the afternoon, the rubber tapper returned to collect his precious viscous liquid.

Making an imaginary cut in a rubber tree. It still produced a profusion of a white viscous liquid.

Changing of the guard at Senauma Falls. Col Hiram had just returned from a four-hour trek looking for a house that supposedly was 'by the river.' Col Angonese, much fresher, is getting ready to go before sunset.

Lighting candles at the Senauma chapel. It is named in honor of a girl who drowned in these waterfalls. Her statue, on right, is revered by the local people. She is the patroness of the falls and protects the people coming down. She is dressed as Our Lady of Aparecida.

Senauma chapel with crosses marking the burial sites of people that drowned in the falls. Roosevelt camped in this spot and describes the crosses.

A small but nasty portion of the Senauma falls. There are actually four falls and several rapids strung over a 12 km length.

Portaging the canoe at Senauma Falls. This was a relatively simple operation, since it weighed only 30 kg (60 pounds).

Roosevelt and Cherrie bathing in the river. Photo by Kermit Roosevelt.

Bathing on beach below Senauma falls. Water was safe from piranhas and stingrays as long as it was shallow, had a sandy bottom, and ran fast.

Splendid sunset that made us forget all our tribulations and uncertainties.

Journey's end at Aripuanan River: Roosevelt and Rondon at the monument marking the baptizing of the River of Doubt as Roosevelt River.

Our team at Aripuanã River: We look a lot cheerier. We could no longer find this marker and a permanent monument should be erected at this point to mark this heroic feat.

Angonese relaxing on power boat after encountering the Aripuanã River. Mission accomplished.

Pelado's bar in Mata Matá, named for fierce fights. The village is an assembly of a few houses by the side of the ferry across the river.

Loading up our gear on Pelado's pickup. He had to fabricate a wooden rack to accommodate our boats.

A stop along the road. The two little children by the fence are Nambikwara Indians.

Miners showing us their discoveries on the ferry over the Madeira River. They claimed to have found tantalum-rich ores and were excited about it, seeking investors.

Saying goodbye to loyal and capable Sergeant Douglas, who helped us along the entire trip.

Roosevelt explaining the exploration at the Explorer's Club in New York. They finally believed him. One can see that he had regained his *avoirdupoids* as Miller euphemistically referred to his girth.

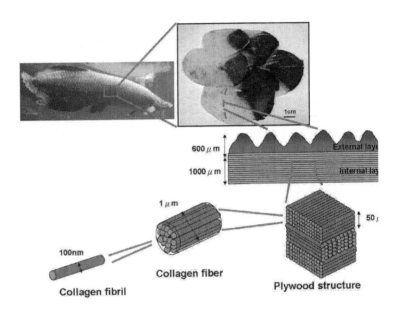

Hierarchical structure of *arapaima* scales that provide protection against piranha attacks. Study by Wen Yang and Vincent Sherman.

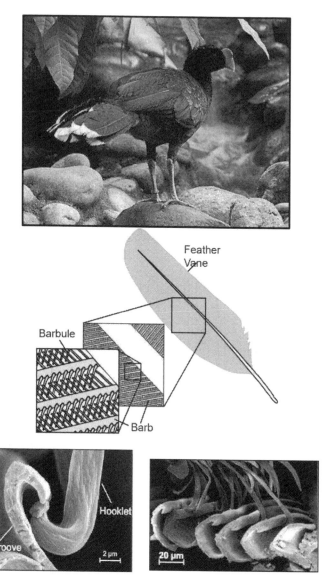

Curassow and structure of feather studied by Tarah Sullivan; the hooklets attach to the grooves and enable the feather to retain its integrity.

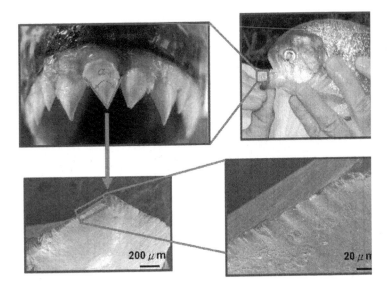

Checking piranha dentition; teeth studied by Albert Lin and Po-Yu Chen; scanning electron micrograph of piranha tooth shows extremely sharp edges and serrations across along the cutting edge.

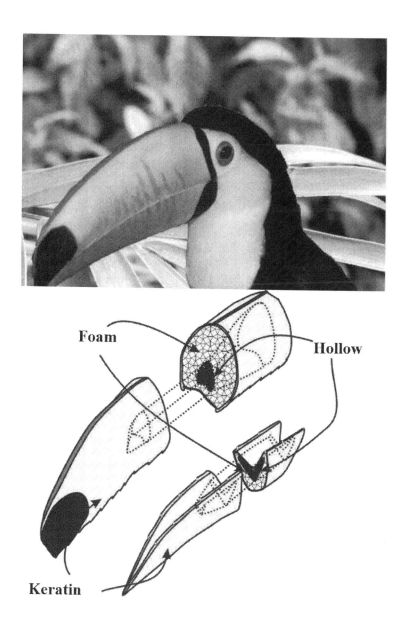

Foam

Hollow

Keratin

Structure of toucan beak studied by Matt Schneider and Yasuaki Seki; it is about 1/3 of its length but only one 30th of its weight; outside keratin sheath covers a bony foam that provides stiffness.

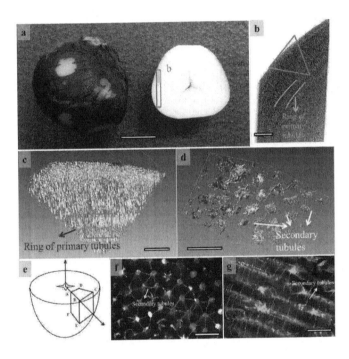

Vegetable ivory studied by Bin Wang and Wen Yang: the Amazon Jarina seed that can be used to produce buttons, has an intricate structure of channels (tubules).

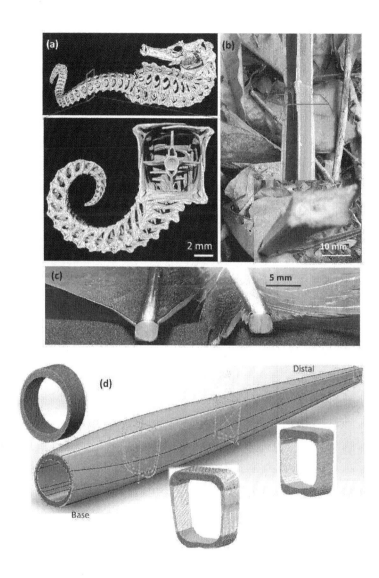

Square shapes in nature: (a) Square seahorse tail, studied by Michael Porter; (b)Square liana from Nambikwara territory; (c and d) Square middle region of feather shaft, which improves the stiffness/weight ratio, studied by Bin Wang. These are rare in nature, which usually favors round shapes.

Made in the USA
San Bernardino, CA
15 May 2017